INTERNATIONAL LEGEND TRIPPING

Robert C. Robinson

Other books by Robert C. Robinson:
Legend Tripping

Other books of Interest:
Bigfoot Nation
Yetis, Sasquatch & Hairy Giants
The Mystery of the Olmecs
Abominable Snowmen
Things and More Things
More Far-Out Adventures
Technology of the Gods
Obelisks: Towers of Power
Pirates & the Lost Templar Fleet
Lost Continents & the Hollow Earth
Lost Cities & Ancient Mysteries of the Southwest
Lost Cities of China, Central Asia & India
Lost Ciies & Ancient Mysteries of Africa & Arablia
Lost Ciies & Ancient Mysteries of South America
Lost Ciies of Ancient Lemuria & the Pacific
Lost Ciies of North and Central America
Lost Cities of Atlantis, Ancient Europe & the Mediterranean
The Enigma of Cranial Deformation
The Crystal Skulls
Ark of God
Vimana

INTERNATIONAL LEGEND TRIPPING

Adventure Outside the Box

By Robert C. Robinson

Foreword by David Hatcher Childress

International Legend Tripping

ISBN: 978-1-948803-27-4

Cover art by Kent Holloway.

Published by Adventures Unlimited Press
One Adventure Place
Kempton, Illinois 60946 USA

www.adventuresunlimitedpress.com
www.wexclub.com

LEGEND TRIPPING
ADVENTURE OUTSIDE THE BOX!

TABLE OF CONTENTS

This book is dedicated to the
Memory of
Ivan T. Sanderson
and
Frank Buck
Two gentlemen that started
me on my path to
Adventure

Editors note: While many dictionaries capitalize the word bigfoot, the publishers have decided that words such as bigfoot, sasquatch, and yeti should not be capitalized since they are common words describing a known animal. Just as wolf, cougar or bear (or elf) are not capitalized, nor should bigfoot be capitalized. There are times, of course, when the word bigfoot should be capitalized, such as in a title or name.

FOREWORD
by
David Hatcher Childress

As I traveled around the world with just my backpack and wits starting in 1975, I knew that I was a seeker, a mystic traveler, one who wanted to explore the world and know the secrets of the universe, to make life a knowledgeable adventure. Little did I know that I was "legend tripping," as Robert Robinson calls it.

Let's face it, science, history and biology can be quite interesting, but it is the undiscovered, the unknown, the fantastic and the paranormal that fascinate us. It is new discoveries and unsolved mysteries that continue to hold our interest. All that Robert Robinson wants you to do is look outside the box and head for an adventure!

In his first book, *Legend Tripping: The Ultimate Adventure*, he took us around the United States and its exciting plethora of myths and monsters, paranormal activity, UFOs and extraterrestrials, lost treasures and mysterious places. Now he takes us around the world to search for mysterious cryptids, explore haunted places and seek legendary lost treasures.

Robinson tells us that there are large hairy creatures roaming all parts of the world like the yeti, the yeren, the alma, and the wildman. He tells us that England might be the most haunted country in the world but there are haunted places in every corner of our planet that include castles, old prisons and hotels. Naturally there are UFO hotspots around the world and Robinson shows us how to explore them for ourselves. He also reveals legends of lost treasure and where to look for these hidden riches. Interesting museums and unusual organizations are also included.

Robinson is an expert on outdoor survival and bushcrafting. His training in the military provided him the expertise that is needed to be a survival instructor and give the sound advice he offers in this book. He was born at Hamilton Air Force Base in California and grew up an Army brat. As such, he had the privilege of visiting numerous countries. After graduating high school at Lansing, Kansas, he enlisted in the United States Army in June 1982 and served for over 21 years as an Airborne Military Policeman.

He was based in numerous countries while serving in the military and developed a keen interest in mysterious and unexplained activities in these places. Upon retiring from the military, Robinson became an investigator with MUFON and founded the Bigfoot Field Search Organization. With this organization he went on numerous expeditions in Florida and elsewhere to find evidence for skunk apes and bigfoot. His wife Tracy accompanies him on his monster hunts and is a paranormal investigator as well, conducting ghost hunts and other investigations into the unexplained. Rob accompanies her on ghost hunts as her tech support. Rob continues to be an investigator with MUFON.

Rob and Tracy were selected to appear on ABC's *Wife Swap* in 2010 as the monster/ghost hunting family. Because they did not want to be labeled as a certain type of investigator, the Robinsons started to refer to themselves as Legend Trippers, and so a new meme was created. They try to conduct at least one monster or ghost hunt a month. I guess you could say that the family that legend trips together, stays together. So, be sure to bring the whole family on your own legend trips.

Sit back and enjoy a wild ride around the world in search of the strange and unusual. The world is full of mysteries of the unexplained and this book will show you not only where to go, but what to take with you. Robinson shares his expertise on fantastic destinations in this great compendium of travel advice and weird sites!

INTRODUCTION

Legends Are Everywhere

Hey Legend Trippers,

As I kid, I was a big fan of the old black-and-white monster movies. My favorite was *The Creature from the Black Lagoon*, which I found out later, was based on an old legend of an aquatic humanoid dwelling in the Amazon basin. So it was no wonder, when I found out mysterious creatures were roaming around that science didn't acknowledge, that I took an interest in it. I later started reading books about the unexplained, with stories about monsters, ghosts, UFO sightings, mysterious and haunted places around the world. I also enjoyed reading about lost buried treasure. My favorite legend is the Oak Island Money Pit.

When I go on book tours or conferences, I get asked a lot of questions. One question I am often asked i: What got you into researching and investigating legends? That I owe to a 1974 documentary movie; it was a movie that changed my life.

My dad took the family to a drive-in theater in Hattiesburg, Mississippi one Friday night. The drive-in was showing a double feature, and to this day, I can't remember the second movie, but I remember the first.

The drive-in was showing Charles B. Peirce's *The Legend of Boggy Creek*. It is considered the first bigfoot quasi-documentary, and today it is a classic.

The movie starts by saying, "This is a true story." Then it goes on to relate the sightings of a large hairy creature seen by some of the townfolk lurking around in the swamps outside the small town of Fouke, Arkansas.

Mr. Peirce superbly created a dark menacing atmosphere with scenes of the murky swamps around Fouke. It is a superbly made movie and uses some of the locals in the incident recreations. Very simply filmed with no expensive special effects, the recreations of the sightings keep the audience on the edge of their seats. It also gave some little kids nightmares.

I can remember that that movie scared me. All the way home, I kept looking into the woods wondering if there was a hairy creature looking at me, and I became intrigued at the idea that strange creatures roam this planet.

While in school, I would check out books by Ivan T. Sanderson, John Keel, and Charles Fort. One of my favorites, which I've read more than once, is John Keel's 1957 book *Jadoo*. It got me hooked on wanting to investigate legends.

Then the hit television show *In Search Of* came on, and that solidified my passion for the unexplained. Every week I would watch Leonard Nimoy introduce a new legend and mystery. The show still stands the tests of time and is a classic.

Another question I get asked is: What was your first legend trip? This adventure started in 1975. During that time frame, my mother, kid brother, and I were living in England. My father, who was in the military, was deployed in the Orient. My mother liked to take us out as much as she could to see the sights of England and Scotland.

One day my mother announced that we were going up to see Scotland, where she was born and raised. My mother was from Edinburgh, but later moved to England when she was in her teens. There she met my father, a US serviceman, and married and went to America.

When my father was deployed overseas to Vietnam or Korea, my mother would take my brother and me back to England to see her family. Even though it was just a year, we visited numerous places like Fountains Abbey, London, and Stonehenge.

But ever since my mother told me about Loch Ness and its legendary monster, I had always wanted to go there. And now I had my chance.

We took off early in the morning with some friends from my mother's work. It took all day, and when we got to the border, I was expecting there to be more of a difference in scenery going from England to Scotland, but there wasn't.

We first went to Edinburgh, where we visited some places from the family's past and then went up to the namesake castle. We sampled Scotland's world-famous dish, haggis. It has a unique taste. Early the next day, we set out for Loch Ness.

We journeyed through the mist-covered highlands; we saw a man playing bagpipes on the way. We then came over a mountain and I saw it. I knew Loch Ness was big, but I didn't expect it to be that big. We stopped to take in the splendor of this impressive sight. The sun was out, so it wasn't as cold as it usually was. For a twelve-year-old, I was surprisingly in awe of how beautiful the area was. There was a light mist in the valley as we came to the town of Fort Augustus.

When we arrived, I quickly piled out of the car and ran down to the Loch Ness viewpoint and looked out at the large lake. I remember not knowing what to expect. I know that I thought that maybe for the creature would show itself to us.

Words really cannot describe how beautiful this place is. The wind came across the water, and I remember feeling excited and cold at the same time.

Later we visited the Loch Ness Monster Centre and Exhibition. This impressive exhibit makes its home in the town of Drumnadrochit. The center featured all the photos of Nessie. It also included the film of John Cobb attempting to break the world speed record on Loch Ness in 1952, which resulted in his boat hitting a wave and crashing. Sadly, Cobb died, and they never could explain the cause of that mysterious wave.

Also, during our brief visit, I remember seeing some *National Geographic* banners on some vehicles. I later found out that Robert Ballard, the ocean researcher who found the Titanic, was leading an expedition to find Nessie. Unfortunately, *National Geographic* invested a lot of money and did not find any evidence of the monster.

When we visited this attraction in 1975, it was pretty much a walk in and walk around museum. Now you have to make reservations and buy tickets to go in, and it also features a cruise on Loch Ness.

Though our visit to this excellent place was brief, it did leave a lasting impression on me. It was the start of my lifelong intrigue into legends and the unexplained.

As a teenager, I read about a large hairy creature seen in Louisiana, Missouri called Momo. I talked a couple of friends into accompanying me on my adventure. We got there but quickly realized that we hadn't brought the right equipment. We didn't bring any camping gear and ended up cutting the trip short. We did, however, get to see the area where witnesses had seen the cryptid. That taught me a lesson about being prepared.

While in the Army, I would check out locations where mysterious events had occurred. I visited numerous haunted castles in Germany and Italy.

Upon retiring from the military, I moved to Florida. I hooked up with the Bigfoot Field Research Organization and started going on monster hunts with them. My wife and I joined some local paranormal groups and started conducting paranormal investigations around the United States.

Through the Internet, I started communicating with other individuals who had the same passion as I had. I found that there are numerous groups out there that conduct monster hunts and paranormal investigations. I love meeting people who like to go and investigate legends the way I do.

On these adventures, I discovered that a lot of people going into the woods to look for a large hairy creature didn't know what they were doing. They didn't know what to look for, and the important thing was that they didn't bring the right gear. I also found this when I participated in some ghost hunts. When it comes to treasure hunting, a lot of people don't know the laws in the country where the hoard is located concerning treasure hunting.

When I realized this I decided to write a guidebook about everything I learned about cryptids and looking for them, haunted places and conducting paranormal investigations, UFO sightings and what to ask the witnesses, and treasure hunting and the laws in different countries. That way, you, the reader, would have a guidebook when you plan your adventures.

I don't pretend to be an expert. Everything I learned was from very talented people who have been investigating legends for years. I'm just passing that information on.

Some of these legends in this book you may have heard of or read about. Then there are some that you haven't.

Today, when I'm not working, I continue to go and investigate legends. As with my first book, I want with this book to share my passion with you for seeking out and investigating legends. I hope my book will stir your sense of wonder about this unexplainable world. Welcome to my world of legend tripping!

Robert C Robinson
Legend Tripper

LEGEND TRIPPING
ADVENTURE OUTSIDE THE BOX!

Chapter 1

Legends around the World

We cannot define it. Nothing has ever been finally figured out, because there is nothing final to figure out.
— Charles Fort

In 1912 Charles Fort compiled over 40,000 notes on unexplained incidents that he had found in books and newspapers in his groundbreaking book *Book of the Damned.* In it were unexplained events involving teleportation, poltergeists, crop circles, and unidentified flying objects. This book was the beginning of paranormal research. He recorded numerous reports of unidentified objects seen flying over different parts of the globe. Later in 1953, the term "UFO" (Unidentified Flying Object) was coined by the United States Air Force to serve as a catch-all for all such reports.

Then in 1955, Bernard Heuvelmans published his book *On the Track of Unknown Animals*. In it, Heuvelmans coins the term for research on unknown animals—"cryptozoology." It was the first book written on the subject of cryptids.

Someone once asked me, "Do you believe in all those legends like bigfoot, the Loch Ness Monster, UFOs, and haunted places?" The simple answer is, "Yes, I do believe that there is truth behind all legends." There are still mysteries that science can't explain. Legend tripping is researching and investigating those legends.

With the success of my first book, *Legend Tripping: The Ultimate Adventure*, I was approached by the publishers to write another one, only this time bigger. I thought, "What could be bigger than legend tripping around the United States?" Then it came to me: What is more significant than the United States? Why the whole world, of course. While I was researching for legends around the United States, I became aware that I was only looking at the tip of the iceberg. There are some awesome legends, i.e., cryptids, haunted and mysterious places, and lost treasures spoken of all over the world.

This great planet of ours is full of unexplained mysteries and legends. I think that the reason that these legends are still around is that they not only scare us but also mystify us and create intrigue.

The yeti, Loch Ness Monster, werewolves in Eastern Europe, flying saucers over Mexico, haunted castles all over Europe, cursed islands, and mysterious ghost lights are all still just as famous today as when they were first rumored.

Contrary to what scientists today have us believe, not everything on this planet is black and white. There is that gray area, and that is where legend tripping comes in.

Some claim that it was the Loch Ness Monster that started the whole cryptozoology craze and not bigfoot. That might be true, but the yeti comes in a close second. There are cryptid creatures located in every corner of the globe.

Most people think that the large hairy giant called bigfoot is roaming exclusively in the continental United States. Because of popular television shows, bigfoot has excellent publicity. But did you know that there are stories and legends of large, hairy, bipedal creatures roaming the forests and swamps in other parts of the world, besides North America?

With this book, we expand our search for cryptids and look at the different kinds seen around the world.

During certain nights witnesses have seen a large canine-type creature walking on two legs lurking around the forests and woods. Terrifying screams echo through the night.

We briefly touched on the werewolf legend, or the dogman, in my first book. Werewolf -type creatures are seen all over the world. Some of the sightings have been researched and documented. Almost every country has a legend of a hairy bipedal creature. Some of the stories of these creatures are terrifying.

Can you believe that in certain parts of Africa, there are reports of creatures that many researchers believe could be modern-day dinosaurs? Expeditions have gone in to find evidence of these cryptids. Some have brought back eyewitness accounts of these beasts.

We will explore some fascinating cryptids that are new to some of you readers. There are stories going back for centuries relating that humans share this planet with some extraordinary and mysterious creatures.

Believe it or not, witnesses are seeing mermaid-type creatures and little people all around the world. You will be astounded to see how many there were. The legends of merfolk and little people go back for centuries. But are people seeing these strange creatures?

There are also sizeable aquatic sea serpent-like creatures dwelling in lakes and rivers around the world besides the Loch Ness Monster. OgooPogoo (also known as Ogopogo) makes its home in Lake Okanagan in Canada. Every day, you can read tales on the Internet of strange alien-like beings that are recorded roaming around various parts of the world.

There are stories of ghosts and mysterious apparitions haunting various locations all over the world. Did you know that England at one time was considered the most haunted country in the world? Ghost hunting got started over in England in the 1960s. Today there are active paranormal groups and organizations all over the globe conducting ghost hunts.

People all over the world report seeing strange objects flying across the sky. While the United States has the most recorded sightings, the United Kingdom and Mexico also have many sightings, as does South America. Alien-like beings have been seen wandering around backyards and forests through the ages in Europe.

Did you know there are lost treasures from pirates all over the Caribbean, worth millions, still not found? There are still millions in gold and artwork hidden by the Nazis at the end of World War II that have not been recovered. Stories have been passed down from generation to generation of buried treasure still out there undiscovered, possibly in our backyards. There are places around the world where mysterious events happen to this day, which defy explanation.

People all over the world, like me, find legends as exciting as they are mysterious. Today legend tripping is gaining popularity as people discover the excitement of going out and looking for them. As I said in my first book, "The best part of legend tripping is that it is not difficult to do, and you can enjoy it with your entire family. Monster and ghost hunting groups are popping up everywhere on the Internet as people get together and search for the truth behind these legends."

Have you ever traveled on a train in another country as it treks by a large wooded area? Did you look into the darkness of the woods and ask yourself, "Is something mysterious out there?" and have you ever thought about what you would do if you saw something that was unexplainable? If you have an adventurous spirit, then you need to go international legend tripping.

So, what is legend tripping, you ask? Wikipedia defines it as "an adolescent practice (containing elements of a rite of passage) in which a usually furtive nocturnal pilgrimage made to a site which is the scene of some tragic, horrific, and possibly supernatural event or haunting. The practice has been documented most thoroughly to date in the United States." Wikipedia has gone back and redone the definition and included the following statement: "Legend tripping is a mostly harmless, perhaps even beneficial, youth recreation. It allows young people to demonstrate their courage in a place where the actual physical risk is likely slight."

That is a better idea of what legend tripping is. Let's break it down as follows. The word "legend," defined, means "non-historical or unverifiable story handed down by tradition from earlier times and popularly accepted as historical," (thefreedictionary.com). Tripping is simply an extension of the word "trip," meaning a physical journey to another place.

Our new definition:

Participate in an adventure to find or find evidence of a creature, place, or event that has not been verified or explained by science and verify the truth behind it.

Now, with that in mind, do you want to be an international legend tripper? Then you need to ask yourself this. Are you one of those unique people who believe that there are still cryptids out there that science has not acknowledged and want to go search for them? Do you believe in the paranormal? Do you want to investigate a haunted castle? Do you think that there is intelligent life on other planets? Do you believe that extraterrestrials have visited us? Do you want to investigate areas where sightings of strange unknown flying aircraft (UFOs) and landing sites are reported? Are you one of those people who want to go search for legendary lost treasure left behind by pirates or smugglers? If you said "Yes" to any of that, then you are a legend tripper.

You've heard the saying 'Think outside the box.' With legend tripping, you '*look* outside the box.' You go out and search for things out of the norm. Let's be real, cryptids and ghosts are not what we call normal. It is why they are called paranormal. If you look up and see strange lights moving in an irregular pattern, and say, 'It's probably a plane,' then you are not looking outside the box. If you say, 'Might be a UFO,' then you are. Legend trippers aren't discouraged by what today's scientists have to say. They know everything isn't always explainable. There are still things out there we don't know. A legend tripper challenges scientists to find the truth behind these legends.

A person who looks for just cryptids is a cryptozoologist, a person who looks for ghosts is a paranormal investigator, and a person who looks for lost treasure is a treasure hunter. A legend tripper searches for all that. They spend every available moment researching and exploring the stories behind the legends.

When you are legend tripping, the passion lies in the thrill of the hunt for the unexplained, the mysterious, and the weird. It is also a chance to experience something out of the norm and exciting.

There are hundreds of videos of cryptid creatures on the Internet today. Ninety percent of them are fake. Today, there are many monster hunters and paranormal investigators out there trying to get the "money shot" (the one photograph nobody, including scientists, can dispute), and to gain a large amount of money for being the person who took it.

Science needs proof that can be examined and then classified. So, unless somebody brings in a live or dead specimen, then the photo or video is going to be ridiculed and branded a fake. The famous bigfoot film is the 1967 Patterson-Gimlin film of a supposed female bigfoot, and is to this day still considered a fake by many. With the paranormal and extraterrestrials, unless you can get the ghost or UFO to show up at the same spot, your photo is going to be called a fake.

But with legend tripping, it's is not about making money and finding fame; it is about experiencing something nobody else gets to experience. It is the opportunity to look for something unique. It's a chance to step out of the typical day-to-day routine of everyday life and look for something that might cause everyone to reexamine how we look at specific scientific theories. Legend trippers are not out to prove science wrong, but some of these legends must have facts behind them.

Where do legend trippers go to explore legends? There are legends in every part of this world. Every country has legendary haunted places. Unidentified flying objects are seen almost daily in every part of the world. Look on MUFON's website to see the daily UFO sightings. Have we documented every known animal on this planet? The answer is, "No." Every year, scientists discover new kinds of animals, new plants, even new planets. Cryptids are seen daily in various parts of the world including bigfoot, Mothman, werewolves, and lake/river serpents. Native Americans have stories of these strange creatures going back centuries, and they are still reportedly seen today. A legend tripper knows where to look.

The author in Fouke, Arkansas.

A legend tripper lives to find weird places and explore them, rather than vacation at a theme park. Legends are all around us; you just need to research and find one and go on a legend trip.

Is everything on this planet explainable? Science will say, "Yes." Well, what I say to that is: have them explain why the rocks sound like bells when you hit them at Ringing Rocks Park in Pennsylvania. Ask them what causes the ghost lights in the Blue Ridge Mountains of North Carolina. Not everything is explainable!

The world around us is full of mystery. Even today, we still don't know what is at the bottom of the oceans. We have theories about the pyramids of Egypt. We still don't know how they were made. Who made the large drawings on the Nazca Plains, out in the desert in Peru, and why? Not every UFO report is explainable. Are we the only intelligent species on this planet or in the universe? Are there large aquatic creatures lurking at the bottom of some of the deepest lakes in the world? If not, what are people seeing? Everyone has heard of the Bermuda Triangle, where aircraft and ships have mysteriously disappeared. But have you heard of the Dragon's Triangle, off the coast of Japan? Stories surrounding the perils of these dangerous waters date back to 1000 BCE.

Every day, people all over the world see animals they cannot identify or have never seen before. Some are seeing a large hairy bipedal animal that walks like a human. A scientist's quick response is they are seeing bears walking on their hind legs. P\ But, people, even experienced hunters, actually see something they cannot identify.

In Ivan T. Sanderson's international best-sellers *Uninvited Visitors* and *Invisible Residents*, he defines strange things seen in the sky as UAOs instead of UFO's. UAO stands for Unidentified Ariel Object. It makes sense because these peculiar objects are not flying with the use of wings or rotors like birds, helicopters, and planes. They are not displacing air but are instead moving through an unknown form of propulsion. To keep it simple, I will still use the acronym "UFO" in this book, since UAO hasn't caught on yet.

I do believe in UFOs and extraterrestrials and that we are being visited by beings not from this planet. As a kid, I read a lot of books on the subject by John Keel and Ivan T. Sanderson. Now, as a legend tripper, I investigate where the last UFO sighting took place to see if the craft shows up again. Sometimes they do and sometimes not. But when it comes to extraterrestrials, what excites me the most is the close encounter of the third kind. You will find the excitement in visiting and exploring supposed UFO landing and crash sites, and locations where legend has it there have alien-like creatures.

There are numerous groups around the world who conduct investigations on strange creature sightings, paranormal investigations, and look for UFOs. If you want to join one of these legend-tripping groups, make sure it is one you want to belong to, and their theories and beliefs are the same as yours. An example is that some people believe that bigfoot is supernatural and is also an extraterrestrial creature with the ability to cloak itself as well as travel into different dimensions and vortices. Other researchers believe that it is an undiscovered earth-born creature that makes its home deep in the forests and swamps.

Most of these groups will allow you to come to an investigation and see what their group is all about. They are excited about having new people along to share in their research. On the flip side, some groups keep everything internal. In other words, if you find anything, you can only share it with them, and the group will announce the finding to the community.

Some books categorize legends and mysteries differently. This book keeps it simple for those who are new to the field of mysteries and the unexplained. All are arranged alphabetically either by legend or location.

The great thing about legend tripping is there are all kinds of legends to look for, and you do not have to limit yourself to just one. These legends have been documented in books and publications before. My purpose is to introduce you to some legends that might be new to you. You will find that each one is just as exciting to look for as the other. In this book, the legends are in four categories:

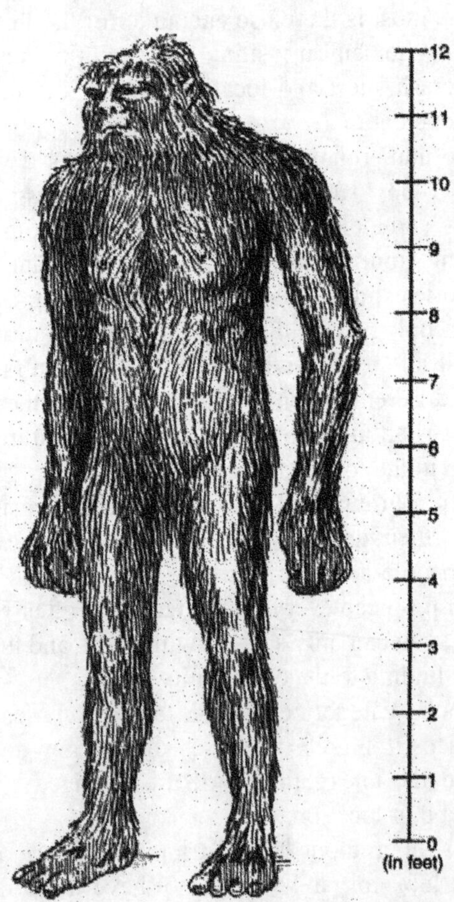

Cryptids (Land Based)
- Wildmen
- Werewolves
- Hellhounds
- Living Dinosaurs
- Little people

Cryptids (Water Based)
- Aquatic cryptids
- Sea Serpents
- Aquatic Humanoids

Paranormal/ Places
- Haunted places

Mysterious and UFOs Locations
- Landing sties

Hidden or Lost Treasures
- Treasures still unfound located around the world

Each chapter will cover all four categories of legends. Since today's information is tomorrow's old news, I will also provide a website on each legend to offer you the most up-to-date information available. Plus, some of the haunted and mysterious

places have specific times that you are allowed to visit.

Like *Legend Tripping: The Ultimate Adventure*, this book is designed as a guidebook. It will go over the different legends, how to plan, what to take, and how to conduct a legend trip. We will go over the various rules and laws of the different countries. Some of these trips can be just a day trip, like looking for ghost lights. Ghost hunts are generally an overnight trip. Some, like cryptid hunting, can take longer. I will go over what I have found is good to take with you on the journey and things to be aware of when planning a legend trip.

I have not been to all of these mysterious places and looked for all these legends. I have been to a few of them like Loch Ness. This book is my bucket list. But who knows, maybe someday I will get to go to all of them.

Here is a quick list of do and don'ts I want to stress to you before we go over legend trips. It's important safety is your primary concern when you're out there exploring.

On a side note: Situational awareness is being aware of one's surroundings and identifying potential threats and dangerous situations. It is probably the most critical thing about legend tripping. In an ever-changing world, you need to make sure you know everything about the area or country you are visiting. I can't emphasize that enough.

International Legend Tripping Do's and Don'ts	
Do	**Don't**
Make a complete plan for your trip but also have a Plan B.	Treat your trip as if it were a walk in the park.
Make sure your shots are up to date before traveling.	Assume there are stores in the area to buy supplies.
Learn all the traditions, customs and restrictions in the country you are visiting.	Mock the culture and people around you. You are a guest in that country.
Let other family members know where you are going and when you expect to return.	Trespass on private property; it's against the law!
Make a note of your passport number; knowing the number will speed up getting a replacement.	Wear new boots for the trips; you need to break them in before hand.
Bring solar-powered cell phone charger for hiking.	Believe the weather reports • Always assume it will rain, so bring wet-weather gear.
Use traveler's checks or credit cards. Keep your credit card numbers and the phone number to call in case they are lost.	Be in a rush to leave – otherwise, you will forget something important.
Carry water and purification tablets.	Drink untreated water.
Dress appropriately for your surroundings as much as you can.	Go near wild animals.
If you get lost, stay put and do not move.	Walk with a bag slung loosely over one shoulder, a thief on a bike will snatch it.
Set aside at least 24 hours to acclimate to the new altitude and temperature.	Visit dangerous locations, or walk-in isolated or dimly lit areas, especially at night.
Always use the two-person rule and have a friend or group with you.	Eat something if you don't know what it is.
Check to see if any shots are required.	Don't take any over the counter drugs in a foreign country.

LEGEND TRIPPING
ADVENTURE OUTSIDE THE BOX!

Chapter 2

Cryptids: Large Hairy Wildmen

There is a famous story about Alexander the Great. After conquering a region in India, Alexander had ten philosophers, or wise men, in his custody. These philosophers caused some unrest in the Indian nation. Alexander stated if they were indeed wise men, they would be able to answer his questions and avoid execution.

He asked one of the wise men, "What animal is the most cunning animal in the world?"

The wise man answered, "The one that avoids man." This wise philosopher's life was spared.

The word "cryptozoology" is defined as "the search for and study of animals whose existence or survival is disputed or unsubstantiated." There is some controversy over who coined the term. Bernard Heuvelmans is credited with it in his book *On the Track of Unknown Animals*, but he states Ivan T. Sanderson was the first to coin the term.

"Cryptid" is a term derived from Cryptozoology for an animal whose existence has not been verified by science. Some animals are no longer considered cryptids, such as the giant squid, which Japanese researchers confirmed through deep-sea video in 2012. It's funny, but when they are still a legend, they belong to cryptozoology, and when proven to exist, they then belong to zoology and biology.

One of the most popular types of cryptid is the large hairy humanoid. Due to numerous television shows the most famous of these is bigfoot, located in the United States.

Around the world, there are similar reports of giant hairy creatures that walk upright on two feet and display other human characteristics. This chapter is focused on these cryptid giants. These are the bigfoot-type creatures seen in the different parts of the world.

These human-like, bipedal creatures are described as being between six and ten feet tall and covered in hair. The hair color varies with different animals. Some of the people who have reported sightings have described them as a hairy Neanderthal. Believe it or not, bigfoot was not the first furry creature to make the news headlines.

A lot of researchers are asking just what these animals are. Are they a hominoid, which describes all apes, including humans? A hominid, which are all modern and extinct great apes?

Russian scientist Dmitri Bayanov coined the term "homin" to use instead of the words bigfoot, sasquatch, almas, and other unknown, upright, hairy primates. Homin means a "non-sapiens hominid," which is any species of early human.

I've arranged the following list of these creatures (homins) reported around the world, in alphabetical order.

1. Abominable Snowman/Yeti, Nepal
https://www.livescience.com/25072-yeti-abominable-snowman.html

There are three famous cryptid legends in the world. Bigfoot, the Loch Ness monster, and one that made front-page news in 1921. Noted explorer Lieutenant-Colonel Charles Howard-Bury led the British Mount Everest reconnaissance expedition into the Himalayas and discovered something unexpected in the snow.

In his book, LTC Howard-Bury relates that at 21,000 feet (6,400 meters), when crossing the Lhakpa La, his team found footprints which in the soft snow formed double tracks rather like those of a bare-footed man. He stated that he believed the track was made by a large 'loping' grey wolf, but his Sherpa guides were adamant that the metoh-kangmi had made them. Broken down, "metoh" translates to "man-bear" and "kang-mi" translates to "snowman."

The term "Abominable Snowman" was first used by Henry Newman, a longtime contributor to *The Statesman* newspaper in Calcutta. Newman interviewed the porters of the Everest reconnaissance expedition. It should be noted that Newman mistranslated the word "metoh" as "abominable," perhaps using artistic license.

Another term for the creature is "yeti." It was first used in 1951 by Eric Shipton when he took pictures of large human-like footprints on Menlung Glacier. His Indian guides related that a yeti made the tracks. The term is now the preferred name used all over the world for this mysterious cryptid.

It is described as an apelike creature who carries a large stone as a weapon and makes a whistling swoosh sound. It was and still is part of the Buddhist traditions of several Himalayan people. The Lepcha people worship this creature, calling it the "Glacier Being." Followers of the Bön religion believed that the blood of this beast had healing powers and used it in certain mystical ceremonies.

Here is a chronological list of the most famous sightings of the yeti:

In 1832, while in northern Nepal, the Court of Nepal's first British Resident B. H. Hodgson reported that his local guides spotted a tall, bipedal creature covered with long dark hair, which seemed to flee in fear. Even though his guides were terrified of the beast, Hodgson concluded it was an orangutan.

In 1889, Major Laurence Austine Waddell wrote in his book *Among the Himalayas* about large human-like tracks that he found. While crossing a pass toward some glaciers, Waddell and his crew discovered large footprints in the snow that crossed their track and headed up toward the higher peaks. The natives in his team told him these belonged to "hairy wildmen" who they believed lived in the snowy mountains. He did go on to say that he felt that the creatures described were purely mythical.

In 1925, N. A. Tombazi recorded a sighting of a large hairy creature that he and his team saw at about 15,000 feet (4,600 m) near Zemu Glacier. He described that creature as having an outline was exactly like a human being, walking upright and occasionally stopping to pull at some dwarf rhododendron bushes. Tombazi related that he and his team watched the creature from a distance of 200 to 300 yards for a few minutes.

Later, when Tombazi and his team descended the mountain, they found the animal's tracks. He described them as "similar in shape to those of a man, but only six to seven inches long by four inches wide."

Sławomir Rawicz, along with some other Russian POW's made a daring escape to India through Tibet and the Himalayas in the winter of 1940. Rawicz stated that as they came over a hill, they found their path was blocked by two bipedal animals. They waited for hours until the animals finally left the area. Rawicz recorded this incident in his 1956 book *The Long Walk*.

In 1948 two members of the Royal Air Force, Peter Byrne and Roald Smeets, both reported finding a yeti footprint in northern Sikkim near the Zemu Glacier. Both were on holiday from a Royal Air Force assignment in India. The sightings took place at different times. Peter Byrne would later become a world-renowned cryptozoologist, conducting searched for the yeti and bigfoot in the United States.

John Keel related in his book *Jadoo*, that in 1949 a Sherpa herdsman named Lakhpa Tensing was torn apart by a yeti on the bleak pass of Nangpa La, one of the highest passes in the world.

In 1951, The yeti became a topic of worldwide fascination when photos of a footprint appeared in every newspaper. The images were taken by English mountaineer Eric Shipton on the Menlung Glacier on the Nepal-Tibet border during an expedition to Mount Everest. The image drew mountaineers, researchers,

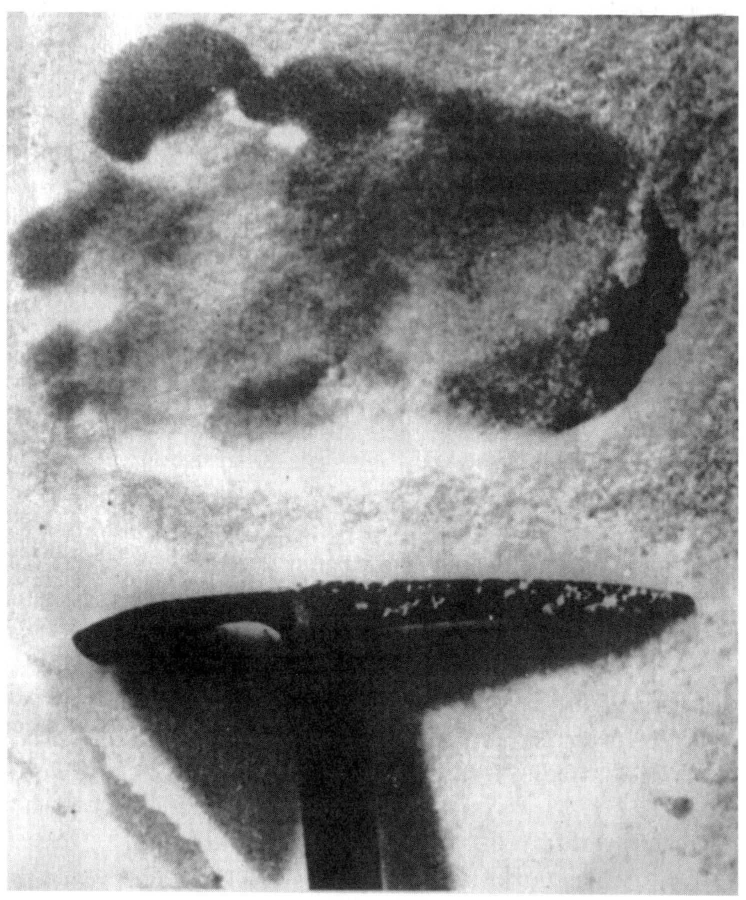

The yeti footprint photographed by Eric Shipton in 1951.

andyyeti enthusiasts to Nepal to attempt to spot the fabled humanoid.

In 1953, Sir Edmund Hillary and Tenzing Norgay, while making their famous assault on Mount Everest, reported seeing large footprints. Hillary later stated that they were probably from a Himalayan brown bear.

In 1954, the mountaineering leader John Angelo Jackson made the first trek from Everest to Kanchenjunga in the course of which he photographed many footprints in the snow. While some were identifiable, some weren't. They were large human-like footprints which could not be identified. Skeptics claimed that these flattened footprint-like indentations were a result of erosion and subsequent widening of the original print by wind and particles.

In 1954 author John Keel detailed his search for the yeti while on assignment in India in his book *Jadoo*. He related that he did see a towering dark figure in the distance; he could not make out if it was a human or something else.

In 1957, wealthy American oilman Tom Slick funded expeditons to investigate yeti reports. He employed Peter Byrne to explore and investigate the sightings. With Byrne, the Slick team collected supposed yeti feces; fecal analysis found a parasite that could not be classified. Cryptozoologist Bernard Heuvelmans wrote, "Since each animal has its parasites, this indicated that the host animal is equally an unknown animal."

Interestingly enough, the expeditions caught the eye of the United States government. Three rules were created for American teams searching for the cryptid: obtain a Nepalese permit; do not harm the yeti except in self-defense; and let the Nepalese government approve any news reporting on the animal's discovery.

In 1986, South Tyrolean mountaineer Reinhold Messner wrote a book, *My Quest for the Yeti*. He said that he had a face-to-face encounter with a yeti, and claimed to have killed one. Messner related the same theory as Sir Edmond Hillary and said that the yeti is the endangered Himalayan brown bear, which can walk both upright and on all fours. Interestingly enough, he states in his book that he heard the animal whistling. There are no bears that are known to whistle.

H. Siiger wrote in his essay featured in the book *Himalayan Anthropology: The Indo-Tibetan Interface* that the legend of the snowman grew because Western visitors sought the help of locals to navigate the terrain. The mountaineers would find unexplained footprints along the way, which could belong to any animal. But the horrified locals would immediately attribute them to the yeti.

In 2013, British scientist Bryan Sykes tested DNA collected from two unidentified specimens from Ladakh and Bhutan and concluded that the animal was related to a polar bear that lived 40,000 to 120,000 years ago in Svalbard, Norway.

Even Europe has reports of large hairy animals roaming the forests. These animals tend to avoid human contact, so sightings are rare. Because these animals live in the woods, their senses are heightened, especially their sense of smell. They usually leave when they smell humans.

2. Almas, Russia
http://www.unknownexplorers.com/almas.php

The almas are known in Mongolia as hairy, bipedal humanoids, as the term alma means "wildman." The plural term almaty is derived from Russian. At the same time, other variations of the name are almasti, almaslar, bnahua, and ochokochi, which translates as the name for a forest deity in the West Asian regions, such as Azerbaijan and Georgia.

They are believed to inhabit the Caucasus and Pamir Mountains of Central Asia and the Altai Mountains of western Mongolia. Sightings of this animal report that they are covered entirely with thick brown to reddish-brown hair and walk upright just like a human. The facial region remains uncovered, but patches of skin are dark.

Unlike the neighboring yeti, they are believed to be more human than ape, but they are just as elusive. Some reports say that it resembles a living caveman. This is not unlike many tales of wildmen in Asia and Eastern Europe.

One of the most famous sightings was in 1420, by world traveler and explorer Hans Schiltberger. He recorded his observation of these creatures in Mongolia in the journal he kept while a prisoner of the Mongol Khan. He described these creatures as hairy, savage humans rather than animals.

A famous story is told of a wild woman named Zana who is said to have lived in 1850, in the isolated mountain village of T'khina fifty miles from Sukhumi in Abkhazia in the Caucasus. Zana was captured and brought back to the village, where she was kept by a farmer named Edgi Genaba. It was reported that Zana had sexual relations with Genaba, and gave birth to several children of apparently normal human appearance. Several of these children, however, died in infancy. Genaba gave away the four surviving babies to other families. Zana died in 1890.

Old print of a Mongolian almas.

Some cryptozoologists have suggested that she may have been an almas, but new DNA evidence indicates that she was a human. In 2015 Bryan Sykes of the University of Oxford reported that he had undertaken DNA tests on saliva samples of six of Zana's living relatives and a tooth of her deceased son

Khwit and concluded that Zana was 100% African but not of any known group, refuting the theory that she was a runaway Ottoman slave.

Another famous story is that in 1941, shortly after the German invasion of the USSR, a detachment from the Russian army captured a "wildman" somewhere in the Caucasus. He appeared human but was covered in fine, dark hair. The soldiers related that their interrogation revealed his apparent inability (or unwillingness) to speak. They later shot the creature as a suspected German spy.

Current sightings of the almas were reported near the southern part of Mongolia, along the Altai Mountains and the Tien Shan pass near the northern border of China.

Theories abound as to the origin of the almas. Some researchers believe they may be a living population of an earlier human ancestor, like the Neanderthals, that may have somehow survived extinction.

The story of the almas opens up an interesting discussion in the bigfoot debate, as some researchers believe sasquatch is actually a species of primitive human, not an ape. So, rather than an ancient Asian ape surviving extinction and populating the world, could it be that an unknown species of humans exists out there undetected?

3. Amomongo, The Philippines
https://www.choosephilippines.com/do/history-and-culture/1983/philippines-bigfoot-amomongo/

This creature is described as hairy, man-sized, and apelike with long nails. The term may have its roots in the Hiligaynon word amó, which means "ape" or "monkey."

Terror gripped residents of haciendas in Barangay Sag-ang, La Castellana, Negros Occidental, Philippines, following the reported existence of a man-sized creature, who attacked two residents and disemboweled animals in the area.

In June 2008, Elias Galvez and Salvador Aguilar reported to Mayor Alberto Nicor and the police that they were separately attacked by a "hairy creature with long nails" one night at Cabungbungan, Aguilar related that he managed to escape from the beast. He was later treated for scratches on different parts of his body, police said. Galvez, on the other hand, who was also attacked by the creature, was rescued by his companions, Nicor told the Daily Star on June 12.

Sag-ang residents described the creature to be about 5 feet 4 inches tall and looking like a monkey. Capt. Rudy Torres confirmed reports of the existence of such a creature, called amomongo (gorilla), by residents. The beast also allegedly victimized chickens and a goat, and ate their intestines, in May 2008. Torres said the creature usually strikes where there are no barangay tanods (village guards or paramilitary elements) around. He called on Barangay residents to be vigilant, especially during night time. People had not been roaming around the barangay at night since the attack against Galvez and Aguilar, Nicor said. Nicor suggested that Barangay residents should put out bait to capture the creature. Barangay Sag-ang is located at the foot of Mt. Kanlaon, which has many caves. The creature could be hiding in one of the caves, Nicor said.

The La Castellana police advised Barangay Sag-ang residents to report to them immediately if the creature is sighted. Inspector Teddy Velez, the town's police chief, said a lot of residents from Barangay Sag-ang reported being attacked by Amomongo around that time.

4. Barmanou, Pakistan
https://1428elm.com/2018/12/09/call-cryptid-barmanou/

This bipedal humanoid primate cryptid inhabits the mountainous region of northern Pakistan and Afghanistan.

Shepherds living in the mountains have reported sightings for centuries.

The barmanou has been seen in the Chitral and Karakoram Ranges, between the Pamirs and the Himalaya. This area is between the ranges of two more-famous cryptids, the almas of Central Asia and the yeti of the Himalayas.

The barmanou is reported to have both human and apelike characteristics. While this creature does look like a bigfoot-type creature, unlike other creatures like this, it has been reported to wear animal skins upon its back and head. There are also stories of this cryptid abducting women and attempting to mate with them.

The barmanou appears in the folklore of the Northern Regions of Pakistan and depending on where the stories come from, and it tends to be either described as an ape or a wild man.

In May 1992, Dr. Anne Mallasseand reported that, during the late evening in Shishi Kuh Valley, Chitral, she heard unusual guttural sounds which she said only an animal with a primitive voicebox could have produced. Dr. Mallasseand was not able to record the audio and never identified what made the sounds.

In 2013, an American soldier reported that he saw with a thermal sensor a heat signature of a gorilla-sized bipedal creature not wearing any clothes. The barmanou has been described as a half-man and half-ape, possibly related to the Neanderthal, that walks upright, makes guttural noises, and emits the odor of rotting garbage.

5. Big Grey Man, Scotland
https://mysteriousuniverse.org/2018/11/the-mysterious-big-grey-man-of-scotland/

Am Fear Liath Moor, or Big Grey Man or The Grey Man of Ben MacDhui is known to stalk climbers on the mountain Ben Macdhui, the second highest peak in Scotland. Because of the high levels of fog there, not many people have seen it.

Legend has it that the Grey Man is the guardian of the mountain, but others believe him to be the guardian of a gate to other dimensions.

This cryptid is reported to be a very tall humanoid, at least 8 feet high. It is covered in short, grey hair, hence the name. Many times the witnesses didn't even see it but still could hear it due to its loud footsteps. Many believe the Grey Man is a relative to sasquatch/bigfoot. It usually stalks its victims until they realize that it is following them, and then it chases them. This is a typical pattern. It stands on two legs and walks (and runs) like an average person.

But more frequently, the Grey Man is encountered in physical sensation, but without an actual physical form. Impressions people have gotten along these lines include vast, dark blurs which obscure the sky, strange crunching noises, echoing footsteps which pursue the listener, an icy feeling in the surrounding atmosphere, as well as a physical sensation of a cold grip on, or brush against, the observer's flesh. There is also a high-pitched humming sound, or the Singing as it is sometimes called, which is associated with Ben MacDhui and the Grey Man.

Additionally, the Grey Man has a potent psychic effect. Visitors to Ben MacDhui report a feeling of overwhelming negative energy. Occasionally this is described as extreme lethargy and despair. More often, it is typified by acute fear, apprehension, and an overwhelming panic, leading to suicidal thoughts or physical flight from the area. Generally, this fear is accompanied by the physical sound of echoing footsteps chasing the observer, and sometimes the tone of a resonant and yet utterly incomprehensible voice which seems to be faintly Gaelic in nature.

6. Chimiset, Africa
https://downthechupacabrahole.com/tag/chimiset/

Known as Chimiset, Chimisit, Chemosit (which mean terms

'devil' in the region's folklore) and Nandi Bear (after a Kenyan tribe), this animal is considered by some to be Africa's bigfoot. However, its description varies from those of sasquatch-like creatures.

Reports of the creature are numerous on the continent, especially in east-central Kenya. It is described as being as large as a man, with long reddish to yellow hair, a short, broad tail, sometimes going on four legs, sometimes on two, and having the general appearance of a vast, very fierce baboon. It is said to be as comfortable in the treetops as it is on the ground, and to attack humans on sight, allegedly being responsible for several killings of men and livestock.

It should be noted that almost every tribe in Africa has a legend of this man-beast, but have different names for it. In Duba (the Swahili and villages along the Tana River), Kerit, Shivuverre (Kakumega country, Kenya), Kikomba (West Africa), Koddoelo (Ngao state, Kenya), Sabrookoo (Kenya/Uganda frontier), Engargiya (Uganda), Gadett (Lumbwa district, Kenya), Ngoloko (Tanzania), Kikambangwe and Ikimizi (Rwanda).

7. Hibagon, Japan

https://mysteriousuniverse.org/2014/12/the-bigfoot-of-japan/

Japan has its own bigfoot and it's called a Hibagon. The crytpid is described as having reddish or black hair, and standing about five feet tall; the head is often reported as being disproportionately large, and shaped somewhat like an inverted triangle. The face is covered in bristles, with a snub nose, and glaring, intelligent eyes. Some reports say that it has white hands and large white feet. Said to resemble a gorilla, like a lot of hairy crytpids, it is reported to be foul smelling.

The Hibagon is reported to make its home in the forests of Mt. Hiba in Northern Hiroshima, from which it takes its name. It also lives in the surrounding wilderness.

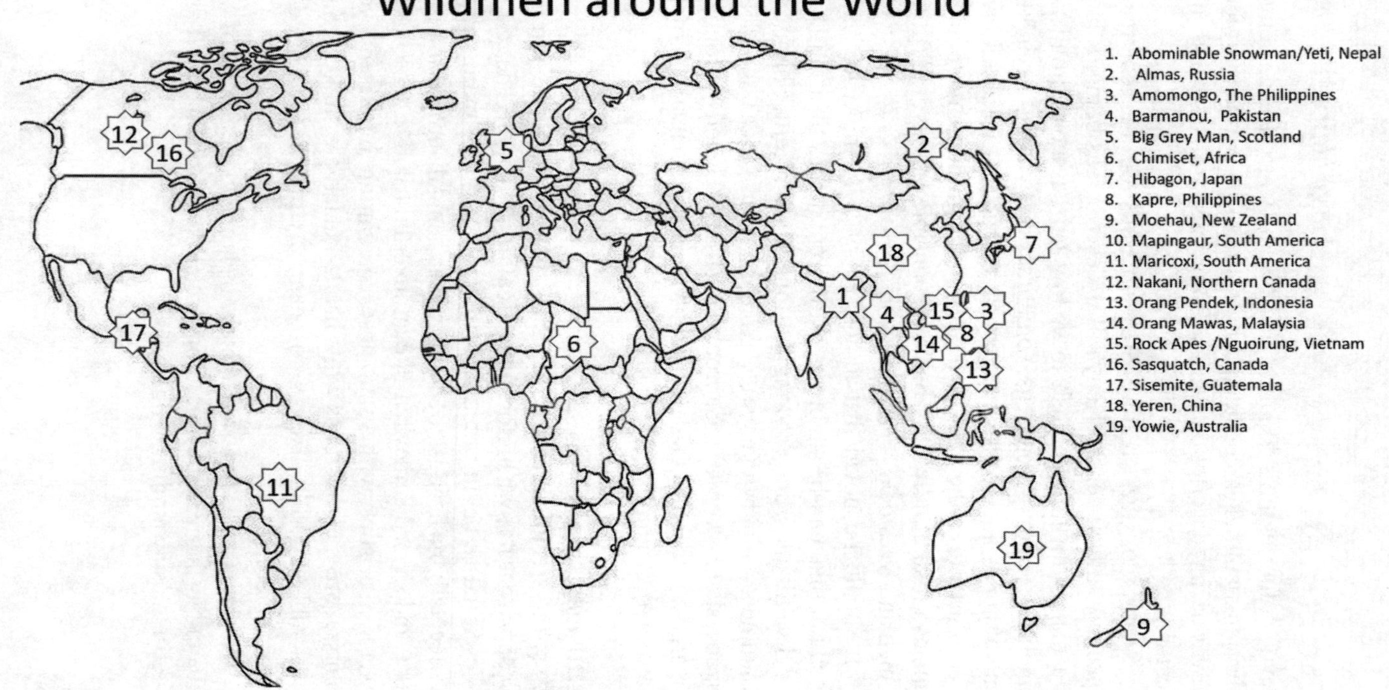
Wildmen around the World
1. Abominable Snowman/Yeti, Nepal
2. Almas, Russia
3. Amomongo, The Philippines
4. Barmanou, Pakistan
5. Big Grey Man, Scotland
6. Chimiset, Africa
7. Hibagon, Japan
8. Kapre, Philippines
9. Moehau, New Zealand
10. Mapingaur, South America
11. Maricoxi, South America
12. Nakani, Northern Canada
13. Orang Pendek, Indonesia
14. Orang Mawas, Malaysia
15. Rock Apes /Nguoirung, Vietnam
16. Sasquatch, Canada
17. Sisemite, Guatemala
18. Yeren, China
19. Yowie, Australia
12
16
5
2
7
18
1
4
15
3
8
14
13
17
6
11
19
9

The first sighting was on July 20, 1970 in the area around Mt. Hiba near the border with Tottori prefecture. A group of elementary school students out picking wild mushrooms were terrified when they saw an apelike creature crashing through brush nearby. Three days after the initial sighting, the furry apelike creature was seen again walking through a rice paddy in the nearby rural town of Saijo. That same year, the Hibagon was spotted again by a utilitys truck driver, who reported seeing a gorilla-like creature on two legs stride across a field near a dam, run across the road, and disappear into the forest. A total of 12 sightings were reported that year, and mysterious footprints were found in the snow that December.

After the wave of sightings in the early 1970s, sightings of the Hibagon dropped off almost completely until 1980, when one was seen fleeing across a river with a bounding gait near the town of Yamano. It was spotted in the same area again in 1981 and 1982. After that, sightings abruptly stopped. There are no reports of the sightings of the Hibagon after this time.

Japan does have a history of nonhuman primate populations. Monkeys are native to Japan. However, so far as I am aware the only large ape who has lived on the islands for any length of time are humans. Scientists feel that since there are no fossil data pointing to populations of these primates in Japan, it is doubtful that one would be living there now.

The Hibagon remains an important and unique part of Saijo and the surrounding area. In addition to selling Hibagon Eggs, a local company features the Hibagon in its logo. Along the highway heading into Shobara (the city Saijo was merged into in 2005) there's even a Hibagon statue to welcome visitors to the area.

8. Kapre, Philippines
http://www.wowparadisephilippines.com/legend-kapre.html

A kapre is a Philippine mythical tree giant or demon. It favors big trees like the balete (banyan), mango, and acacia, and you will sometimes find it sitting under their shady boughs.

The term "kapre" was derived from the Arabic phrase "kaffir," meaning a non-believer in Africans. It is also related to the Spanish term "kapfre." According to historical accounts, the early Moors and Arabs used that term to signify persons who are non-Muslims and who possess a dark complexion. By having contact with the Moors, the term, later on, finds its way into the language of the Philippines via the Spanish in their more than three centuries of colonizing the Philippines.

One account described a tall as (8 to 10 foot) brown hairy male with a beard that was fond of smoking. A strong scent of tobacco is what humans notice when they believe there is a kapre in their presence because it is invisible unless it wants to be seen.

Scores of people from the countryside have reported sightings of a mysterious creature atop a big tree, usually an acacia, bamboo, narra, banyan (known locally as balete), or mango. There have been kapre sightings which locals are now attributing to a bigfoot-type creature.

9. Moehau, New Zealand
https://hauntedauckland.com/site/moehau-new-zealands-bigfoot/

Also called the Maeroero, this large hairy creature prowls the Coromandel Ranges. The name "Moehau" is the Maori name for the highest peak in the mountain range at the tip of the Coromandel Peninsula. This cryptid is reported to be the size of a normal man, with an apelike face, long shaggy hair, and extremely long fingers and sharp fingernails or claws. Reports say this animal is very aggressive and might be responsible for the deaths of prospectors, who were found mauled. In 1882 a woman was abducted from her home and was found with a broken neck.

In 1972 two pig hunters reported that they saw a large creature approximately 150m away from them. They later found huge human-type footprints 35cm long.

In 1983 two trampers reported a group of seven of these primitive people in the vicinity of Lake Waikaremoana. These beings included, said the two men, three juvenile females, and a young male. The humanoid creatures were dressed in animal hides. The witnesses stated that they watched the creatures for several minutes above a gully as the strange creatures moved along the edge of a rocky creek.

In 2001 Rex Gilroy, an Australian yowie expert, travelled to New Zealand and found three fossil hominid footprints in the Karangahake Gorge, enough information to convince him there is indeed something to the Moehau Man stories.

On a remote forest track in the Urewera National Park, on the east coast of the North Island, Gilroy's team uncovered a number of faded tracks in a patch of soil, which led them a few yards away to discover two that were clearly visible and worth casting. These left and right foot impressions measured 29.5cm in length by 13cm in width across the toes, with a 10cm width at mid-foot and 7.5cm width across the heel, making the owner about 5 feet 6 inches (about 1.68m to 1.83m) in height.

10. Mapingaur, South America
https://www.gaia.com/article/does-the-legendary-mapinguari-of-south-america-exist

This hairy beast is one of the most unusual cryptids in the world. I'm not sure it even belongs in the wildman category or is even a primate creature at all. But because it is a large hairy animal, I decided to include it here.

Making its home in the jungles of the Brazilian Amazon and possibly Paraguay, the mapinguari is described as a red-haired, slope-backed man-like creature with massive claws and exceptionally foul-smelling. But what makes this animal stand out from the rest of the cryptid wildmen are two unusual features. There are reports that the beast's feet are facing backward and that its mouth is located on its stomach.

Some cryptozoologists speculate, wading through the folklore, that these animals must be a form of giant ground sloth. Cryptozoologists Bernard Heuvelmans and Ivan T. Sanderson theorized that the animal was some sort of undescribed primate.

The giant ground sloth is believed to have gone extinct long ago, but is it possible there is still a population deep in the jungle? There are more than eighty mapinguari sightings and seven accounts of the beast being killed. This cryptid has featured in many television shows on the unexplained.

11. Maricoxi, South America
https://mysteriousuniverse.org/2019/06/percy-fawcett-and-the-mysterious-man-apes-of-south-america/

Jungles of the Amazon Basin have long been the source of tales of strange creatures and legends. There have been sightings of large, apelike creatures prowling the wilderness. It would make sense, as any bigfoot population in North America undoubtedly could migrate down to South America.

The most well-documented encounters with these mysterious creatures come from famed British explorer Colonel Percival H. Fawcett. Fawcett was known to write extensive journals of his travels. They were later compiled into books by his son Brian Fawcett after the explorer vanished into the jungle during an ill-fated expedition to find a mysterious Lost City of Z.

The journals, published in 1917 titled *Lost Trails, Lost Cities*, and there is an entry about a spectacular tale of Fawcett's encounter with the Maricoxi. In his meticulous notes, he wrote that his expedition was surrounded by hairy man-like beings, one of whom eventually drew a bow and arrow on Fawcett.

The explorer then pulled out his revolver and fired a couple of shots, which sent the large hairy tribesmen retreating behind trees.

Arrows started raining down on them as the expedition made a hasty retreat back into the jungle. Fawcett's expedition did not have any more run-ins with the wildmen.

12. Nakani, Northern Canada
https://www.mysteriesofcanada.com/nwt/nakani-the-wildman-of-the-north/

Nahanni Butte in the Canadian Northwest Territories is the reported home to Nuk-luk, translated from Inuit as "Man of the Bush." This beast differs from the classic sasquatch in that local legend describes it to be much more like a Neanderthal-type creature than an ape, though it is purported to have long hair, a broad and stocky musculature and an odd smell.

The earliest known report of Nuk-luk outside of Inuit culture was in 1964, but local Eskimo stories suggest that the creature(s) have been living in the area of Nahanni Butte for more than 3,000 years.

There is indication in early reports of Nuk-luk that it has adapted a culture of its own, wearing crude boots and using stone tools, but there is very little real information due to the extremely remote locale.

In the 2018 book *Legends of the Nahanni Valley,* author Hammerson Peters details the sightings from the past to present of this largely unknown cryptid.

13. Orang Pendek, Indonesia
https://www.wildsumatra.com/orang-pendek/

The natives of Sumatra have long believed in this cryptid, known as the orangpendek, which means 'little man.' The orang-pendek seems to have a large potbelly and may be dark grey, dark black, yellow, or tan. The animal is described as being bipedal, standing between 3 to 5 feet in height, and having very long hair on its head.

In 1923 a Dutch settler in Sumatra reported that he saw one in a tree. Even though he was armed, the settler related that couldn't bring himself to shoot the stange animal because it resembled a human.

Orangpendek is definitely an example of a bizarre bigfoot-like critter and there may be more similarities than we think.

Could it be a kind of pygmy version of bigfoot, or perhaps a related species that went down some different evolutionary path?

Even more intriguing is the idea that the orang pendek could actually be some kind of human ancestor, perhaps a relic population of the tiny "Hobbit" humans found on the island of Flores. Whatever it is, Sumatran natives see something strange in the jungles, and it appears to be a bipedal ape.

14. Orang Mawas, Malaysia
https://www.independent.co.uk/news/world/asia/the-unknown-world-how-i-tracked-bigfoot-through-the-malaysian-jungle-5335503.html

There is a legend in Malaysian folklore of the orang mawas, which is said to inhabit the jungles of Johor in Malaysia. Also know as the Sakai, it is described it as being an apelike creature about 10 feet tall, bipedal, and covered in reddish-brown or black fur. It has been reported feeding on fish and raiding orchards.

Sightings of it are pretty regular, and go back to 1871! The most famous sighting, however, was in 2005, when three workers supposedly saw a mawas family of two adults and a child on a jalan-jalan (walk about) in Kampung Mawai, Kota Tinggi.

Another famous incident occurred in 2014, when hundreds of massive, strange footprints were discovered all over a tar road in Endau-Rompin.

On the subject of large hairy beasts of Southeast Asia, the famous animal collector Frank Buck tells in his book *Bring 'Em*

Back Alive of acquiring an eight-foot orangutan in Singapore. He relates that the giant ape was first brought to his attention by Ali, his Malaysian guide and partner. Ali said that some farmers were at Singapore harbor trying to sell it and that is was the largest orangutan he had ever seen. "Orang" means Man in Malya, and "Utan" means Forest, thus the Man of the Forest. Frank found the farmers at the harbor. The giant primate from the forest was sitting in a large bamboo cage. The farmers told how they had captured the beast.

This animal had attacked and killed some of the villagers in the area. They found it sleeping at the top of a tree. They then put a tub of water at the base of the tree in the hopes that the forest giant would come down from its nest and drink the water. At first, nothing happened. Then one day, the large primate came down the tree and moved past the tub. The next day it took notice of the tub and started drinking the water. The villagers then started putting in some native alcohol called arak. Each day the orangutan would come down and drink the water, and each time the villagers would increase the amount of arak until finally, it was pretty much all the native alcohol.

At last, the giant primate, after consuming the tub of arak, fell from the tree when it tried to go up, dead drunk and fast asleep. The villagers quickly built a large cage with reinforced bamboo and loaded the man-beast into it. They then loaded the cage onto a cart and moved it to Singapore. Frank saw the man-beast and knew he had to have it. After a few rounds of bargaining, he finally got the farmers to agree on a price.

Later the ape was loaded onto a ship destined for the United States. When out at sea, the primate escaped from its cage. It was caught, but later the animal became sick and soon died. In accordance with the shipping company's policy, the large dead primate was thrown overboard.

The orangutans are three extant species of great apes native to

Indonesia, Borneo, Sumatra, and Malaysia. They are closely related to humans, having 97% of DNA in common. It should be noted that the usual size of an orangutan is six feet at the tallest. This primate was eight feet tall. Was this animal just a freak of nature, or something else?

The people of the region know the difference between this creature and an orangutan.

There have been many sightings of the creature, which the local Orang Asli people call hantu jarang gigi, which translates

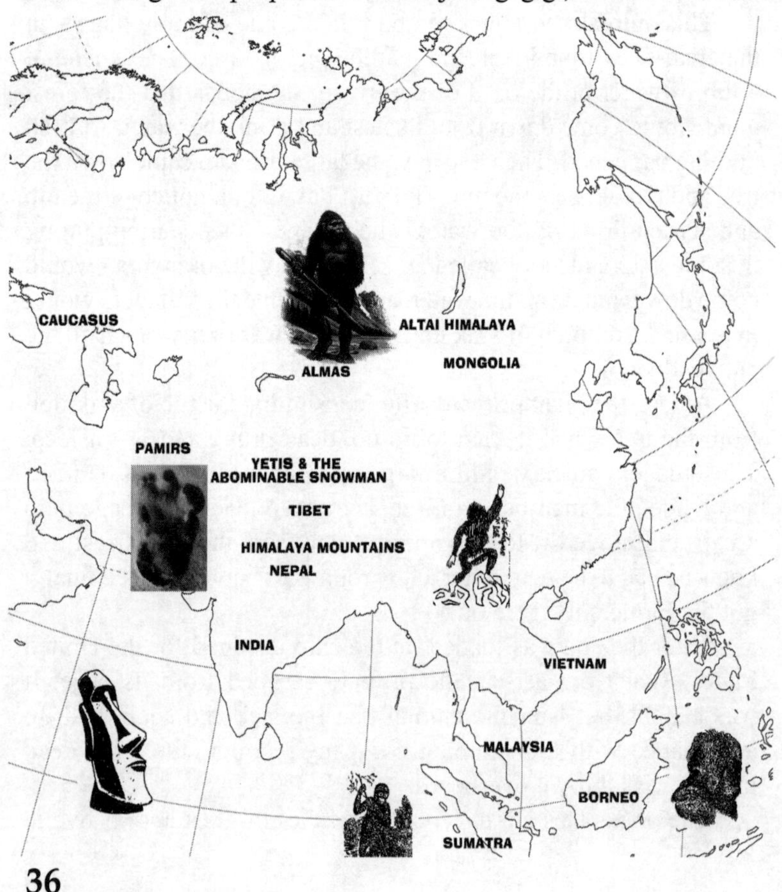

as 'snaggle-toothed ghost.' Recorded sightings date back to 1871, and there is some speculation that the creature may be a surviving Gigantopithecus. Anthropologists believe that the orangutan is the descendant of Gigantopithecus.

Frank Buck journeyed many times into the heart of the Malaysian jungle. I find it hard to believe that he would not have heard of the orang mawas. Unfortunately, with the carcass being thrown overboard, we will never know just what the villagers caught.

This cryptid beast was featured in the first episode of Josh Gate's *Destination Truth*. In the episode, his team was able to find tracks of an unknown bipedal animal.

15. Rock Apes /Nguoirung, Vietnam
https://mysteriousuniverse.org/2016/01/the-mysterious-rock-apes-of-the-vietnam-war/

These animals is also known as the Vietnamese Wildmen, or "Forest People." Their appearance and legends are similar to those of the Wildman of China; they are described as being approximately six feet tall and completely covered with hair except for the knees, the soles of the feet, the hands and the face. The hair ranges in color from gray to brown to black. The creatures walk on two legs and have reportedly been seen both solitary and moving in small clans.

Along the Laotian border, the beast is called khi-trau, meaning "buffalo monkey" or "big monkey."

While "rock apes," or "batututs" as they are called in Vietnam, are nowhere near as well-known as the aforementioned cryptids, sightings of these mysterious creatures by American troops in the jungles of Vietnam throughout the Vietnam War were surprisingly numerous, with many witnesses giving extremely detailed accounts of sightings.

One particular hill in Vietnam was the site of so many rock

ape sightings that it became known as Monkey Mountain. While no corpses of these strange creatures were ever recovered, or any clear pictures taken of them, the fact that sightings of them were so widespread and shared throughout the war makes them worthy at least of an investigation.

Rock apes were so named because of their supposed propensity for throwing rocks—usually in retaliation, though, after rocks were thrown at them first. They were also said to have tossed grenades hurled their way back at the throwers, on occasion.

Described as being solidly built, with long limbs and protruding stomachs, the rock apes or batututs were said to live in troupes, rather than living a solitary existence, and their habitat was confined to remote areas of the jungle, far from human habitation—areas that the Vietnam War opened up.

16. Sasquatch, Canada
https://bc.ctvnews.ca/bigfoot-in-b-c-canadian-writer-shares-sasquatch-stories-1.4547796

Native American stories and legends about this large hairy animal go back for centuries. During the 19th and early 20th centuries, newspapers around Canada featured accounts of hairy wildmen seen by locals, sometimes giving warnings. Its name and presence come from legends told by the Native First Nations of Canada's Pacific Northwest.

J.W. Burns, an Indian agent assigned to the Chehalis Band, now known as the St'ailes First Nation, was the first to write about this cryptid. He researched the Sasq'ets sightings among community members and collected numerous tales for a story in *Maclean's* magazine in 1929.

It should also be noted that Burns was the first to coin the term "sasquatch" in the 1930s. The word is believed to be an Anglicization of the Salish word Sasq'ets, meaning "wild man" or "hairy man." The St'ailes people claim a close bond with Sas'qets and believe that the beast has supernatural powers and can move between the physical and spiritual realms.

Sasquatch sightings go back as far as the 1800s when prospectors and miners journeyed to the Yukon from the Klondike Gold Rush. Some of these men of adventure came back with tales of a significant hairy being living in the mountains. In British Columbia, over 200 sasquatch sightings have been reported in the area of Harrison Hot Springs, Pitt Lake, Whistler and Squamish, Hope, Mission, and on Vancouver Island.

Two well known researchers from Canada, have made a major impact on the studye of these large hairy crytpids. The first one is René Dahinden, who is was perhaps Canada's best-known sasquatch researcher. Dahinden immigrated to Canada from Switzerland in 1953. During his research he collected hundreds of footprint casts and interviewed hundreds of witnesses along the West Coast of North America. Dahinden continued to research the sasquatch all the way up to his death in 2001.

The second one is John Green. The BC-based author and authority on sasquatch compiled a database of over 1,300 sightings in North America between the early 19th century and 1995. Green

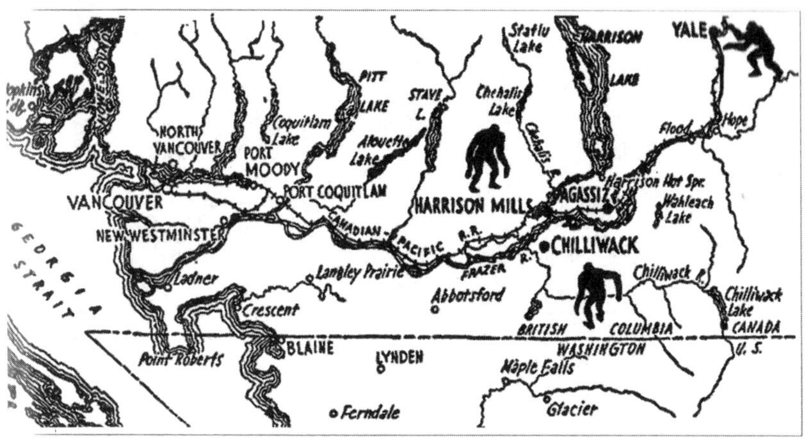

A map of sasquatch sightings from a 1934 Canadian magazine.

related that according to his data and witness accounts, the animal can move extremly fast and is powerful. This crytpid has the ability to overcome extreme obstacles by striding through dense brush, ascending steep banks, and hurdling large objects. Some of the reports said that sasquatch is also able to swim.

Green retired in 1995 but stayed active in cryptzoology conferences. Green passed in 2016.

One of the famous sasquatch sightings was covered in an 1884 article in Victoria's *British Colonist*. The article describes the capture of a juvenile "half man and half beast" near Yale, BC. The strange animal was named "Jacko." It was described as "resembling a human covered in thick, glossy black hair." The creature was found unconscious on a set of railway tracks. Upon awakening the animal attempted to run away but was corraled on a rock shelf. One of the men dropped a rock on its head, knocking it out.

A couple of days later, the newspaper ran a letter to the editor from J.B. Good. In the letter, Good wrote that he had heard stories

A 1990 postage stamp issued by the Canadian government.

of "wildmen of the woods" reported by groups out hunting or fishing. This story was featured prominently in movies and on the 1976 television series *In Search Of.*

Later, author Jerome Clark, through research, revealed the Jacko story might be a hoax. Clark noted that a newspaper, the *Mainland Guardian of New Westminster*, wrote, "Absurity is written on the face of it." John Green also found that several contemporary BC newspapers did not take the alleged capture seriously. Still, it may be a valid story.

Another giant hairy legend from the woods of Canada is the windigo (or wendigo), but Native American legends don't always describe it as an animal; the belief is that the windigo is a creature that transforms from a human after eating human flesh, and has evil intentions.

Many cryptozoolgoist beleive that the stories of the windigo stem from sightings of a real creature like bigfoot. Native Americans, who believe it to be some kind of spirit beast, have expanded on the abilities of the creature.

The Bigfoot Field Research Organization (BFRO) has over three hundred recorded sightings of the sasquatch on their database.

On a side note: The term sasquatch gained popularity when it was featured in the popular 70s television show *The Six Million Dollar Man*.

17. Sisemite, Guatemala
https://www.belizeadventure.ca/get-to-know-belizean-folklore/

Also known as sisimito, this large hairy creature is reported from the Guarunta Mountains of Central America and nearby wild areas in Guatemala. They look like apemen, and are often described as having a gorilla-like body, covered in darkish hair that reaches to the ground. Their screams are loud and piercing. The Chortí Indians have a name for its cry, marikonet, which loosely means, "We'll get you." They prefer hilly or mountainous country with few human inhabitants.

According to the Chorti, these creatures abduct human women. Young girls were always warned not to stay late at the river when washing clothes.

The natives also believe that the sisemite has supernatural powers and is appointed as a kind of guardian of the wilderness. It will attack hunters in order to protect wildlife.

A Mayan carving at the ruin of Xunantunich, Belize, is said to show a sisemite.

The last known sighitng was in 1940 when a man reported to the police that a sisemite abducted his wife.

18. Yeren, China
https://www.thestar.com.my/news/regional/2018/08/26/dreamers-crackpots-or-realists-the-diehards-on-the-trail-of-chinas-bigfoot

This creature lives in the forests of China and is described as something very close to bigfoot in size and appearance. What's interesting is that the yeren hails from the general area of the world where Gigantopithecus, the ancient giant ape, is believed to have gone extinct.

Also called the Chinese Wildman, reports of this creature go back for generations. Again, like the sasquatch in North America and the yowie in Australia, stories often contain a touch of mysticism, making it tough to discern if the yeren is a flesh-and-blood creature or some kind of spiritual being dreamed up by local cultures.

19. Yowie, Australia
https://www.ancient-origins.net/unexplained-phenomena/australian-yowie-mysterious-legends-tribe-hairy-people-003605

From the outback of Australia, the aboriginals have related

tales for centuries of a giant creature that roams the woods and forests of the eastern Australian states. In parts of Queensland, the beast is known as the quinkin; in parts of New South Wales, they are called the ghindaring. Some legends say that the yowie is an apelike hominid. In others, it is more like a primitive human living in the outback.

With legends come questions. So, where did this beast come from? Australia is thought to have been isolated for millions of years. This means whatever factor may have driven the yeti or sasquatch to evolve and migrate across Europe, and North America can't be responsible for the yowie. The top areas for yowie sightings in Australia are the Blue Mountains and Mount Kembla in New South Wales, and the Sunshine Coast, Gold Coast, and Conondale National Park of Queensland.

The first reported sighting was in Sydney in 1790; there were several other sightings reported in the area in the ensuing decade. Later, in the 1870s, accounts of "indigenous apes" appeared in the *Australian Town and Country Journal*.

In November 1876 the journal reported sightings of a strange creature near the Wyangal Dam in mid-western New South Wales. The article went on to say that a young shepherd, out with his dog and sheep, had seen the creature coming down a mountain towards him. He and his dog quickly left. His family did not believe his tale until another sighting took place in the area. It was during a camping trip. A woman was left alone while the others of the group went night fishing. She was preparing a meal on a fire when she saw a sizeable human-like animal with long red hair approach her. The woman immediately started screaming, alerting the others. They quickly arrived to see the strange animal exit back to the rocks.

In 1977, the *Sydney Morning Herald* reported that residents on Oxley Island near Taree had recently heard screaming noises made by an unknown animal at night.

In 1994, Tim the Yowie Man claimed to have seen a yowie in the Brindabella Ranges.

In 1996, while on a driving holiday, a couple from Newcastle claim to have seen a yowie between Braidwood and the coast. They said it was a hairy creature, walking upright, standing at a height of at least 2.1 meters tall, with disproportionately long arms and no neck.

In August 1997, mango farmer Katrina Tucker reported having been just meters away from a hairy humanoid creature on her property in the Northern Territory.

In Nov 1998, Darryl Campbell was driving along the Arnhem Highway on the Adelaide River floodplains at 10 pm when he sighted a yeti-like beast in the bush. He said, "It was like a bloody big gorilla or ape." He went on to relate that the animal was crouched down on the ground and hobbled along, holding grass and other junk in its hands. It stood about the height of a man. He pulled his vehicle over where a group of European tourists had also stopped. They, too, had seen the beast. Campbell and the group of tourists reported the sighting to Transport and Works Department traffic controllers at the Adelaide River bridge.

In August 2000, a Canberra bushwalker described seeing an unknown bipedal beast in the Brindabella Mountains. The bushwalker, Steve Piper, caught the incident on videotape. That film is known as the 'Piper Film.'

In March 2011, a witness came forward claiming that he had filmed the creature and taken photographs of its footprints. The witness reported seeing a large hairy creature in the Blue Mountains at Springwood, west of Sydney, to the New South Wales National Parks and Wildlife Service.

In May 2012, a United States television crew claimed it had recorded audio of a strange unknown animal in a remote region on the NSW-Queensland border.

In June 2013, a Lismore resident and music videographer

claimed to have seen a yowie just north of Bexhill.

In September 2016, video footage emerged of a creature bearing a striking resemblance to the mythical yowie as it makes its way through the woods in Australia. The video, which depicts a dark beast walking through dense forest in New South Wales, was reported in the publication *The Sun*.

In June 2019, the *Daily Mail* reported that a family living in the Currumbin Valley was being terrorized by a yowie. The visits started in November 2017, when the family claimed the first encounter happened one Sunday evening at about 9.30 pm when the mother was sitting on the back deck. She heard loud noises in the bush. She moved to the railing and saw the creature. The animal was walking when the wife bumped something causing the animal to stop. It turned from the waist, looked in the witness's direction, and snorted loudly and quickly twice. The witness then immediately fled inside her home. The creature returned that night and made loud gorilla-like sounds.

INDIANS FEAR THE SASQUATCH HAVE RETURNED

Hairy Giants from the Hills Again Terrorize Chehalis as They Used to Long Ago—Visits Recalled.

HARRISON MILLS, March 2.—The fearsome "Sasquatch" have returned. Indian women in the Chehalis reservation are watching their youngsters closely these days, keeping them indoors at night, terrifying them with stories their old folk used to tell, of hairy giants who come down from the mountains and kidnap naughty children.

Men of the tribe are keeping their rifles handy, watching for unusual movements in the forest, and when their dogs bark at night they leap from bed, run to the window and peer out, expectantly. For the Sasquatch have returned.

There is no longer any doubt about it. Suspicions were aroused some time ago that the dreaded wild men of the Chehalis hills were "on the prowl" again. But there was no proof. And then, one night this week, Frank Dan SAW a Sasquatch! Saw it with his own eyes, clearly. There is no doubt about it now. Ask Frank Dan.

A 1934 article in the Canadian magazine *Macleans*.

Chapter 3

Cryptids: Werewolves and Other Land-based Creatures

With cryptozoology gainilng in popularity, more legends are starting to also gain in popularity. In the headlines are eyewitness accounts of the dogman or werewolf.

I briefly talked about the werewolf/dogman legend in my first book, *Legend Tripping*. Not knowing what group to put this canine cryptid, I gave the dogman/werewolf its own category.

A werewolf, also known as a lycanthrope (from the Greek lykos, "wolf," and anthrōpos, "man"), is a mythological or folkloric human with the ability to shapeshift into a wolf.

If you were a monster kid of the '70s like I was, you got to enjoy the Saturday afternoon Creature Double Feature and watch the old black-and-white monster movies. I loved Universal's *The Wolfman* starring Lon Chaney Jr. Since then, many more werewolf movies followed including the 2010 remake of *The Wolfman* starring Benicio del Toro. These movies have set the mold for what werewolves look like and their and nasty behavior. Marvel Comics in 1972 ran a popular series called "The Werewolf by Night." I was a big fan of that comic book.

The werewolf creatures that witnesses are reporting today are described as a large canine-type creatures walking upright on their hind legs. And like their movie screen counterpart, they too have a nasty temper. Do these terrified witnesses see a bear or maybe a bigfoot-type creature? In the United States, the North American Dogman Project has hundreds of sightings on record of these canine cryptids.

I find it sometimes hard to fathom that there is a wolf-like creature prowling the woods. Is this animal a flesh-and-blood creature that has always been hiding in the woods, or is it something supernatural?

Linda Godfrey's best-selling 2003 book *The Beast of Bray Road* is credited with starting the new interest in the werewolf legend.

There are legends of these creatures fanning back centuries and they have been seen all over the world. Legends of the werewolf have been found predominantly in folklore across Europe for centuries. Still, no one can say with certainty at what point in history legends of this beast originated.

Most researchers believe the werewolf was first mentioned in print in *The Epic of Gilgamesh*. In the story, Gilgamesh jilted a potential lover because she had turned her previous mate into a wolf.

In France, there is a legend that in 1521, Pierre Burgot and Michel Verdun allegedly swore allegiance to the devil and claimed to have an ointment that turned them into wolves. After confessing to brutally murdering several children, they were both burned to death at the stake.

Montague Summers' 1928 book *The Werewolf* states the origin of the werewolf myth traces back a few thousand years. Summers goes on to say that the Greeks adopted the idea of lycanthropy from an ancient Phoenician cult, which originated in 1200 BC and had existed until 539 BC.

Almost every country in the world has its legend of the werewolf. As you will see, this creature is an international historical mystery.

Here are some of the werewolf legends from around the world:.

1. Loup-Garou, France

https://www.werewolves.com/le-loup-garou/

Precisely at what point in time the myth of loup-garou originated is not known, but in 1198 Marie de France wrote "Bisclavret." In it, she relates the story of a hapless baron who, because of this spouse's betrayal, is trapped in wolf form.

In 1214 in France, Gervaise of Tilbury told Emperor Otto IV that the people of Auvergne had all transformed into wolves during the full moon.

In the 16th century, France was in the grip of lycanthropic terror. Over 100 years, a werewolf was suspected of killing more than 30,000 people. France brought the legend of the loup-garou to both Canada and the United States. There are terrifying tales of encounters with this beast in the cajun swamps of Lousiana.

2. Nahual, Mexico

http://mexicounexplained.com/the-nagual/

In Mexico, there is the legend of the nahual or nagual, pronounced na'wal. The belief in a Mexican werewolf or nagualism, varies from region to region. The legend of the nahual did not come about with the Spanish colonization of Mexico. Stories of man-beasts go back at least 2,000 years to the were-jaguars of the Olmecs.

According to some Mesoamerican Indian legends, the nahual is a guardian spirit that resides in an animal, such as deer, jaguar, eagle, or mountain lion. In other regions of Mexico, it takes on a more supernatural version. Legend has it that witch doctors and magicians are shapeshifters and transform themselves into an animal to cause harm.

Conceptualizations of the nahual vary from place to place, and have also changed over time. Today with the recent surge in werewolf sightings in the United States, the Mexican nagual has generated interest from cryptozoologists.

3. Luison, South America
https://www.smithsonianmag.com/smart-news/argentina-has-superstition-7th-sons-will-turn-werewolves-180953746/

The Guarani indigenous people of Paraguay believe that there are seven monsters. One of these is known as luison. It was originally described as a horrendously deformed monster, with no features of a wolf, and was known as the God of death and night.

During the European colonization of South America, the lusion myth eventually mixed with European werewolf legends. Today, these creatures are said to be half man and half wolf.

The legend of the luison is known mainly in parts of Argentina, Brazil, Paraguay, and Uruguay. People of these countries firmly believe that the seventh son of a family of all boys can turn into a luison during a full moon night. So strong was this belief that in Argentina, President Juan Domingo Perón, made it law that all seventh sons of a family be baptized.

4. Faoladh, Ireland
https://earthandstarryheaven.com/2015/05/13/irish-werewolves/

There is a large werewolf that lurks on the Emerald Isle. But unlike most werewolf legends where the beast leaves a long trail of dead bodies, some of the legends about this one depict the cryptid as a guardian spirit who protected children, wounded men, and the lost.

In Ireland, there is a 12th-century folktale called "The Werewolves of Ossory." The story is about a priest who is traveling from Ulster to Meath, accompanied by a boy. One night in the woods, they saw a wolf approaching. The priest became terrified. He couldn't believe what he was seeing and hearing. As it came nearer to them, the creature began speaking of God. The terrified priest asked the wolf what kind of creature he was that had the shape of a wolf but was able to speak like a man. The canine creature told the priest that he was a native Ossory. A saint named Natalis had cursed all the natives for some ancient sin. This curse compelled a man and a woman, to be chosen at random, to take the wolf form. They would remain in that canine form for seven years. Afterward, two new people would take their place, and the prior two would return to human form.

There was only one other wolf creature like him, and it was his wife, and she was very sick and dying. He needed the priest's help in his wife's absolution—after all, they were just ordinary human beings under the wolf skin. The priest reluctantly followed the wolf.

The priest hesitated upon seeing the ailing wolf. Seeing his discomfort, the creature assured him he wouldn't commit blasphemy by giving the dying wolf viaticum (final communion). The male wolf peeled the skin of his ailing wife from the head down to the stomach. Underneath the wolfskin was a weak old woman. The priest gave her viaticum. After the priest finished, the male wolf rolled the wolfskin back over her body, and the woman returned to wolf form. This story is a documented incident rather than a mere myth.

In May 2016, the *Irish Mirror* reported that residents of Hull, England had reported several sightings of a mystery "werewolf," which had terrified locals. Reports related that the 8 foot "beast," half-man half-creature, was lurking around industrial estates, and had allegedly been spotted eating a dog. The locals believed that the legendary Old Stinker was the culprit and sparked a hunt for the creature.

Since the 18th century, legend has it that a werewolf creature called Old Stinker prowls the Yorkshire Wolds near Hull. Around Christmas a few years back, there was a sighting of the beast at an old water channel called the Barmston Drain.

A terrified woman reported that she witnessed a canine creature standing on its hind legs. The whole incident left her shaking.

5. Ratman, England
https://cryptidz.fandom.com/wiki/Ratman_of_Southend

In the town of Southend-on-Sea, Essex, there is the legend of the Ratman of Southend. The legend says that on certain nights, a rat-like creature appears in the pedestrian underpasses.

The origin story of this legend tells that one night, a group of teenagers beat an older man who was using the underpass to escape from the rain. They beat him half to death and stole his blanket, his only real source of warmth for the cold night. The teenagers left him there, dying from his injuries. He finally succumbed to hypothermia. Then numerous rats, the vermin that inhabit the area, nibbled and gnawed on his stiffening corpse.

Soon after, the townfolk reported hearing high-pitched squealing and the sound of nails dragging along the walls. Whether or not this was evidence of a real ghost or cryptid creature prowling the night, this story and the weird noises led to locals dubbing the beast the Ratman of Southend.

Another version of this story tells of a town mayor who got a local woman pregnant. Legend has it that the church cursed the unborn child.

Nine months later, a grotesque child was born. Described

as having an elongated snout and worm-like tail, the rat child grew and developed a taste for flesh. Then the mayor constructed the underpass with a concealed entrance to a chamber to hide his monstrous offspring. Only at night, the Ratman emerges to indulge its hunger.

There is a similar story in the United States of the Jersey Devil, another cursed child who escaped to the New Jersey Pines Barrens.

6. Bat Beast, England
https://www.cryptopia.us/site/2010/03/bat-beast-of-kent-england/

On the evening of November 16, 1963, on Sandling Road in the county of Kent, two witnesses, 17-year-old John Flaxton and 18-year-old Mervyn Hutchinson, reported the sighing of a strange extraterrestrial being.

Walking home from a party with several other friends, the two witnesses noticed what appeared to be a large, glowing orb hovering high in the air. Described by the witnesses as being a few meters in diameter, the self-illuminated ovoid object hoveredabove a field. They watched as it descended behind the trees and settled into the foliage of the woods at Sandling Park.

Moments after the craft landed behind the trees, the teens noticed a shaking in the brush, and a strange creature emerged.

The boys stated that the animal was approximately 5 feet tall, with large webbed feet, and wings protruding from its back—but it was headless. In Hutchinson's own words: "It didn't seem to have any head. There were huge bat wings on its back." As a side note, this matches the description of the Mothman creature seen in Point Pleasant, WV, in 1967. Like the Mothman in West Virginia, the Bat Beast has seemed to vanish with time.

7. Owlman, England

https://www.spookyisles.com/cornish-owlman/

In England, there are reports of a large flying cryptid, resembling an owl, stalking, and terrifying a rural Cornwall village churchyard and woods after dark. Known as the Owlman, sightings of this flying cryptid go back as far as 1976, and it has been seen as recently as 2011. The creature is described as being a 6 foot tall hybrid human with grey/dark brown feathers and large eyes that glow a fiery red. It has a wingspan of about 10 feet and has clawed feet. Witnesses relate that it makes a loud hissing and screeching cry.

The first sighting of the Owlman took place on April 17, 1976. Two young children, June and Vicky Melling, observed the cryptid hovering over the tower of Mawnan Old Church.

The children immediately told their parents what they saw, and the police were summoned. Each child, separated from the other, was asked to draw what they saw. Both drawings depicted an owl-like being with clawed feet.

It was seen again at the same place on July 3, 1976, by two other girls. Sally Chapman and Barbara Perry were camping near the church when they saw large being in a tree, standing on a branch. They later described a "a big owl with pointed ears, as big as a man" with glowing eyes and black, pincer-like claws." The girls thought it was a person in a costume until the creature leaped into the air and flew away into the night.

Incidents have continued, with the cryptid being seen near the old church, and strange red lights being spotted above the church. According to local legend, a "loud, owl-like sound" could be heard at

A drawing of the Cornish Owlman.

night at Mawnan church during the year 2000.

On August 3, 2019, ghosthunter Mark Davies claimed to have caught the infamous character on camera. While conducting a ghost hunt in the spooky graveyard next to the church, Davies was prowling with his camera. He was holding his 'spiritual detector' and panning the camera around when a large ghostly figure appeared in the corner of the frame.

When he went to investigate, the apparition had vanished and he could find no more trace of the Owlman. Today researchers continue to investigate around Mawnan church. Some conduct ghost hunts while others continue to look for the giant flying cryptid.

8. Aswang, the Philippines
https://mythology.net/monsters/aswang/

According to legend, the aswang is a flesh-eating, shapeshifting monster, a demented cross between a werewolf and a vampire. During the daytime, it appears as regular person, usually a woman. Legend has it that during the nighttime, this cryptid will shift into eerie predatory forms and go hunting for human prey, preferring children and pregnant women above all else. aswang comes from the Sanskrit word asura, meaning "demon."

In addition to shapeshifting, aswangs also can transform the appearance of other objects. It's common for an aswang to convert plant material into a doppelganger of one of its victims, to hide the evidence of its feeding habits from locals.

9. Mapinguari, Brazil
https://cryptidarchives.fandom.com/wiki/Mapinguari

Whether you go east or west (as long as you go just a wee bit north) from Australia, you'll end up in the Brazilian home of the mapinguari, a sloth-like humanoid that rivals the Florida skunk ape for the smelliest bipedal beast.

Some reports say the mapinguari has a large mouth in the middle of its stomach. So either there's a really weird critter roaming the Amazon, or somebody licked one too many psychedelic toads.

10. Hellhounds

These ferocious black canines with glowing eyes have been the stuff of legend for centuries. Legend has it that if someone stares into a hellhound's eyes three times or more, that person will surely die.

As a youth growing up in England, I heard stories of these terrifying beasts that come in the night and kill helpless victims. In Great Britain, you will find numerous books on the subject.

I wasn't sure if this beast is a cryptid or a paranormal entity, which would put it in the ghost category. According to legend, this paranormal beast is a monstrous dog, leashed to the spiritual world. In some parts of the globe, legend has it that they were created by ancient demons to serve as heralds of death and are called "Bearers of Death." In different parts of Europe, the Hellhound guards the entryways to the afterlife and.

The Hellhound is mentioned first in Walter Map's 1190 book *De Nugis Curianium* and the Welsh myth cycle of the Four Branches of the Mabinogi.

There are three separate species of these beasts. There is the shapeshifting demon hound; the large shaggy black dog; and the black canine that appears only at certain times in specific locales.

In 1577, reports were made of a massive demonic dog that had killed multiple people of East Anglia, England. The beast was said to be 7 feet tall, with glowing red eyes; it is known as the Black Shuck.

In Yorkshire, England, it is called barguest and is said to prey on lone travelers in the city of York's narrow back alleys. The barguest is a shapeshifter.

In the highlands of Scotland, there is a belief in the cu-sith or green 'fairy dogs.'

In 2013, at Leiston Abbey archaeologists, working in ruins excavated the skeleton of a huge dog that would have stood at least seven feet tall and weighed around 200 lbs. Buried in a shallow grave in the Abbey, scientists and historians think it would have been placed there around the same time as the most famous Black Shuck story seems to have occurred.

Primarily a British phenomenon, legends about hellhounds or phantom black dogs, have been reported all over the globe.

In Guatemala, legend has it that a big black dog called El Cadejo terrorizes travelers who walk late at night on rural roads.

In China, a giant black demon-dog named tiangou is blamed for causing eclipses by eating the sun or the moon.

In Japan, a wolflike demon, called okuri-inu, is said to follow men and women who travel by night. If the traveler has a pure heart, the okuri-inu will protect him from other monsters. If, however, the traveler is evil, then the hound will devour him.

Witnesses have related stories of seeing these nightmare beasts in graveyards and cemeteries at night. The hellhound has been seen numerous times throughout history, in different places around the globe. The most recent sightings occurred in the United States and Germany, all adjacent to cemeteries.

Dinosaur Cryptids

Sir Arthur Conan Doyle, the creator of Sherlock Holmes, published a 1912 novel called *The Lost World*, set in the remote Venezuelan jungle where dinosaurs still survive in modern times. Doyle thrilled readers with Professor George Challenger, as he and his team braved the land of dinosaurs. Dino-revival films and books such as *Jurassic Park* were inspired by Doyle's idea of dinosaurs still roaming our planet.

Scientists have ruled out that there are any dinosaurs alive today, but remember this: There are regions in central Africa, specifically the Likouala Swamp, an area which covers about 49,000 square miles, that remain 80% unexplored. Reports of dinosaurs continue to pour out from these locations. Some witnesses have claimed to have seen them in the last century. Could there be descendants of these giant lizards still hiding in small pockets of uninhabited jungles around the world?

I debated where to put the subject of living dinosaurs—in this chapter or the chapter 5 aquatic cryptids. Since some of these creatures are seen on land and in rivers, I listed them in this chapter.

11. Kongamato, Zambia, Central Africa
https://www.genesispark.com/exhibits/evidence/cryptozoological/pterosaurs/kongamato/

Deep in the bush of east-central Africa lives a beaked, flying creature said to resemble a pterodactyl. In the 1932 book *In Witchbound Africa*, Frank Welland describes a large, reddish creature with leathery wings, devoid of feathers, called a kongamato. It means "overwhelmer of boats" in the language of the Kaonde people of the North-Western Province.

In 1932, world-renowned cryptozoologist Ivan T. Sanderson organized an expedition to find evidence of the kongamato in Cameroon.

Sanderson later recorded his experience with the flying cryptid. He wrote that he and others had made camp near a river. That night, Sanderson saw a giant, fruit-eating bat in the trees. He shot it with his rifle, and the bat fell into the river. Sanderson waded out to get it. Due to the darkness, he lost his balance on a rock and fell. Just as he stood back up, his companion, George, yelled: "Look out!" Sanderson looked up to see a black thing the size of an eagle coming at him. He said that he could see the head with sharp teeth. Sanderson quickly submerged as the animal flew by. He then promptly made it to the bank where his companion was standing, ready with the rifle. They both heard a hissing noise, and they looked up in the night sky and again saw the flying beast coming toward them. They both dropped to the sand as it flew by. They then watched as it soared into the darkness of the night.

When Sanderson and George made it back to their camp, they asked their native guides about the animal. They said it was "Olitiau" and immediately fled, leaving Sanderson and his friend to make it back by themselves.

In 1958, journalist Maurice Burton wrote in the *Illustrated London News* that there had been several reports of a pterodactyl-

A kongamato attacks a boat in this drawing by Tim Bertelink.

like creature in Africa. He goes on to say that the Bangweulu Swamps might be one of its habitats.

Dr. J.L.B. Smith wrote about these flying cryptids in his 1956 book *Old Fourlegs*. He wrote, "A man had seen such a creature in flight close by at night near Mount Kilimanjaro, Tanzania. I did not and do not dispute at least the possibility that some such creature may still exist."

On April 2, 1957, J.P.F. Brown reported seeing two of these creatures near Lake Bangweulu, Zambia. Brown had stopped at a location called Fort Rosebery while driving back to Salisbury from Zaire. It was about 6:00 p.m. when he got out of his vehicle to retrieve his canteen from the trunk. Looking up, Brown saw the two creatures flying slowly and silently directly overhead. He related that these prehistoric-looking creatures had long tails, with narrow heads and a 3-½ foot wingspan.

The Awemba tribe claim that these flying creatures make their home in caves in cliffs near the great Zambezi River.

As recently as 2010, the Genesis Park staff mounted an exploratory trip deep into the Bangweulu Swamps in search of the creature. They interviewed Zambian fishermen and conducted all-night stakeouts. Unfortunately, they found no evidence of the kongamato.

12. Kasai Rex, Angola, Central Africa
https://cryptidz.fandom.com/wiki/Kasai_Rex

On February 16, 1932, J.C. Johanson, a Swedish rubber,plantation overseer, observed a colossal creature in central Africa. Hunting in the Kasai Valley (now the border of Angola and the Democratic Republic of Congo), he and his bearer encountered this monster. Johanson described it as sixteen yards long and said it was devouring a rhinoceros when the two men came upon it. Johanson is supposed to have taken pictures of the creature. The animal fled back into the swamps upon hearing the camera's clicking sound.

The photo shows a Komodo dragon superimposed onto the picture of a dead hippopotamus. If this is the real photo that Johanson took or one the press released on the wire is unknown.

The creature Johanson and the bearer saw is referred to as Kasai rex by researchers, who believe it is likely a surviving species of a theropod dinosaur, such as a Tyrannosaurus rex. Logical speculation by zoologists is that it a species of enormous monitor lizard or a terrestrial crocodile.

The local natives refer to the creature as a chipekwe. It is a Bemba term used to refer to any dangerous animal. The closest English equivalent would be "monster."

13. Mokele-Mbembe, Congo River Basin, Africa
https://www.genesispark.com/exhibits/evidence/cryptozoological/apatosaurs/mokele-mbembe/

For over two hundred years, there have been reports of a strange creature lurking in the remote Congo River basin of Africa. The region is the reputed home of the mokele-mbembe, an amphibious dinosaur-like creature said to be up to 35 feet long, with brownish-gray skin and a long, flexible neck. Central Africa is unique in that it is the only place where many people believe dinosaurs may still exist. Natives from the Congo believe that the cryptid lives in caves that it digs in riverbanks. The local natives say that it feeds on elephants, hippos, and crocodiles.

Captain Freiherr von Stein zu Lausnitz was the first to describe the animal when he was sent to explore Cameroon in 1913 by the German government.

In 1920, a 32-man expedition from the United States found large, unexplainable tracks on the bank of a river. The team recorded that roars were heard that bore no resemblance to any known animal. Tragically the four-member team was killed when their train derailed.

Famed Cryptozoologist Ivan T. Sanderson headed an expedition into the Congo in 1932 to look for the kongamato. He and his team found hippo-like tracks along the banks of the Congo River. His native guides told him that mokele-mbembe made the tracks. Sanderson wrote that he saw something swimming that was too large to be a hippo, but the creature disappeared before he could determine what, exactly, it was.

In 1992 a Japanese film crew flew in and recorded aerial footage of something large swimming in a lake. Some researchers call it the "best evidence" for mokele-mbembe, while for others, the jury is still out. Some investigators see the head of a living dinosaur, while others see a crocodile, elephant, or even men in a canoe.

I recall seeing a segment on mokele-mbembe on the 1980s American television show *That's Incredible*. The segment showed supposed actual film footage of the cryptid. I have looked all over the Internet for this rare piece of film, but to no avail.

14. The Gbahali, Libera, Africa
https://cryptidz.fandom.com/wiki/Gbahali

In Liberia, there is a little known but large creature that resembles a Rauisuchian Postosuchu. There is not a lot known in the western world about this cryptid. Reports describe it as 30 feet long, with a snout shorter than a croc's, and somewhat longer legs. Although Postosuchus supposedly died out over 200 million years ago, Liberian hunters do not consider it a legend, but a real creature they have caught and eaten. A picture of the extinct animal Postosuchus was shown to witnesses by researchers, and the locals said it was the gbahali.

In 2017 this little-known cryptid was featured on television. The *Animal Planet* television episode "Expedition Mungo" did a segment on the gbahali. The investigation included eyewitnesses and the location of this creature. In the end, the researchers concluded that it is an enormous crocodile.

15. Ninki-Nanka, Gambia, Africa

https://allaboutdragons.com/dragons/Ninki_Nanka

In West Africa, legend has it that a dragon-like creature makes its home in the Gambia River. Natives call the animal ninki-nanka and describe it as being up to fifty feet long, with the body of a crocodile, a long neck, the head of a horse, and horns. The natives warn that the animal is enormous and dangerous. Tales of the ninki-nanka eating children that wander away from the village have spread from tribe to tribe in Africa.

In 2006, researchers from the Centre for Fortean Zoology (CFZ) journeyed from England to the Gambia to find proof of the beast. For two weeks, they interviewed witnesses who had claimed to see it. While the expedition received a lot of press, they failed to find evidence of the ninki-nanka. There is no physical or photographic proof of this cryptid, only eyewitnesses.

16. Bunyip, Australia

https://cryptidz.fandom.com/wiki/Bunyip

According to legend, there is a large creature lurking in swamps, billabongs, creeks, riverbeds, and waterholes in the land down under. It is called the bunyip, which means devil or evil spirit, from the Wemba-Wemba/Wergaia language in the Victoria region. Different Aboriginal groups across Australia have their own stories of this beast.

With this cryptid, witnesses can't seem to make up their mind what it looks like and seem to have trouble describing it. Some describe it as looking like an enormous starfish, and others claim it looks like a snake with a beard. Some even describe it as having a dog-like face, a crocodile-like head, dark fur, a horse-like tail, flippers, walrus-like tusks, and a duck-like bill.

The Aborigines coined the name bunyip and related stories of the cryptid to the white settlers. Then during the 1840s and 1850s, a large number of bunyip sightings by settlers were recorded, especially in Victoria, New South Wales, and South Australia.

The first written account of the bunyip was in July 1845 when fossils found near Geelong were said by an Aboriginal man to be from a bunyip.

To date, no expeditions have researched this cryptid. With an inaccurate and changing description, some researchers don't know what this animal is. In contrast, some researchers believe that it is a species of megafauna that lived about 50,000 to 12,000 years ago. The Aborigines believe the animal is real and that they are still prowling the swamps and tributaries of New South Wales.

17. Fairies or Little People
https://www.celtic-weddingrings.com/fairy-stories/are-fairies-real

Everyone has heard tales of these magical little creatures, and most people today don't believe that they exist, hence the term "fairy tales," which refers to any story that not only is not true but could not possibly be true. Believe it or not, some witnesses will swear that they have seen these strange little creatures with their own eyes. In this section, when I refer to fairies, I will be exploring the legends of all little people.

Throughout the world, from nearly every culture, there are tales of little people. Ireland and Germany have a long history of sightings of elves, pixies, and trolls. There are stories of fairies and little people in America, but Native Americans tell stories of them as nature spirits and guardians. There are also legends of gnomes making their home in the Catskill mountains.

The Native Americans tell stories of encounters with the little people. They speak of how the little people helped children or taught shamans how to heal.

The belief in fairies is worldwide. The term 'fairy' comes from the word 'fay,' which in turn derives from the old French word 'feie.' This word came from the Latin word for Fates 'fata.' The Fates were supernatural beings that played a significant role in the fortunes of humans.

In the 14th century, writers wrote that these tiny beings were capable of enchantment and illusion. They either lived underground or in prehistoric cairns, forts, and earth mounds. As a result, features such as fairy hill, fairy mounds, and fairy forts received their names.

The exact origin of fairies varies according to culture, with different countries each having their unique tales. Although they are commonly associated with the United Kingdom and Ireland, countries around the world have their version of these magical creatures. In Great Britain, there are several fairy legends. In Ireland, legend has it that these little creatures are spirits of the dead who returned to provide warnings and wisdom. In Wales, they are called the Tylwyth Teg, and these 'ancestor' spirits were over 6 feet tall. Not a very little person. In Cornwall, they are shapeshifters, but they become smaller with every transformation. In Scotland, at the Isle of Skye, the belief in the existence of fairies (also locally

spelled faeries), or "the little people," goes back to prehistoric times.

Most people believe that fairies are tiny winged creatures like Tinkerbell. But, there is a large variety of fairies, both good and bad. Here is a list of the better-known fairy types from all over Europe.

Goblins: This type of fairy is ugly, bad-tempered, and tends to live in dark places. There have been goblin sightings caught on camera. Some resemble the goblins from the Harry Potter series. Are these alien creatures? Some cryptozoologists think so.

Hobgoblins: Part of the brownie tribe, these little creatures live on farms, and because they love the warmth of the hearth, they may enter the home to get near one. They can become a nuisance, if that situation arises, but they are generally good-natured.

Brownies: These little creatures like to attach themselves to a house. They live in a dark corner of the home. They can also live in a hollow tree near the home. Brownies are helpful and keep things tidy. You are supposed to leave out a bowl of cream as a reward.

Pixies: This fairy is associated with England's West Country region and is known as the Piskie in Cornwall. Even today, people in these regions almost universally believe in Pixies/Piskies. You will find 'pisky pows' on the roofs on some of the homes, to ensure these fairies have a dancefloor of sorts. These mischievous creatures are capable of doing good or harm to humans.

Elves: When most people think of elves, they conjure up images of these magical creatures that work for Santa Claus at the North Pole. Elves have been a popular subject in fiction for centuries, ranging from William Shakespeare's play *A Midsummer Night's Dream* to the classic fantasy novels of J.R.R. Tolkien 300 years later.

In Scotland, these little creatures are called trolls. In Norway, they believe that there are Dark Elves and Light Elves.

Over in Iceland, 55% of people surveyed in 1970 believed that elves existed, or there was at least a strong possibility of their existence.

Dwarves: This particular fairy is associated with Icelandic and Indian lore; dwarves typically lived within the earth and mined it for precious stones and metals. The magical rocks they unearthed gave them wisdom and the ability to become invisible.

In 1920, there was an odd twist to the fairy legend, when five strange photographs appeared in *Strand* magazine. The pictures, accompanied by an article by Sir Artuor Conan Doyle, the famous author of the Sherlock Holmes stories, show a young girl with tiny fairy-like beings flying around her. Some readers accepted the images as genuine, while others believed that they were fakes.

The photographs were taken in 1917 by Elsie Wright (1901–1988) and Frances Griffiths (1907–1986). The girls were living in Cottingley, England, at the time. The young girls claimed they saw

One of the Cottingley fairy photos.

the little people by a stream, which their family did not believe. Elsie borrowed her father's camera, went back to the small narrow river, and took five photographs. Her father dismissed the figures as cardboard cutouts, while her mother Polly believed they were genuine. The two girls insisted that they were real.

After years of controversy over the photographs, in 1980 Elsie and Frances admitted that the pictures were fakes, made using cardboard cutouts of fairies copied from a popular children's book of the time. Frances, however, has maintained that the fifth and final photograph was genuine.

One of the Cottingley fairy photos.

Chapter 4

Monster Hunt: Land-Based Cryptids

One of the things I enjoy the most is going out camping and looking for legends. I will camp at the location of a cryptid sighting. I also like to camp in areas that have paranormal activity.

I get asked, "What it's like to go hunting for monsters?" I compare it to a roller coaster ride. It is both scary and exciting at the same time. It is also one of the most accessible and most popular legend trips to do. Today more people all over the world are forming groups and researching legends. In this chapter, I will refer land-based cryptid legend trips as monster hunts. Also, in this chapter I will refer to large hairy bipedal cryptids as bigfoot-type creatures.

In my first book, I related my first legend trip/monster hunt that I organized on my own. I was in high school, and after reading *Creatures of the Outer Edge* by Loren Coleman and Jerome Clarke, I wanted to go check out some of the legends near me. I talked two friends, Rob and Phil, into going with me on a road trip to check out the legend in Louisiana, Missouri. I had read about some sightings of a bigfoot-like creature called Momo prowling along the banks of the Mississippi River. On a side note, Louisiana is about twenty-five miles from Hannibal, the birthplace of Mark Twain.

It turned into an overnight trip, and because we didn't properly prepare ourselves for our excursion, we ended up sleeping in the car. Long story short, the townfolk were not too cooperative.

Most of the residents didn't believe in bigfoot. We talked to some local teenagers, and they were kind enough to show us where the sighting occurred. We walked around the river banks that night, hoping to see it. Unfortunately, we didn't see Momo or anything weird or strange. We did have a good time and enjoyed the freedom of going out on our own and going on a real adventure.

As for my first monster hunt, I want to point out that I did things wrong on this adventure. First and most important, I didn't plan out my trip; it was spur of the moment thing. With night coming on, I realized that we did not have any camping equipment. We weren't prepared to spend the night. It ended up costing more money than I anticipated.

Second, I didn't realize investigating cryptid sightings was not going to be easy, and a lot of people did not believe in these legends. As the expression goes, "Lesson learned!"

Don't do a monster hunt or any other legend trip on a whim. Research and preparation will make a successful monster hunt. There is nothing worse than going to the woods and seeing something weird and forgetting your camera. You'll find as you go out on any kind of trip that when you forget something, your adventure comes to an abrupt halt.

Now there are some cryptids that you're not going to be able to research. Some countries will not allow foreign visitors to conduct research. Some countries are going through political unrest, and it's dangerous for international visitors. Research the country you plan on going to and make sure you're allowed to conduct research there.

An example, in Africa, you have to be approved by the state government to conduct any research. You have different permits for each country in Africa. Not mention that some governments are unstable, and tribal warlords rule some areas. The governments of China and Russia will not allow you to research at all. They have denied a lot of television shows access to film in these countries.

Serving in the military, I learned that you need to have everything planned out before going out. I lay out all the equipment and check and make sure all my electronic devices work. I usually keep most of my gear in a footlocker, so I have everything needed kept centrally located, so I don't have to run around looking for everything. I've compiled a quick list of equipment you'll need at the end of this chapter and a more detailed list of equipment in Chapter 15.

You'll need to decide where you can conduct research. You can't just jump in your car and drive to the first wooded area and hope a wildman or a werewolf is hiding nearby. You're probably asking, "Where can I find the research data for my monster hunt?" The answer is, "It's everywhere on the Internet." There are hundreds of sites and books on the subject. The most up-to-date information on cryptids and paranormal is on the Internet. That is why I have websites attached to the different legends. What is current today is old info tomorrow.

When I get notified of a sighting, I immediately check the map to see where it occurred. I also look to see where the nearest town is, and the closest water source (i.e., river, stream, or creek). Research has shown these animals like to travel along waterways. A lot of sightings are near a water source. My theory is some of these creatures travel using favored water landmarks to guide migration. A typical pattern of most bigfoot-type creatures is travel primarily at night, to avoid human contact. Check all the details of the sighting to see which direction the animal moved. Consider the time of the year and make a guess where the animal is traveling. If you research past sightings in the area, you might be able to pinpoint the general area where is animal is at or going.

Every animal on Earth has a behavior pattern. Humans down to insects have some kind of pattern to the way they live. When you read about past sightings, you can see a general profile these creatures seem to be displaying. Sightings of these cryptids are usually at a particular time of the year and in specific places.

On a side note, cryptids will immediately flee the area, upon being seen. You probably won't have any sightings or activity in that area for a while.

Researching these legendary creatures, I have found they are mostly nocturnal and nomadic. In other words, they mostly move around at night and do not stay in one place but move from one location to another, generally following a water source, such as a river. There are some who believe these animals do stay in one area where they will probably encounter low human contact.

When it comes to other cryptids like werewolves, their behavior is still being studied and hypothesized about by cryptozoologists. The only thing they have determined is these creatures seem to be nocturnal. With that in mind, use the same process to look for these cryptids as you would looking for bigfoot, but remember these particular cryptids could be dangerous. Treat this cryptid like a wild canine animal. Do not go looking for them alone.

Dinosaur-type cryptids are hard to research due to their location. Permission from the country's government is needed, which they usually don't grant. There are a lot of stories and data on them, but very few pictures or films.

As far as looking for the little people, you need to see where they were last seen and plan a campout in the area, provided you have permission.

The best time of the year to make a cryptid legend trip is spring or fall. I highly recommend you do not do it in the winter. While in the military, I attended cold-weather training, and it was not a pleasant experience. If I do go on a trip to the extreme cold, I make sure I have the right kind of tent and sleeping bag. I also make sure I have a heat source, i.e., camping stove and wood for a campfire.

When it comes to clothing, make sure your team brings the right kind of gear for extreme cold; your legend trip companions are not going to have a good time if they are cold. It's impossible to get them away from the campfire. If you even think it is going to be cold, bring the right kind of clothing and camping gear.

Dangerous situations can arise when camping in the winter, hypothermia being the worst of the threats. When that happens, the legend trip comes to a halt, and you need to seek medical attention. It happens more to people who have never done any wintertime camping. It is alright to research during the daytime, but unless you have the proper equipment and training, winter camping overnight is not advised.

If you go in the summer, you run into the heat, and you will have to deal with the mosquitoes and other irritating insects. If you do decide to go on a cryptid hunt in the summer, you may end up staying at lodgings where you will pay more in the summer. Also, if it is scorching and you don't have a pool nearby, your team may become miserable and will lose interest in the legend trip quickly.

Living in Florida, a tropical environment, there are things that I do and prepare for whenever I go out into the jungle. First, I always take someone with me. If I am going camping, I take my waterproof bag, and I always have a second set of clothing, which I keep in a zip lock bag. I keep my self hydrated with water that I filter/purify myself. I like to take an energy bar or snacks with me. I wear headgear and make sure I have sunscreen. My tent and hammock both have built-in mosquito nets.

Bigfoot hunters in the U.S. primarily do their monster hunts at night, when animals are more active. Most sightings have taken place in the evening because these animals enjoy the security of the nighttime darkness to move around. These large hairy cryptids have been seen many times at night, crossing a road or highway. Daytime is right for looking for evidence such as footprints and broken branches, but these are smart animals, and they continually stay alert to avoid humans. When most animals come into contact with humans, they immediately leave and never return. You might get a whiff of its lingering odor. I used to wonder how these animals can smell us when they stink so badly. The smell is quite overpowering. But I've learned these animals have heightened senses. In other words, they hear, smell, and see better than humans.

When monster hunting, one thing to consider is if there is a water source nearby. By "water source," I mean a flowing body of water, such as a river or creek. These animals usually stay close to rivers and streams. Rivers provide a route for them to travel without being detected as well as a source of drinking water.

When trying to predict the next sighting(s), consider the nearest water source. My theory is these large hairy creatures, and other bipedal animals hang around lakes at night but do not stay long. Rivers and creeks seem to be their comfort zone areas. Also, there are fewer mosquitos around flowing water than stagnant water. Roger Patterson filmed his now-famous bigfoot footage at Bluff Creek.

The next thing you need to consider when determining a good expedition location is whether it is away from the general population. Like I said earlier, bigfoot seems to avoid human contact as much as possible, so look for a wooded area away from towns and cities. There are many national forests in the U.S., and the great thing is most of them have had bigfoot sightings. Yosemite National Park has had some bigfoot sightings. Scenic locations where there are sightings are especially exciting.

Never—and I mean never—go rucking or hiking by yourself. A lot of bad things can happen when you are by yourself. You always hear stories about people who strike out alone and go missing. If you can't find anybody to go with you, then wait till you can. I cannot stress this point enough. Never go into the woods by yourself. Also, check that there are no designated hunting areas in the location. If there are, then make sure everybody is wearing orange. Usually, if hunters are present, then bigfoot won't be. Remember, it usually stays away from humans.

For scout masters and venturing crew guides, most Boy Scout camps have stories of bigfoot sightings and haunted areas. You should look into this when you are planning your weekend outing and make it part of the experience.

Conducting a Witness Interview

It doesn't matter what country you're in, if you do come into contact with a witness, there are things you need to know about conducting an interview. As a military policeman, I learned some useful interviewing techniques I now use with legend tripping. I know legend tripping is supposed to be fun, and it can be, but when it comes to probing deep into a legend, you need to take it seriously.

On a side note, if you're legend tripping in another country,where you do not speak the language, you need to have a device to help you translate both sides of the conversation, or someone to assist who speaks that language.

It has been my experience that when a person sees bigfoot or a ghost, it is a life-changing event for them. They become emotional after the sighting and sometimes when they are recounting it to you. They are very sure about what they saw and generally don't add to their stories. In other words, if I ask the witness if they saw what the animal's eyes looked like, they either did, or they didn't. They don't say, "I think they were brown in color." They will say either "I didn't get close enough to see them," or "It was dark outside." They know what they saw, and there is no doubt. Now some will say, "I can't believe I saw it."

But you also need to remember even good people lie; sometimes, they do it to try to make sense of what they saw. In other words, they will add things so they don't look stupid about what they saw. Some people like the attention and some like to make legend trippers look foolish, as if they will believe anything.

Whatever the outcome with the witness, do not become aggressive if you feel the witness is lying. Let the person tell the story and then thank him or her. Then go over the story with your team or family and explain your conclusions about the interview after the witness leaves.

I often refer to my experience and describe how I conductemy interviews. The first thing I would do when I arrived at a scene was to gather up the witnesses. I would separate them and interview each one in a different location. Do this to ensure that the witnesses cannot hear each other.

Make sure they are comfortable (either standing or sitting) and let them tell their stories without interrupting them. If I had questions, I would write them down and wait for the witness to finish. If I suspected a witness was lying, I would have him/her tell me the story again. I would then ask my questions, and then ask him to tell his story again. A liar cannot retell a story without changing it. The only exception to this is when the event took place more than a week earlier. Then, witnesses have had time to get their stories straight.

It's the same with monster or ghost hunting. If you have more than one person who saw something, try to separate them and talk to them individually. It is a great idea to make a list of questions before the interview. If they can't describe what they saw, do not help them. In other words, don't put words in their mouths. If they saw something, they will be able to tell you what they saw. Always look at them with your full attention. Occasionally nod in acknowledgment and encouragement. Try not to show any emotion except attentiveness. If you show signs of disbelief, like rolling your eyes or shaking your head, they are liable to stop their story and that could end the investigation.

Don't go into an interview thinking you've got a hoaxer. Let the person tell his or her story. Body language can show you if a person is lying. Most people look up when answering questions. Those who I believe have had a real sighting will look you in the eye when they tell you their story. Have a map available so they can show you exactly where the sighting occurred. Have them use a marker so you can get an idea of the size of what they saw. You can do this for both a cryptid and a ghost investigation. If people see something strange, they will be able to describe what they observed in detail. If they did not get a detailed look at the cryptid, they should at least be able to show you where they saw it.

When it comes to questioning a witness, there are different styles of questions. These are as follows:

- Open-Ended Questions: questions do not limit or direct the answer. An example would be, "Tell me what happened to you," or "Tell me everything that happened that night."
- Closed-Ended Questions: questions require a brief answer or a yes or no answer. An example would be, "What time was it when you saw it?" or "Were you alone during this time?"
- Follow-Up Questions: questions probe deeper into the event after the witness tells his or her story. An example would be, "Where exactly did you see this thing?"
- Direct Questions: reserved for a witness who might be lying. An example would be, "After you saw it, what exactly did you do?"
- Control Questions: questions bring you back in control of the questioning. An example would be, "Before we finish, I would like to go over a few of your answers that I am not clear on."
- Leading Questions: questions used to guide the witness through the interview. I frown on this type of questioning. A witness might not be able to identify the thing positively, but through leading questions, you can have the witness believing he or she did see something. This type of questioning is useful in law enforcement, but not when it comes to legend tripping. I've seen

this technique used a lot by monster hunters.

• Confrontational Questions: questions are accusatory, typically being confrontational when you believe the witness is lying. Since legend tripping should be fun and exciting, I highly discourage this type of questioning. It would be best not to challenge the statement. Just because you think the witness is lying doesn't make it so. When you resort to this type of questioning, there is no going back to being friendly.

The first time you interview a witness, it will be best to use what is called the oblique approach. This method is suited for an interview in which the witness tells the story without prompting. Let him/her tell the story while you're silent but attentive. When witnesses are telling me about their sightings, I like to nod, maybe smile, and I will say things such as, "OK" or "I'm listening." Try to keep eye contact.

If I write down the story, I like to go over it with the witness and make sure I heard it right, which works as another method to detect if the witness is lying. If you are interviewing a child, always have the parent present. It will make everybody more comfortable during the interview. The only drawback is sometimes the parent will interrupt the child. If this happens, be patient and keep your attention on what the child is saying. If a witness becomes emotional, be patient and wait for him to compose himself. I like to say, "I believe you saw something." It will help the witness compose himself more quickly and continue with the story.

Another side note: Working with television production companies, I have observed that a witness will change or embellish their sighting if they are being filmed, with the possibility of being on television. Sometimes it's not their fault. The television interviewer will try to get them to say certain things to make the incident more exciting.

Don't get discouraged if you interview a witness who is lying about a sighting. It happens. It shows you what to look for, and it's good training.

Physical Evidence

On a legend trip, one of the goals and, admittedly, one of the exciting parts is finding tangible evidence. What can be more exciting than looking on your camera and seeing a strange apparition floating along in a dark room, or looking on your game camera and seeing a large hairy animal walking past? You go out into the woods and, lo and behold, you find some large footprints are not from a bear, a deer, or a panther. You just might have found some prints made by a bigfoot! You might find some strange hair on a fence where somebody saw the creature go over it.

There are two kinds of proof you want when you go legend tripping: video proof and physical proof. With both monster and ghost hunting, you want to get video proof. With monster hunting, you also look for physical evidence or evidence of the animal's presence.

Base Camp

When you arrive at the area where you are going to conduct your research and investigation, you are going to set up your base camp. If you are visiting another country, make sure you understand all the rules for camping. They may be different. Some countries are serious about leaving trash around and will impose hefty fines for not cleaning up your debris. Some countries make sure you leave the camp area the way you found it with no evidence that you had been there.

You may not know this, but it is essential to set up the base camp the proper way. I have a checklist to make sure I set up everything we need. Again, you can do it the way you want, because everybody is different. This checklist has worked for me, and I've been doing this for many years.

I like to pick an area for my base camp with numerous areas to investigate, not just one. I have gone to locations full of hunters, so you need not only one destination but many, just in case one of them has human activity. Check to make sure it is not private property. Try to find posted campsites. They often have bathrooms and trash bins. If the area is full of campers, it might be a good idea not to tell everybody you are bigfoot hunting.

When you arrive at your actual campsite, the first thing to do is unload your camping gear and get your base camp set up. I like to first put up a tarp, just in case it rains when we are unloading our gear, and it makes an excellent shade area when there aren't any others.

If you are the team leader, then you need to make sure everybody gets the camp set up before it gets dark. Do not go wandering around yet; wait until later. It is essential to get all your gear set up, especially the tents. Do not set up near a lake, because the mosquitoes or other insects will drive you crazy. Rivers are different, because the fish eat the mosquitoes, otherwise, make sure you have the mosquito candles ready. When the sun goes down, they come out to play. You need to have the bug spray ready.

The first thing to set up is the tents. Find the right spot and put them up. After you've got them up, put down some ant repellent around each tent. Fire ants love tents. If you brought cots, then get them up and assembled. The next thing is to inflate your air mattresses if you brought them. When you put your sleeping bags out, don't unroll them. They attract bugs and snakes. Get your light source, i.e., lanterns, ready in each tent. Then get your eating area set up. I always keep the food locked up in the back of the car. I keep the cooler there as well. It keeps bears and raccoons and other pesky animals away from the food.

I also get a garbage bag set up away from the tents. When you go out at night, make one stop a trash point so that you won't have garbage around the area at night. Raccoons can destroy a camp, so make sure you get rid of the trash or secure it in a vehicle for the night.

Get your folding chairs set up. I usually put them near the campfire. You don't want to sit on the ground. If the campgrounds have a trash drop-off point and bathrooms, then go find out where they are. If I do bring my family, my kids always find the bathrooms the second we get to the campgrounds. I guess it is a standard family ritual after a long trip.

The author in a one-person tent.

Start gathering up wood for a fire if you are permitted. Make sure you can have a fire. In some countries, during the dry part of the year, it is prohibited to have a campfire. Make sure you have your lanterns ready. In most countries, it is against the law to chop down trees. You can incur an expensive fine. Search for dead wood and make sure you get plenty of it. Dry wood burns fast, and it can be a problem when you run out in the middle of the night. Make sure you collect a good supply. Even if you think you have enough firewood, you don't. You will require three times as much as you feel you need. You can never have too much wood, and if you leave it in a nice pile, somebody else can use it. Also, watch out for snakes when you are gathering up wood. They like to hide in deadfall.

Lay of the Land (Area Reconnaissance)

Now you've got your base camp set up; it is time to scout around the area and see what's out there. Get your map out and, with your team, plot where you want to look. Also, you might want to check and see where the nearest hospital is, just in case. If you have a GPS—and most cell phones have it on them—then find out where the nearest emergency personnel are located, such as the Ranger Station. You need to see what else the area has to offer in terms of things to see and do. Since monster hunts are at dawn or dusk, you have a whole day to fill. Your legend hunting team will appreciate having something to do. Swimming, hiking, and canoeing are great family-friendly activities to do during your downtime.

Go and scout the area. In the military, this is called reconnaissance or "recon" for short. You should take the team with you when you go over the research area. It's easier than going back and explaining it on a map. Something can get lost in the translation. You might have members who do not have land navigation training. Make sure everybody knows what they should look for, such as tracks in the dirt broken branches or weird branch configurations.

The author cooking on a camp stove.

There are things you need to be on the lookout for to let you know one of these cryptid animals is in the area. First and foremost, look for tracks. Look for loose soil or muddy areas where tracks are easy to see. Looking near rivers or streams is an excellent idea. You also need to look to see if there are any torn-down branches. The theory is bigfoot tears down branches to either mark its trail or warn others of human activity. People have found what they claim to be bigfoot nests, which might be something to look for as well. Be aware of strange branch configurations. These are broken tree branches arranged in a pattern usually interwoven with each other off the ground, referred to as stick structures. I observed one of these configurations while on a bigfoot expedition. A couple of years ago, during a monster hunt on the Georgia/Florida border, our research team found a stick structure miles from any human habitat or roads.

You need to be conscious of smells. These animals during certain parts of the year give off a pungent aroma, which most of the time will catch you off guard. You'll be walking through the woods when the smell will hit you like a tidal wave, and you'll stop dead in your tracks. The smell is terrible. It reminds me of a dead wet dog.

You need to realize the area in the woods or forest where you are conducting your legend trip is this animal's home, and it knows the woods better than you do. Its senses are a lot more acute than a human's. In other words, it can hear and smell you when you enter the woods. Do not have any misconceptions that these animals just sit around and wait to be seen. They are very intelligent species. If they were stupid, we would see them a lot more.

There is a ninety-five percent chance you are not going to see bigfoot or other cryptids. Now you are asking, "Then why search for them?" My answer is, "The five percent." If you don't look, you're never going to see them. Only patience and determination pay off in this field. As of this writing, I have witnessed glowing eyes and a large shape in a thermal. I have seen physical evidence, such as large tracks and strange stick structures. Something is out there. I realize there is only a slight chance I will get a good look at it, but I believe if I continue to look, my efforts will eventually pay off. Plus, I enjoy the thrill of the hunt.

Safety Considerations

When you are in the woods, be careful of what is around you. In the eastern part of the country, which is very hilly, there are a lot of cliffs, which are challenging to see, if you're going lights out during a hunt. There have been numerous accidents with hikers. I recently read an article about some hikers who found an injured person who fell from a cliff next to a waterfall. Because it was night, he didn't see the end of the ledge and fell and broke both his legs. Luckily the hikers came by the next morning and found him. He had to be airlifted by helicopter.

Conducting your legend trip in the swamplands, you will need to be exceptionally vigilant. In the swamplands, cypress trees grow their roots to the side and up. With the swamplands flooded ninety percent of the year, the roots will grow up above the waterline. These roots are called knees. They look like stalagmites and can be sharp. These are especially dangerous at night, which is why my team and I stay on the dirt roads once darkness falls. I have heard many stories of hunters falling and becoming impaled on them. Also, there are sinkholes which you can't see, and you can't tell how deep they are, which presents a dangerous situation. Make sure you go over all of this with your team before you enter the area.

Also, during this time frame, you need to choose a rallying point—a designated area for everyone to meet back up again after the hunt. You need to decide where to set up observation points (O.P.s) and where to place your trail cameras. Daytime is the best time to find an O.P. Use trail markers or orange 550 cord to mark your O.P. (trail markers work best because you can see them at night).

It is also an excellent time to see if you can find footprints and stick structures. If you do find prints of known animals, such as deer or raccoon, show them to team members who are new to the woods so they can learn something about the animals in the area. As I stated earlier, loose soil or muddy regions are where you're going to finds tracks, especially near rivers or streams. Stick structures are usually easy to see. They stand out pretty well in the forest. Take plenty of pictures of them and mark where you find them on the map or GPS.

Making Castings of Footprints

One of the most popular things to look for during a bigfoot legend trip is footprints made by the cryptid creature. Recently I attended a cryptozoology conference and talked with Cliff Barackman. Cliff is one of the hosts of the popular television show *Finding Bigfoot* on the Animal Planet channel.

He commented that a footprint is not the shape of the foot. It's the shape of the damage done to the ground by the foot. That is why all bigfoot prints look different. There are different kinds of terrain which affect the impression, and also how long it has been there.

If you or somebody on your team finds a footprint you cannot identify, then you need to make a plaster cast of it. Here are the steps you need to do to make a successful casting. The items list is in Chapter 15. You need to keep all the cast-making items in one location. I keep all the casting material in plastic storage tubs. You can also use these tubs to store the finished castings.

If this is the first time you have ever done any casting, then I recommend you start off using plaster casting powder. It is inexpensive, and you can find it at any home improvement or hobby store. There are other casting powders, but some dry fast.

You can also use foam, but you'll need to put something on top of it. I have experimented with other materials, and I come back to plaster.

You will likewise require a pail or a large, durable, and sturdy plastic bag. And you will need plenty of water to mix into the casting powder. To make a barrier around the print, you will need a large plastic or bendable copper strip about two inches by twenty-four inches or two pieces of two-inch by thirteen-inch. You will also need some hairspray.

First, you need to take a picture of the print. Take a bunch of pictures. Make sure you have something in the image to compare to the size, such as a ruler or even a dollar bill. It helps to give an idea of the size of the print. Then scout around and see if you can find more tracks. You need to find all the footprints you can. Unless this creature is one-legged, there should be more than one print. If it has a right foot, it has a left foot. It is better to get both left and right footprints. When a person finds only one print, it automatically seems suspicious. If you brought out plenty of casting powder, you need to cast as many of the tracks as you can. Use small sticks with orange tape to mark the prints; this way, everybody in the party will know where they are and won't accidentally step on them.

You then need to move some of the large items like branches away from the print. Leave the tiny twigs or leaves, because they might have hair on them for analysis. Set up the barrier around the impression. Make it at least one inch from all the borders of the print.

A track immersed in water can be a challenge. There are different ways to remove the water without damaging the track. You can build a channel and drain the water away. You can utilize an oven baster. It looks like a large eyedropper, and can carefully remove the water. Do not be in a rush when you do this. When the water is removed, let the track dry.

Once you have the print ready, make sure the barrier is set up and not going to move. I put small sticks on the outside of the barrier to keep it in place. I like to use the sticks with the orange tape on them, so they have a dual use. Next, take the hairspray and spray the print and around the print. Use a generous amount and let it dry. The hairspray acts as a kind of glue and will keep the print intact, especially if it is in the sand.

You then need to get the casting powder ready. First, put your rubber gloves on, and then put the powder in the pail or plastic bag. Remember, you are casting a larger than typical human-style footprint; you will use a lot of the powder. I recommend four cups of powder and three cups of water. Then, wearing rubber gloves, use your hand to mix it up. Make sure you mix it well and get rid of all the clumps. It should have a soup-like consistency. Now carefully and slowly pour the mixture into the print. I recommend starting at the heel and working your way up to the toes. Some people like to add branches into the back of the print to add strength. I have never done that, and all my castings have come out strong and stable. Do not try to push the mixtures around with your hands; it will damage the print. Let it dry and start on the next print.

It will probably take about an hour to dry. Do not mess with it during the drying period. After the hour is up, first check the top of the casting to see if it is all the way dry, which you will recognize when the cast is hard as a rock. Rainy or damp weather can affect the time it takes for the plaster to set. If you are in the swamps, it will take longer to dry because of the moisture in the air.

When you are satisfied the casting is dry, carefully pick it up. Take a soft brush and thoroughly clean the loose sand or dirt off the print. I always take a picture of it after I do this. Then wrap the print with bubble wrap and secure it in a container where you know it will not get broken. Large plastic tub containers are ideal. If you get more than one print, make sure you use plenty of bubble wrap to protect them.

To be able to do this correctly and effectively, you need to practice making casts. If you do it for the first time when you find a track, you are going to end up ruining it. Sometimes I will do a casting of a known animal just to keep in practice. Have your family do it as well. It's kind of fun to do. Messy but fun. My kids love doing castings of prints. They feel like they're a CSI agent solving a crime. A word of caution: the plaster casting mixture can ruin your clothes if you get it on them, so be careful. It is a pain getting it out of your hair. My stepdaughter found out the hard way.

Setting Up Trail/Game Cameras

Set up Trail (game) cameras during the day. You need to think about where to set up these cameras. You've got to remember you are not trying to photograph deer or wild pigs. You are dealing with an ingenious animal that shies away from human contact. You are going to have to put the camera deep in the woods away from roads. You will not have good results if you put it in an area that has a lot of human traffic.

Be careful: I have found game cameras out in the boonies that were left out there by owners who forgot where they placed them. Make sure you put a lock on it. Some people think because they put the camera up deep in the woods, nobody will see it or take it. I am here to tell you from experience you may think you have the perfect hiding place, but some hunter or kid riding his ATV will see it and take it. When I set up cameras, I always secure them with a lock, and I mark where I put them with my GPS, so it is easier to recover them. They cost a lot, and you don't want to lose them out there.

The best place to set them up is on game trails. These are paths animals have cut through the grass and continue to use. They are not hard to see during the day. I put camouflage netting around the camera to help hide it. I spray anti-scent on it to mask my human odor. Even with anti-scent, it will take at least two weeks for the human scent to go away completely, so be prepared to leave your camera out for a while unless you are just making a weekend legend trip. Set up some kind of trail marker close by so you can find them to retrieve later. Do not put the trail marker right next to the camera; otherwise, your camera will be gone.

I also put a camera in an area where I want the animal to go, or I think it will go. In other words, I will place the camera in the area I want to walk around in the evening. I know if this animal is about, it will leave when it knows we are there. Looking at a map of the area, I try to guess which direction this animal will go, and I put my camera there, so when it moves through that location, it will go by my camera, trip the beam, and get its picture taken.

Make sure you know how to use your trail camera before you set it up outside. You will want to set up your camera in the night vision mode. If the flash on the camera goes off, every animal in the area will see it and stay away. Some cameras have timers; if yours does, make sure you don't have it set, otherwise, the batteries will run down faster.

If you are going to look in multiple areas, then make sure you have at least two people on each team, including an adult. The teams need to know their prescribed distance (five hundred feet is usually the best distance) before coming back to the rally point. Each team will have a working radio with fresh or extra batteries or a cellphone. I instruct the teams to always return to the rally point when they can't get reception on the radios. In other words, if they can't pick up anybody on the radio, then turn around and come back. If they see panther or bear tracks, then they are to call it in and return to the rally point. I go over all of this with everybody before each team moves out to their assigned area or path.

Dangerous Animals

I want to bring up the subject of dangerous animals that are in the woods. I am not an expert on animals, but I do know there are dangerous animals out there. You probably have heard stories about attacks on humans by animals. There is some truth to those stories. It is imperative to understand this land is the animal's home, and they will protect it. Do not underestimate any kind of wildlife, even small foxes and armadillos.

While out in the woodlands, there are dangerous animals you need to know. The most dangerous animals are bears, large wild cats, wild pigs, alligators, snakes, and certain insects. They are incredibly unsafe and need to be avoided at all times. I will go into detail on each animal. Every team member must know what animals are in the area.

Bears are known all over the world. But there are only eight different kinds of this animal.

North American Black Bear. It is the most common bear in North America, ranging from the State of Florida north into Canada and Alaska.

Brown Bear: Located in Alaska and Western Canada

Polar Bear: Located throughout the Arctic region, these are the largest bears in the world

Asiatic Black Bear: Located in eastern Asia, including Afghanistan, Bangladesh, Bhutan, Cambodia, China, India, Islamic Republic of Iran, Japan, Democratic People's Republic of Korea, Lao People's Democratic Republic, Malaysia, Mongolia, Myanmar, Nepal, Pakistan, Russian Federation, Taiwan, and Vietnam.

Andean Bear: Also referred to as the Spectacled Bear. It is located only in the Andes mountains of South America.

Panda Bear: located in the mountain ranges in western China, biologists believe this animal is a member of the raccoon family.

Sloth Bear: In Sri Lanka, India, Bhutan, Nepal, and Bangladesh.

Sun Bear: The smallest species of bear, it is located southeast Asia: Brunei Darussalam, Cambodia, China, India, Indonesia, Lao Peoples Democratic Republic, Malaysia, Myanmar, Thailand, and

Vietnam.

Reports of bear attacks have been on the rise as urban sprawl continues to soak up habitat. If you go to a place where there are reports of roaming bears, I recommend you look for somewhere else. Bears can be particularly aggressive, especially in the fall before hibernation, as well as in the spring when waking up hungry from a long winter's nap. Bears are typically solitary animals. They can be active during the day (diurnal), but are very active during the night (nocturnal) or twilight (crepuscular), particularly around humans. They will come into camps when they smell food.

Bears have an excellent sense of smell. Bears may, at times, look slow-moving because of their heavy build and awkward gait, but they can move quickly and are adept climbers and swimmers. Bears use caves and burrows as their dens. Bears hibernate for an extended period during the winter months. Bears should be considered dangerous and should be left alone. Carry bear mace when you go into woods or swamps. This highly-concentrated pepper spray is also effective on large cats, wild boar, and even snakes—more on bear mace in Chapter 15.

Another hazardous animal and one you don't hear a lot about are the large cats. Mountain lions, pumas, and panthers are located in many habitats, from Florida swamps up to the Canadian forests. Believe it or not, these large cats are all basically the same animal and can be extremely dangerous. Because these cats are seldom observed, people do not take the proper precautions when they are out in the woods. I was fortunate enough to see one in the wild, from the safety of my car.

Panthers are on the endangered species list. These cats do avoid humans but have been known to stalk a lone hiker. Again, travel in pairs or groups when out in the woods. It is a dependable safety strategy. Relocate your research to a different location if there is a reported panther sighting. Their tracks are easy to distinguish from other animals with a distinctive "M" shaped pad and three lobes on the rear of the heel (dogs only have two lobes). Their claw marks do not show on the track.

In the United States, the Montana Fish, Wildlife, and Parks Department came up with some great tips on what to do if you ever encounter a large cat such as a mountain lion or panther. They are as follows:

- Avoid the animal if at all possible; in other words, do not approach it.
- Do not run or turn your back. Make eye contact, and if you have children, pick them up while maintaining eye contact with the animal. If you have sunglasses on, then take them off.
- Try to appear larger than you are by opening your jacket and by raising and waving your arms.
- Speak firmly and try not to sound afraid (I know this is easier said than done).

Bottom line: if you see these animals, leave the area and make your legend trip somewhere else. Remember, personal safety is a priority.

Black panthers are jaguars or leopards and live in the hot, dense tropical rainforests of South and Southeast Asia. Found mainly in southwestern China, Burma, Nepal, southern India, Indonesia, and the southern part of Malaysia, black leopards are more common than light-colored leopards.

There have been reports from time to time of black panthers roaming around the Florida swamps, but Florida Fish and Wildlife will tell you this is false. They state that people who say they have seen them are, in fact seeing the black bobcat. Following severe storms, zoos and rescue centers have reported losing animals, including black panthers. Though these animals shy away from humans, they can be dangerous when encountered.

There is the legend of the Phantom Cat. There are reports of sightings, tracks, and predation in several countries, including Canada, Britain, Australia, Germany, France, Spain, Ireland, New Zealand, Finland, Denmark, the United States, Italy, and Luxembourg. Scientists believe that these reports are nothing more than mistaken identity or a cat that has gotten loose from a zoo.

Wild pigs (also known as wild hogs, wild boar, or feral swine) are a "suid" native to much of the Palearctic and was introduced in the Americas by European explorers. Human intervention has spread it further, making the species one of the widest-ranging mammals in the world, as well as the most widespread suiform, and it has become an invasive species in part of its introduced range. The animal originated in Southeast Asia during the Early Pleistocene and outcompeted other suid species as it spread throughout the Old World.

Wild or feral boar will eat almost anything and are extremely dangerous. A mother boar will aggressively protect her young, and all wild pigs will defend themselves when they feel they are cornered or injured. They have rock-hard snouts, which they use to burrow in the ground for insects. Wild boars usually come out at dawn and leave when humans show up. They are incredibly fast-moving animals. If you hear them out there, have the bear mace ready. Wild boar cannot climb trees, so if you come into contact with this aggressive pig, immediately seek shelter in a nearby tree.

There are only two countries on earth that have alligators: the United States and China. In the United States, alligators dwell in the southeastern part of the country (i.e., Florida, Georgia, Alabama, Mississippi, Louisiana, and Texas. These reptiles are extremely dangerous and should be avoided at all times. When they attack humans, they will get ahold of a limb and drag them into the water. They will then do a death roll, which twists the limb off and drowns the victim. They are especially aggressive during the mating season which is April through May. I recommend you do not plan any of your legend trips where these animals habitat.

A park ranger advised that if you find yourself lost and there is a shallow body of water you must cross, then you must do the following. When you start moving through the water, drag your feet along the bottom. This will kick up the mud and silt, which will camouflage you. If you do kick an alligator, because they can't see you, they will think it is another alligator and move. During the mating season, alligators will attack anything that touches them. Only undertake this as a last resort.

Snakes

When it comes to snakes, there are hundreds of dangerous species around the world. The Inland taipan is considered the most venomous snake in the world. I cannot stress enough to leave all snakes alone if you come in to contact with them, even the non-venomous ones.

While Brazil has the most snakes, Australia has the most poisonous snakes in the world, with 60 species, followed by Columbia with 50 species.

Here are the top ten dangerous and venomous snakes from around the world. You will probably never have a run-in with most of these reptiles, but it doesn't hurt to know about them.

Inland Taipan: Found in Australia, this member of the elapid family (which includes cobras) is the deadliest snake in the world today. Most of the taipan species are found along the northeast coast of Queensland, as well as the southern sector of Papua New Guinea. The taipan's venom contains high levels of neurotoxins, which cause paralysis of the victim's nervous system and clot the blood, preventing an adequate flow of blood through the blood vessels.

Mojave Rattlesnake: Found in the desert regions of the southwestern United States as well as central Mexico, this pit viper possesses the most poisonous venom of all rattlesnake species. They are cold-blooded reptiles and will sun themselves near logs, boulders, or open areas. They inhabit mountains, prairies, deserts, and beaches. They can accurately strike at up to one third their body length. Their venom is neurotoxic (it affects the nervous system), leading to everything from seizures to death. Rattlesnakes use their rattles or tails as a warning when they feel threatened.

Philippine Cobra: It inhabits the low-lying plains and forest regions of the Philippines near sources of fresh water. Cobras are quite stocky and have a hood that they raise when threatened. The cobra's venom is composed of a postsynaptic neurotoxin that directly affects the respiratory system of its victims. These Cobras also possesses the ability to spit its venom at victims, causing severe damage to the eyes.

Death Adder: Located in Australia and New Guinea. This snake has a viper-like appearance, but it is a member of the elapid family of snakes, which includes cobras and black mambas. The death adder's venom is a highly toxic neurotoxin that causes paralysis, as well as a complete respiratory system shutdown.

Tiger Snake: found in the southern sector of Australia and Tasmania. It likes to stay in coastal regions, wetlands, and marshes due to the abundance of prey in these sorts of environments. The tiger snake is quite aggressive when startled, and will flatten its body to raise its head above ground level. Its venom is a combination of highly potent neurotoxins, coagulants, myotoxins, and hemolysins.

Eastern Brown Snake: Found in Eastern and central Australia and southern New Guinea, they inhabit nearly all environments, except for dense forests. Out of 35 reported snake-bite deaths between 2000 and 2016 in Australia, 23 were by the eastern brown snake (University of Melbourne, 2017).

Russell's Viper: also known as the chain viper, is a venomous snake from the Viperidae family and is found in Southeast Asia, China, Taiwan, and India. They stay in grasslands or brushy areas and around farms. Their venom is neurotoxic (it affects the nervous system), leading to everything from seizures to death.

Black Mamba: It resides in Sub-Saharan Africa and is known to live in both the ground and trees. This snake is 6 feet to 10 feet in length and can move extremely fast. Its venom is composed primarily of neurotoxins and it will deliver multiple bites when it strikes.

Blue Krait: Also known as the Malayan krait, it is in the elapid family with cobras. It is found predominantly in Southeast Asia, including Indochina and Indonesia. It is fond of water sources and can be found near rivers, lakes, and ponds. Unlike most snakes, it is primarily nocturnal in its hunting habits.

Fer-de-Lance: Also called a Bothrops asper, this is a highly venomous pit viper species, ranging in distribution from southern Mexico to northern South America. It is the most dangerous snake of Central and South America and has caused more human deaths than any other American reptile.

They can be found in a wide range of lowland

habitats, often near human habitations. Natives of the area refer to it as the two-step snake, meaning you take two steps and die after being bitten by one of them. Its hemotoxic venom spreads through cells and blood vessels, causing swelling and blisters, and destroying tissue as it moves.

Insects and Spiders

There are dangerous insects you need to know about. The most dangerous insect in the world is the **mosquito**. They carry a variety of nasty pathogens. According to the World Health Organization more than 1 million deaths are caused by mosquitos every year. The Anopheles mosquito can transmit malaria, and they are found all over the world. These insects are most active at two times: just before dawn and dusk, right after it gets dark.

Ants are found everywhere, and there are a variety of them that are dangerous. The bullet ant, which also the largest, inhabits the rainforests of Nicaragua and Paraguay. A bite from these ants feels like being shot and is 30 times more painful than the stingof a wasp or a honey bee.

The fire ants build their colonies on the ground in soil and sand, very close to your feet! They will sting the intruder repeatedly. The venom of fire ants can result in an allergic reaction.

In the Congo, the driver ant is a dangerous insect to watch out for. Also known as army ants, these insects are extremely mean and will attack anything in their path. They travel in colonies of 2 million individual ants.

When it comes to flies, there are two that are dangerous to humans. The first one is the South Amerian bot fly. These insects are parasitic organisms, and lay their eggs in mammals. These eggs turn into larvae and will dig their way out from underneath the skin. To extract the larvae with tweezers is painful because the larvae have tiny barbed spines that anchor them in place.

The next fly is the African tsetse fly. These dangerous insects inject potent toxin with each sting. In Africa, half a million people have lost their lives due to an attack of these insects.

Another dangerous insect is the scorpion. They like to hide under rocks, in woodpiles, or under tree bark (hence the name bark scorpion) during the day, while at night they come out to actively hunt for prey. These scorpions prefer to be upside down, so this means many stings are from someone reaching under an object with their hand. The annual number of scorpion stings is estimated to be in the thousands. A sting from a scorpion should not be taken lightly; seek medical attention immediately. One of the most dangerous scorpions is the black spitting thick-tail scorpion. It makes it home in the deserts of South Africa. A sting from this insect will cause extreme pain, paralysis, and even death.

With spiders, the Brazilian wandering spider is considered the most venomous in the world. Located in northern South America, with one species in Central America, they are highly defensive and nocturnal hunters.

The next is the black widow spider. These are one of the most recognizable, and most feared, insects and they inhabit the entire United States. The females usually measure between ½ to 1-½ inches in length, are a glossy black color, with the signature red hourglass marking on either the top or the bottom of the abdomen (or none at all). Their venom is strong enough to drop a cow. Although human deaths are relatively rare, a Colorado resident died after being bitten 19 times on the foot in 2011. The good thing is these spiders are not aggressive, so in other words, if you leave them alone, they'll leave you alone. Accidental encounters cause most bites when spiders are in places like woodpiles, trash dumps, sheds, gardens, and under rocks, or if they get trapped in a sock or shoe. If someone gets bitten, it can take over 30 minutes for symptoms to take effect. Watch for redness and swelling, and an overall "achy" feeling, weakness, vomiting, headache, and nausea. Always seek medical attention as soon as possible.

The next dangerous spider is the brown recluse. This spider is challenging to identify from other non-hazardous types since it has no discernible markings on the body. However, they sometimes have a violin pattern, which cellar spiders and pirate spiders can also have. The best way to identify them is by their eyes; if you can get close enough to see them, these spiders have six eyes instead of eight. Their range is from Texas to western Georgia and from Louisiana to southern Iowa. These spiders are not as aggressive as their name suggests and tend only to bite if trapped in clothing, gloves, or bedding.

If someone does get bit, it usually isn't even felt initially. Pain and itching can follow within 2-8 hours, pain worsens over the next 36 hours, and a visible wound will develop within a few days. Immediate treatment is to place an ice pack on the bite area and seek medical attention. Do not cut open the wound and squeeze the puss out; this will only make the bite area worse. If left untreated, the tissue around the bite becomes infected and rots. I have been bitten by one of these, and it took weeks for the bite to heal up. I didn't even know I had gotten bitten until I went to the hospital for a large swollen bump on my leg. I now have a permanent scar from this encounter.

When it comes to bees, the most notorious and deadly is the African honey bee, also called killer bees. In 1957, a Brazilian beekeeper accidentally released some, and they spread through most of South America, Central America, and up into Mexico. They have now been located in the southern United Sates. These honey bees are much more aggressive than the European honey bee that lives in the United States. Killer bees, as a swarm, will chase a victim over a mile and attack within a quarter-mile of their hive (which can be underground). Their sting has the same potency as a European honey bee, but since they attack in much larger numbers, it makes them much more dangerous. One to two deaths per year are usually credited to killer bees.

When I was down in Panama, my group had a run-in with these insects. We ran a couple of miles before the bees stopped attacking. Luckily nobody in my team was severely stung, and better yet, no one was allergic. If you happen to run into a nest of Africanized bees, don't make any sudden movements, keep animals away, and avoid waving around jewelry or other flashy objects.

On the other hand, if the bees begin to attack, run! And don't stop running until you're sure they are not swarming after you. Try to protect your face from being stung, run into the wind, and head towards the nearest shelter such as a house or tent—don't jump in the water, since the bees will wait for you to resurface. It is a good idea to know if any members of your group are allergic to bees or any other stinging insects.

The next dangerous insect and one everyone has had some kind of encounter with is the wasp. There are over 100,000 species of wasps, but the two most common are the yellow jacket and the hornet. The hornet is larger than the yellow jacket, but the most obvious difference is their color. Yellow jackets are yellow and black, while hornets are white and black. Hornets make their nests in trees, whereas yellow jackets make theirs in the ground. This accounts for the fact that most yellow jacket stings occur on the bottom of exposed feet. Hornet stings are usually more painful than yellow jacket stings. Again like bees, multiple stings can cause shock and sometimes death. If you see them, leave them alone.

The Hunt

After you finish the recon, head back to camp and get ready. There you will eat dinner and wait for the early evening. Make sure everybody helps with the camp chores and cleans up. When it is time to move out, get the teams ready, load up the vehicle(s), and drive to the research location. Before you head out, always double-check the radios, flashlights/headlights, and survival necklaces. Once you get to the rally point, park your vehicles so it is easy to get out. This can be a challenge at nighttime.

When members of the team depart, instruct members to keep their video cameras on record. You never know when something will happen, and when it does, it happens quickly. If you're not all set, by the time your camera is up and running what you wanted to film is gone, or the noise has stopped. If this happens and you don't get anything, erase the recording. Each team should stay on their paths or dirt roads. I know the woods look pretty inviting during the day, but once the sun goes down, everything looks different. It is better to stay on dirt paths, and roads are easy to see at night, so it will be easy to backtrack to the rally point. Each team will move to their O.P. (observation point) and wait and listen.

Have some of the groups do wood knocks or call blasting. There is a theory that a bigfoot will alert other bigfoots humans are in the area by knocking on wood. I have heard these knocks. You can never be one hundred percent sure it is bigfoot making these sounds. I know some people who take a baseball bat to do the wood knocks. If you do the wood knocks, make sure every team knows it is happening; otherwise, one team will do a wood knock, and another team will hear it, thinking it's a bigfoot, and do a wood knock back. Then you'll have two teams thinking they've got a bigfoot in the area.

"Call blasting" is where you take a recording of a supposed bigfoot scream or howl and play it on a loudspeaker and see if you get any response. I have tried this technique. I don't set up an elaborate sound system to do the call blasting. I simply put the recording in my vehicle sound system or outdoor speaker, turn up the volume, and wait. Sound travels farther at night, so as long as everybody is silent, the call blast will go out. If you do get a callback there are a couple of caveats. First of all, you won't know one hundred percent if it is a bigfoot making the call, and second, what if these cryptids are communicating to others to stay away from the area? The call you recorded in the first place may have been a cry of warning.

When I first started writing this book, I was not a big fan of humans attempting to make bigfoot yells or screams. I thought for some time that it was a waste of time when people tried to imitate a bigfoot yell. It reminded me of a person meowing to a cat. The cat looks up at the human and doesn't even twitch an ear at the sound. The cat is thinking, "Why is this human trying to sound like us?" With these bigfoot-type creatures, I thought the effect was the same. These animals are smart, and I'm pretty sure they can tell the difference between a human and one of their own.

But on one of our late-night outings, we had a young female investigator, April, do some screams, and oddly enough, we heard something call back. You can get more positive results if female members do the screams. The big guy has a thing for the ladies. Some investigators swear these screams provide positive results. Many bigfoot investigators with whom I've been on expeditions like to do the yells when we're out in the woods. Again I'm going off of my own experiences when I go out monster hunting.

You can now buy game calls that will broadcast animal yells. You can record bigfoot yells and broadcast them with the game caller. It will save you from losing your voice.

If you can afford it, a thermal imager is a great tool to use when looking for bigfoot. These expensive devices will scan an area and pick up heat signatures. In other words, if there is something alive and giving off heat, this device will pick it up. It works great at night when you can't see your hand in front of your face. Thermal imagers come in a variety of designs, but they are all expensive. Production companies rent the thermal imagers you see on these monster hunting and paranormal shows. As I said, they are great for monster hunting, but they are expensive.

When I was in the military, there was a huge one used to scan the outside of the base to make sure nobody was trying to infiltrate us. I keep looking at the online auction sites for one at a reasonable price. No luck so far, but I'll keep looking.

After the teams have walked around for a couple of hours, I usually call them in when twilight fades, and it gets dark. An exception to the rule is if a team starts to see or hear things. If you or one of your teams hears something, then have everybody stop what they're doing and listen. Remember, always keep the video camera in record mode. You can talk into it and explain where you are and what time it is. There is a theory bigfoot is attracted to a child's voice. So have your children act like they are taping a television show and you never know, you might hear something. Again, it makes the kids feel like they are part of the investigation.

When you get all the teams back, inventory all the gear. If your team is late getting back as, a safety measure, call on the radio and let the base know you have stopped and are listening for something. Give them your location as well. It only takes a couple of seconds to do this. If a team does not show up at the prescribed time, don't panic. First, call them on the radio and see where they are at. On the way back, a team may hear something and stop to listen. If they don't answer (radio/cellphone) and it has been a while, then send out only one team with a member who knows the area.

When you are out in the woods and your team radio stops working, you need to come back to base or the rally point immediately. You can't depend on your cellphones. Sometimes they lose their signal deep in the woods. This is something all of your teams need to know: if your team gets lost, first stop and then contact the base and tell them the situation. If at night, have every team member turn on their light, and form a circle pattern, facing out and flashing away from the center. That way, when the search party comes looking for the team, they can be easily seen. You are probably thinking this will blow the whole legend trip and scare the bigfoot away, with all the lights flashing everywhere. Oh well, never jeopardize safety for the experience.

If you have night vision goggles, turn them on. They magnify any kind of light source, and you can see quite a distance away. It will make it easier to find the lost team. If you have done your briefing right and every team went to and stayed in their assigned zone or road, you will pretty much know what area they are in. Also, call out to them and see if the lost team can hear you. Sound travels better at night. Make sure only one team is calling out to them. If all the teams do this, then you won't be able to hear the lost team when they reply.

If the worst happens and you can't find them, call the police. A search and rescue team will come out, and they often have helicopters equipped with thermal heat-detecting devices and will be able to find the lost members. When the police arrive, give them the location of where the team is supposed to be, which will provide them with an area to start their search. In the whole time,I have been legend tripping; I have not lost a team. I always ensure each team has an experienced person with them, stays on the road, and has a working radio.

When all the teams are back at the rally point, do a quick debriefing to find out what all the teams saw or heard. Make sure they know where it was that they listened to the noise or saw the object. Draw a sketch because things look different in the daytime, and your team might not remember the exact spot in daylight. That way, you can go back in the morning and search for the area in daylight. You might find some evidence, such as footprints.

Once you finish your debriefing, have everybody load up the vehicles. Assign an order of march for each team. In other words, the first vehicle has a team member who knows the area and then have everybody follow that person. I like to be in the last vehicle; that way, if any vehicle breaks down or something goes wrong, I am there to fix it. If a vehicle breaks down, you may have to tow it with your vehicle.

When you get back to base camp, you get everyone together and go over the night's events. You talk about what you saw and heard. Go over all the pictures and recordings. If you or any of your team found footprints, you need to make plans to go to that location and make castings of the tracks.

Last but not least, here is a quick packing list for your legend trip. A more detailed list is in Chapter 15: Tools of the Trade.

Monster Hunt Packing list:

- Camping gear, including tent(s), sleeping bag(s)
- Lanterns, and cooking stove
- Fuel for cooking stove
- Water and items to clean water
- Food
- Trash bags
- Canteens
- Knife/machete/shovel
- Camera—one that has I.R. capabilities
- Flashlights/headlights/light sticks
- Batteries for all equipment devices
- Game camera—it is better to have more than one, so you can put them in multiple places
- Outdoor clothing, including snake boots
- Sunglasses
- Rain gear—GORE-TEX is great because it also keeps you warm
- Bug spray/sunblock—bring a lot of it; you'll need it
- Anti-scent spray—start spraying this on your equipment before you leave on the legend trip
- GPS—this is good to use when you set up your game cameras; you can mark where you put them with the GPS
- Bionic ear device
- Evidence kit including footprint casting material
- Fishing gear
- Binoculars

Here is what I carry in the backpack I use for day trips. I carry this with me all the time in the back of my vehicle:

- Survival kit
- First-aid kit—include poison ivy cream, moleskin for blisters
- Foot powder (cold weather)
- Petroleum jelly (hot weather and swamps)
- Extra socks
- Canteen with cup
- Flashlight (two)—always carry a headlamp and an extra flashlight
- GPS (with extra batteries)
- Compass—in case the GPS stops working
- Poncho (for use as a poncho or shelter)
- Rain gear
- Backup knife
- Water purifier pump
- Plaster casting kit
- Fermion chips (keep in sealed, durable container)
- Binoculars
- Trail camera
- 550 parachute cord
- Marking kit
- Bear mace
- Machete
- Food (beef jerky, trail mix, peanut butter crackers, and an MRE)
- Solar wrap used to recharge a cell phone or GPS
- Toilet paper/baby wipes (you will need them)
- Sunscreen/bug spray
- Map of area
- Camera with night vision

Chapter 5

Cryptids: Aquatic Beasts, Serpents and Aquatic Humanoids

The ocean was magical to her; its depths and mysteries were boundless, its call irresistible.
—Jeff Mariotte

The very idea that there are still undiscovered creatures in our oceans, seas, and lakes boggles the mind. With most of the oceans mapped out, it seems hard to believe that some unknown fish or creatures could have escaped detection. But the fact is, scientists today still don't know how many species exist in the oceans.

Aquatic cryptids are in a category all by themselves and deserve an entire chapter. As is the case with land-based cryptids, like the teti, there are well documented aquatic cryptid sightings around the world, with the Loch Ness Monster being the most famous.

One of the most popular books on the subject of aquatic cryptids is Bernard Heuvelmans' *In the Wake of the Sea-Serpents.* Heuvelmans concluded there were unknown animals still in the oceans and seas, and tentatively identified nine possible species into which those sufficiently described might be classified. He also stated that 600 claimed sightings were made of unknown animals, and about 10% were hoaxes.

International Legend Tripping

In this chapter, I will give a brief overview of some of the most famous and a few of the little-known aquatic cryptids reported around the world. If I miss one you know of, I do apologize.

I also want to touch on a legend that is centuries old but doesn't get a lot of publicity. That is the legend of mermaids or aquatic humanoids. Not all mermaid legends depict these creatures as a shimmering version of femininity often seen in pop culture. Are they a lost civilization of Atlantis that has adapted to breathing underwater? Some today people have sworn that they have seen these aquatic beings in every ocean in the world.

As a kid, my favorite movie monster was the Gill-man from Universal's 1954 movie *The Creature From the Black Lagoon*. I later found out that there is a real legend of a half-man half-fish creature that dwells in the Amazon River known as the Igpupiara. It is one of the oldest myths ever recorded in Brazil and is mentioned in the letter of St. Vincent written by the priest Joseph of Anchieta, in 1560. This creature was later the subject of in the 2017 film *The Shape of Water.*

Some aquatic cryptid legends I will only briefly mention because there isn't a lot of data on them or sightings, but I do include websites to get the most up-to-date information. Some sea serpents have only been seen once, so eyewitness statements are all that is available, and evidence and documentation are rather thin.

As I said at the beginning, the most famous aquatic cryptid in the world is the Loch Ness Monster. Located in the northern part of Scotland, sightings of this lake creature have been recorded for centuries. Still, nobody has gotten a good picture of it. The famous "Surgeon's Photograph" of the monster seemed to be proof of its existence but was later reported in the news to be a fake, though new research on the photo has caused some debate on it. Yet the legend continues and inspires the imagination—and fictional movies, such as *Water-Horse*. This family movie tells a creative and beautiful story about the possible origins of this famed creature—more on this cryptid later in the chapter.

In the 1980 book *All About Dragons*, author Bengt Sjögren wrote that present beliefs in lake monsters are associated with kelpie legends. Sjögren went on to say that stories of lake monsters were originally meant to keep children away from the loch. Sjögren wrote that the kelpie legends have developed into descriptions reflecting a modern awareness of plesiosaurs.

There are three kinds of aquatic cryptids. They are the sea serpent, the lake/river monster, and the aquatic humanoid. Bipedal swamp cryptids seem to have more in common with other bipedal cryptids, and I put them in my chapter on land-based cryptids.

Sea Serpents

For centuries, man has been reporting strange creatures in our ocean depths. There are legends of giant aquatic reptile beasts attacking and sinking ships. When man first journeyed across the waves, when a ship went missing, sea serpents were blamed.

Today, with 71 percent of the earth covered in water, there are aquatic creatures still unknown. When it comes to sea serpents, unfortunately, many aquatic beasts are often seen once and never again. Today there are still reports and videos of large unidentified creatures in our oceans and seas witnessed by dependable observers.

Not all sea serpents make a solo appearance then disappear. In British Columbia, there is a sea serpent creature known as Caddy that is seen frequently. These unknown sea serpents living off the coast of British Columbia are a popular figure in Canadian cryptozoology. Cryptozoologists believe the creature to be a Cadborosaurus, named after Cadboro Bay where most of the sightings have occurred. Sightings of this sea serpent report the creature to be up to 30 feet long and sometimes showing front and rear flippers. The descriptions given by witnesses are consistent and have been reported for ages. In 2009 a video of this sea serpent surfacing in the water was taken by an Alaskan fisherman in Cadboro Bay. In the film, you can see a large object moving through the water.

Author/Cryptozoologist John Kirk has done some of the best research on this aquatic cryptid to date and has written books on it.

Another type of aquatic cryptid creature that resides in the ocean and seems to be making more appearances is the giant squid. Though technically not a sea serpent, this massive creature, at first, was thought to be an old sailor's legend called the Kraken. Now it is science fact: giant squid and possibly octopuses are living in the deepest part of our oceans. With the changing water temperatures in the oceans, more sightings of these large eight-limbed mollusks are being reported.

In Oct 2013, a giant squid washed ashore on La Arena Beach in Spain, and in May 2015, another one appeared on a beach of New Zealand's South Island.

Sometimes reported sightings are misconstrued, creating excitement only to end with a "logical" explanation. For example, in 1937, the body of an unknown animal was found in the stomach of a whale captured by the Naden Harbor whaling station in the Queen Charlotte Islands, a British Columbia archipelago. Samples of the animal were brought to the Provincial Museum in Victoria, and it was identified as a fetal baleen whale.

Lake/River Monsters

Here is a list of but a few lake/river monsters seen around the world.

Nessie, Loch Ness, Scotland
http://www.nessie.co.uk/

If we're going to talk about lake monsters, I think it only fitting that we start with the most famous of cryptids. That is undoubtedly the Loch Ness Monster, often referred to as simply "Nessie." This aquatic cryptid is known the world over and has been in numerous movies and books. Every year people report seeing something unusual in the waters of Loch Ness. To date, there have been over 1,113 sightings of Nessie. To the cryptozoology world, The Loch Ness Monster has evolved into a worldwide icon.

To start with, reports of these mysterious creatures date back to ancient times. There are stone carvings by the Picts depicting a mysterious beast with flippers. A monk claimed to have seen Nessie in the seventh century. One of the first and most famous accounts appears in a biography of St. Columba from 565 AD. According to that work, the monster had attacked one swimmer and was going after another when Columba intervened, ordering the beast to "go back." It obeyed, and over the centuries, only occasional sightings are reported.

Loch Ness is around twenty two and a half miles long and between one and one and a half miles wide, with a depth of 754 feet. The bottom of the loch is as flat as a bowling green. Seven major rivers, the Oich, Tarff, Enrich, Coiltie, Moriston, Foyers, and Farigaig feed into Loch Ness, plus numerous burns, with only one outlet, the River Ness. This flows 7 miles through Inverness into the Moray Firth 52 feet below the loch surface.

The whole Nessie craze started in 1933 when construction began on the road (A82) that runs along the north shore of the loch. Many researchers believe that the drilling and blasting caused the monster to rise up from the depths and into the open.

The first sighting to make the headlines was on May 2, 1933. The newspaper *Inverness Courier* ran a story of the incident reported by a local couple. In the story, they claim that they saw "an enormous animal rolling and plunging on the surface." The story of the "monster" (a moniker chosen by the *Courier* editor) was a top headliner in Great Britain. A circus in England offered a 20,000 pounds sterling reward for the capture of the beast.

But it was in 1934 when Nessie made the headlines worldwide. London surgeon R. K. Wilson was traveling along A82 when he saw something strange in the loch. He stopped, got out his camera, and managed to take a photograph of what appears to show a slender head and neck rising above the surface of the water. It became known as the Surgeon's Photograph.

Sixty years later, it was said to be a hoax conceived by Marmaduke Wetherell, a journalist ridiculed for finding "Nessie footprints" on the shore.

Some cryptozoologists have found inaccuracies in the hoax

The 1934 "Surgeon's Photograph" of the Loch Ness Monster.

story and believe that the photo is genuine.

In 1962, the Loch Ness Investigation Bureau was formed and conducted a ten-year observational survey. They recorded an average of 20 sightings per year.

In 1975, an expedition formed by the Academy of Applied Science led by American lawyer Robert Rines used sonar and underwater photography in Loch Ness. The result was a photograph of what appears to show a giant flipper of an aquatic animal.

In September 2019 Researchers from New Zealand extracted DNA from water samples from the Loch Ness in an attempt to catalog all the living species in the loch. The test results showed no evidence of prehistoric marine reptiles or a large fish such as a sturgeon. They did find a significant amount of eel DNA. The researchers stated that what people see and believe is the Loch Ness Monster might be a giant eel.

The most recent sighting occurred on January 18, 2020. Eoin Fagan once again caught something on video from his webcam at 1558 hours. The video shows an unknown moving object rising from the water and then a few seconds later disappearing again in the loch.

Morag, Loch Morar, Scotland.
https://www.scotclans.com/scotland/scottish-myths/scottish-monsters/morag/

There is another lake monster in Scotland, and this one lives in Loch Morar, an inland loch around 70 miles to the southwest of Loch Ness. Separated from the sea by only a quarter of a mile, it is much smaller than Loch Ness at only 11 miles long by around a mile and a half wide, but it is the deepest freshwater body in the British Isles with a maximum depth of 1,017 feet. Nevertheless, it is a large enough body of water to hold a secret.

The first recorded sighting of "Morag" was in 1887, while in 1948, nine people in a boat reported that they saw a 20-ft-long creature in the loch.

In 1969 two men claimed to have hit Morag with their boat. One of the men then hit it with an oar while his companion opened fire with a rifle. The animal descended into the depths.

Sightings of Morag are rare due to the situation of the loch. It is far more remote than Loch Ness, and only has one small single track road for access at one side.

On August 25, 2013, vacationer Doug Christie reported seeing 'a big black shape... just like a bit of a submarine, all black and smooth.' Christie said he couldn't believe his eyes when he saw it. Christie saw it with his wife, Charlotte. They were staying for a night at the B&B owned by Barra-born Michael MacNeil when the sighting occurred.

Ogopogo, Okanagan Lake, Canada.
https://www.tourismkelowna.com/plan/about-kelowna/history/ogopogo/

Next to Nessie, this Canadian lake monster is the best known lake monster throughout the world. This aquatic cryptid gained international fame in 1976 when the television show *In Search Of* did a whole episode on this cryptid.

Ogopogo is described as being one to two feet in diameter with a length of 15 to 20 feet. It is dark and multi-humped, with green, black, brown, or gray skin. The head is snakelike or even resembling an alligator.

Located about 250 miles (400 kilometers) east of Vancouver, Lake Okanagan is 84 miles (135 km) long and between 2.5 and 3 miles (4 and 5 km) wide, with an average depth of 249 feet (76 m).

Ogopogo has its roots in Canadian Indian legends of a beast called N'ha-a-itk (also spelled Naitaka). Legend has it that whenever Indians ventured into the lake, they brought chickens or other small animals to kill and drop into the water to assure a safe journey. They also believe that Rattlesnake Island on Lake

Okanagan is the home of this cryptid.

Because the lake has been searched several times, most thoroughly in a 1991 expedition with a remotely operated vehicle and a miniature submarine, there has been more evidence produced on this cryptid than any other lake monster.

The best evidence for the existence of this creature is the 1968 film footage shot by a man named Arthur Folden. Folden reported that he noticed "something large and lifelike" in the distance out on the calm water and pulled out his home movie camera to capture the object. It was studied by experts who found no evidence of tampering.

The first recorded sighting was in 1926 when about thirty carloads of witnesses saw it at Okanagan Mission beach. On July 2, 1947, several boaters saw the monster simultaneously.

To date, there are over 200 sightings by credible people, including a priest, a sea captain, a doctor, and police officers.

On a side note, Lake Okanagan and Loch Ness are both on the same longitude line, and are both large deep lakes.

Memphre, Lake Memphremagog, Canada
https://www.mysteriesofcanada.com/quebec/lake-memphremagog/

Like Scotland, Canada has more than one lake monster. One of the lesser-known ones is called Memphre. This cryptid is often described as much like the Loch Ness Monster. While Memphre's existence is disputed by many scientists, sightings continue with it last seen in 2005.

Champ, Lake Champlain, Canada and the United States
https://www.lakechamplainregion.com/heritage/champ

This large beast is said to reside in the depths of Lake Champlain in Essex and Clinton Counties in New York. The beast is nicknamed "Champ" and is known as America's Loch

Ness Monster. Lake Champlain is 125 miles long and, though averaging a depth of 64 feet, it is 400 feet deep in its deepest point. Situated between New York and Vermont, it extends six miles into Québec. The Abenaki and the Iroquois tribes have legends dating back hundreds of years about this aquatic creature. The Abenaki have stories of their horses being mysteriously pulled under by the creature they call Tatoskok.

On July 24, 1819, a boat captain reported he saw a creature black in color, about 187 feet long with a head resembling a sea horse. The witness's story relates the monster reared more than 15 feet out of the water on Bulwagga Bay. He went on to say the monster had three teeth, a white star on its forehead, and a red-colored belt around the neck. He related all this detail, yet he was two hundred feet from the creature.

In 1873 a *New York Times* story reported that a railroad crew had seen the head of an enormous serpent in Lake Champlain. At the time, Clinton County's Sheriff Nathan H. Mooney reported an enormous snake or water serpent, 25 to 35 feet long. Later in August, the steamship *W.B. Eddy* ran into Champ, and nearly capsized, according to the tourists on board.

Showman P. T. Barnum, hearing the reports, offered $50,000 for the monster—dead or alive. As anyone can guess, nobody collected the reward.

In 1981, Sandra Mansi presented a photograph of Champ that she took while on vacation with her family on July 5, 1977. The photo does show what appears to be a large Plesiosaurs-type animal in Lake Champlain.

The 1977 photograph of Champ.

Muyso, Lake Tota, Colombia
https://theculturetrip.com/south-america/colombia/articles/everything-you-need-to-know-about-the-monster-of-lake-tota/

The Muisca, who inhabited the Altiplano Cundiboyacense, for centuries have believed that there is a monster living in Lake Tota in Colombia. This legendary aquatic animal is known in many works as diablo ballena "the devil whale."

The earliest reference to this creature was made by the conquistador Gonzalo Jiménez de Quesada. He described the monster as, "A fish with a black colored head like an ox and larger than a whale." The locals refer to the cryptid as "a monstrous fish," and even as "a dragon."

Yacumama, Peruvian Amazon River, South America
https://www.livinginperu.com/terrifying-legends-peru-3-yacumama-sachamama/

The Amazon River is a dark, forbidding river sluggishly twisting its way through Brazil and eight other South American countries. The river is so vast and largely remote that no bridge passes over it.

There are two legends of the enormous serpent believed to live in the Peruvian Amazon Rainforest.

The first one is "Yacumama," which means "mother of water." Legend has it that this cryptid serpent could suck up any living thing that passed within 100 feet of it.

Another legend, which is said to be older, is that of the giant serpent called the Sachamama which lurks in the same general area. Different Amazonian tribes have different names for their legends.

Many sightings by natives have included descriptions of the serpent having sprouted horns on its head. This peculiar feature comes up in many reports coming from independent observers up and down the Amazon.

Some researchers have theorized that the Yacumama could be a prehistoric version of the modern-day caecilian. There was a prehistoric ancestor of the modern-day anaconda that grew up to 50 feet in length and weighed in at 2,500 pounds called the Titanoboa. This enormous serpent thrived in the tropical jungles of South America some five million years after the extinction of the dinosaurs.

Herpetologists shrugged off the talk as myths and references to the great aquatic boa, the anaconda. However, natives describe leviathans so huge that the anaconda is small in comparison.

During the year 1906, the world-famous explorer Major Percy H. Fawcett shot and killed a gigantic sixty-two-foot anaconda while traveling up the Amazon River. His Indian guides related that there were even more enormous serpents deeper in the jungle.

In 2009 Mike and Greg Warner mounted an expedition in search of the monstrous snakes in the jungles of the Amazon. The expedition recorded mammoth trails of giant snakes and took testimonies of natives who claimed to have seen the Yacumama, but no hard evidence of the cryptid snakes were found.

Today there are countless hotels, tourist agencies, restaurants and other places named for the giant snakes. There is even a large statue of the legendary serpents. Sightings persist as strongly as ever; in the urban center of Pucallpa, it seems that everyone has either sighted or knows someone who has sighted a Yacumama.

Lagarfljót Worm, Lagarfljót, Iceland. https://guidetoiceland.is/connect-with-locals/regina/lagarfljotsormurinn-serpent-in-lagarfljot-lake

The Lagarfljótsormur or Lagarfljót worm is an Icelandic lake monster purported to live in Lagarfljót, a lake by the town of Egilsstaðir. Sightings of this lake cryptid have been logged since 1345 and continue to this day. In fact, in February 2012, a farmer named Hjörtur Kjerúlf took a video of what appears to be a long object moving in a snakelike motion across the current of the river feeding into the lake.

In 2014 a government investigation carried out by the Fljotsdalsherao municipal council in Iceland ruled that a sea serpent named Lagarfljotsormurinn, which legend has it inhabits Lake Lagarfljót, actually exists.

Lariosauro, Lake Como, Italy
https://www.italymagazine.com/news/italys-lake-como-has-monster-called-lariosauro

Lake Como, located in Lombardy 30 miles north of Milan, is one of the deepest European lakes, at about 410 m (1,200 feet) at the deepest location. This glacier lake is also said to be the home of a legendary lake monster. Lariosauro, which means 'lizard from Lario," made the headlines in Europe when it was spotted on 18 Novmeber1946. Two hunters near Colico, on the north shore of Como Lake, related that they observed a creature with very harsh reddish scales travel for a length of ten to twelve meters near the shore. They quickly fired in the direction of the "thing" with their rifles. The creature quickly moved off to the center of the lake, disappearing with a sharp hissing sound.

The name Lariosauro comes from the prehistoric reptile "Lariosaurus balsami," whose fossilized remains were found by the lake. It was seen numerous times in 1950 and as recently as 2003, with many witnesses describing it as a giant eel.

Lake Tianchi Monster, Lake Tianchi, China
http://www.cits.net/china-travel-guide/Urumqi/heavenly-lake.html

The first reported sighting was in 1903 when a strange large creature attacked three people in the lake. The unknown beast escaped back in the depths after being shot six times.

Between 21 and 23 August 1962, a person using a telescope

A Chinese newspaper drawing of the Lake Tianchi monster.

reportedly saw two of the monsters chasing each other in the water. More than a hundred people reported the sightings.

Lake Van Monster, Lake Van, Turkey
https://mysteriousuniverse.org/2019/03/the-mysterious-lake-monster-of-turkey/

Stories of something strange inhabiting Lake Van go back centuries. The first documented sighting was in 1889 when three men journeying through the area on their way to Ahlat stopped and set up camp at the lakeshore. The story goes that they made their way to the water's edge, to clean up. Suddenly an enormous serpent came surging up from the depths. The beast grabbed one of the men and began to drag him into the water. The two remaining men tried to fight it off with fire but to no avail. The creature then bolted into the lake's depths with its still screaming victim. The victim's body was never recovered.

Seen by over a thousand witnesses, this lake cryptid is described as a reptilian beast 50 feet long, with mottled skin and spikes, spines, or triangular humps present on its back. Van Gölü Canavarı ,or more commonly just Lake Van, is an impressive body of water, covering a surface area of 3,775 km, 119 kilometers across its widest point, and with a maximum depth of 451 meters. A church on a lake island called Akdamar Island carries an engraving of one of the creatures in the lake dating back to 915 AD. A supposed short video of the Lake Van Monster was filmed in 1997 by 26-year-old Van University teaching assistant Unal Kozak.

In 2017, a team of archaeologists investigating the lake monster legend discovered a castle buried deep beneath Lake Van in Turkey.

Nahuelito, Nahuel Huapi Lake, Patagonia, Argentina
https://www.patagonia-argentina.com/en/enigma-nahuelito/

Nahuelito is named after the body of water that is her domain, Nahuel Huapi Lake, which covers 318 miles at the foot of the Patagonian mountains. There have been sightings of Nahuelito since 1910 when George Garret, who was the manager of a sailing company, came forward claiming to have seen the creature.

Descriptions of this cryptid have varied from a giant water snake with fishlike fins to an overturned boat. The creature's estimated length is from 15 to 150 feet. Nahuelito is said to surface only in the summer when the wind is still, and the topwater is warmer.

Aquatic Humanoid Cryptids

When people hear the word mermaid, they immediately think of Disney's 1989 movie *The Little Mermaid*, which is considered one of the best animated movies in history. But few people have read Hans Christian Andersen's 1837 book *The Little Mermaid*. In the original book, the young mermaid has her tongue cut out, and gets burned hard by the prince when he chooses another woman. She eventually dissolves into sea foam instead of saving her own life by ritualistically stabbing said prince through the heart and bathing in his blood.

Many countries and culture have their versions of mermaids, from a snake water goddess to a fish with a monkey mouth. Some are benevolent, some ambivalent, and many are openly hostile to the weak humans who cross their paths. In Scotland and Ireland, an ancient legend says that these aquatic creatures live in an underwater kingdom called Finfolkenheim and, during the warm summer months, go to the island of Hildaland. This land would only appear for a moment before disappearing, making it impossible for humans to find.

In the 1840s, P.T. Barnum introduced the Fiji Mermaid to an astounded crowd. Later it was revealed to be a taxidermy fake with the head and torso of a small monkey grafted onto the body and tail of a fish. It was bizarre and strange.

In 1610 Capt. Richard Whitbourne reported that he had seen a mermaid in Newfoundland's St. James harbor.

In 1830 in Scotland, a young boy killed a mermaid by throwing rocks at it; the creature looked like a small child but had a fish's tail instead of legs. The villagers supposedly gave it a funeral and buried it in a small coffin.

In 2007 in the Israeli town of Kiryat Yam, witnesses claimed to see an alleged mermaid, said to resemble a cross between a fish and a young girl. The aquatic creature is said to appear at sunset and perform tricks before disappearing for the night.

A Fiji Mermaid created from two animals.

Witness Shlomo Cohen stated that she was with her friends when suddenly they saw a woman weirdly lying on the sand. She first thought it was just a sunbather, but when she and her friends approached, the creature jumped into the water and disappeared. What shocked them the most was that the human-looking creature had a tail.

Here are some of the famous aquatic humanoid legends from around the world.

Scotland's Selkies

Legend has it that these creatures are gentle creatures who live their lives as seals while in the water and shed their skin to become human on land. Still, they're frequently equated with mermaids because, in Gaelic stories, they are associated with maighdeann-mhara, or "maid of the sea." Selkie legends usually end in tragedy; the folktales almost inevitably feature a selkie's sealskin getting stolen and the selkie getting married and having children with a human, only to find its old sealskin later and get called back to the sea.

A statue of a Selkie.

Ireland's Merrows

Female merrows, with their long green hair, are similar to traditional sirens—the beautiful, half-human fish of mythology. Male merrows, however, are considered hideous and frightening, more fish than man. And they're cruel—so cruel that merrow women were said to have relationships with human men often. The offspring of these unions might have scales and webbing between their fingers. Merrows frequently become tired of the land and try to find a way to return to the sea—with or without their human family. A magical cap called a cohuleen druith enables merrows to live under water.

Faroe Islands Seal Woman

These tiny islands are located halfway between Norway and Iceland and are part of the Kingdom of Denmark. It is here that for hundreds of years, a famous legend told of the Kópakonan. Kopakonan means seal woman, and the legend goes that seals could come ashore and shed their skins once a year on the Thirteenth Night. In the village of Mikladalur, a young man, upon learning about the legend, goes to see for himself. While laying in wait, he watches as many seals swim to shore, shedding their skins to reveal their human forms. The farmer steals the skin of a young selkie woman, who, unable to return to the water without her skin, is forced to become his wife. The man locks the woman's skin in a chest, keeping the key to the lock on his person at all times, so she may never gain access. The two stay together for many years, even producing several children.

Then one day, the man accidentally leaves his key at home. When he returns to his farm, he finds that the sealskin and his wife are gone. He knows that selkie wife has returned to the ocean.

The legend goes on to say that while the farmer is out on a hunt, the man kills the selkie woman's selkie husband and two selkie sons. The enraged selkie woman uttered a curse. She stated that, "Some shall drown, some shall fall from cliffs and slopes. It will continue until so many men have perished that they will be able to link arms around the whole island of Kalsoy." Even today, when a death occurs, it is said to be because of the seal woman's curse.

The people of Miklasadur had a statue of the Kopakonan installed in the Mikladalur Harbor on Kalsoy, one of the Faroe Islands, on August 1, 2014 to commemorate the legend. The 9 foot bronze and stainless steel statue, created by Hans Pauli Olsen, is designed to withstand 13-metre waves.

Norway's Finfolk

Probably the least like a traditional version of a mermaid, finfolk are shapeshifters of the sea. Considered nomads who can alternate between living on land and at their ancestral home—Finfolkaheem—finfolk tend to have an antagonistic relationship with humans. They often abduct humans for their spouses, making them more servant than a partner. Finfolk also have an affinity for silver, and one might be able to escape their grasp by throwing a silver coin their way.

Netherland's Mermaid

In 1403, in the city of Kampen, a dike had a crack in it, opening it up to the sea. Water began to flood into the river. After making repairs, citizens from Kampen claimed that they saw a mermaid swimming in the river in town. At first, people were scared, but the woman continued to swim without bothering anyone. The people eventually decided to capture this woman and bring her on land, where she transformed into a human with two legs. She could not speak, but they cleaned her up and forced her to go to church and become a Christian. Many times she attempted to escape and jump into the water but was always caught. There are no other stories about what happened to her.

Russia's Rusalka

Often translated as "mermaid," these water nymphs of Slavic myth were initially considered benevolent because they came out of the water in the spring to water crops. But the mythology also has a darker side: Rusalka are thought to be the spirits of girls who died violently, and thus they frequently lure men and children to their watery deaths. Their translucent skin gives them a ghostlike appearance, and they'll sometimes use their long hair to trap and entangle their victims.

New Zealand's Marakihau

Most tales of mermaids have been passed down through spoken tales and pictures—and in New Zealand's Maori folklore, they can also be seen on carvings. A little more intense than a mermaid, the Marakihau is a taniwha (guardian) of the sea. It has a human head and the body of a very long fish, as well as a long, tubular tongue that is often blamed for destroying canoes and swallowing large quantities of fish.

France's Melusine

A feminine spirit found in many medieval European folk stories, the Melusine has a serpent tail and occasionally sports wings. The legend describes her as a willful maiden who attempts revenge on her father on behalf of her mother. Her mother punishes her with a serpent's tail.

There are varying legends of Melusine in France, Germany, Luxembourg, and Albania.

Melusine is mainly connected with France as the French royal house of Lusignan claimed to be decedents of her. Images of this sea fairy are seen all over the world—especially on the coffee cups of Starbucks, which has a Melusine-like mermaid as its logo.

Brazil's Lady of the Waters

The idea of mermaids in Brazil comes from the tale of Iara, the "lady of the waters." Iara was initially known as a water snake, but through folklore became an immortal woman with green eyes and brown skin, which was known to lure sailors to her underwater palace, where they became her lovers. Many believe that Iara is responsible for any accidents in the Amazon, especially those where men disappear.

Amazon's Yacuruna

The indigenous people living in the Amazon rainforest believed in aquatic creatures called yacuruna. A yacuruna resembled a human, except that the head, hands, and feet were on backward. Other stories claimed that these humanoids simply had webbed hands, feet, and green skin. Legend said that a human captured by a yacuruna would begin to transform into one, starting with their eyes rolling backward. A shaman would have to reverse the curse before it was too late. Some believed that the yacuruna were an advanced civilization and that they were the source of a shaman's medical knowledge. The Universal movie monster in *The Creature of the Black Lagoon* is based on this cryptid.

Japan's Ningyo

Vastly different from the Western version of a beautiful mermaid, this monster found in Japanese folklore is described as a giant fish with a human face and a monkey's mouth, and sometimes even horns and fangs. In a strange twist of fate, anyone who eats the Ningyo will have eternal youth and beauty—but catching one often brings terrible storms and misfortune to entire villages.

A temple in Fukuoka, Japan is said to house the remains of a

A page from an old Japanese book depicting the Ningyo.

mermaid that washed ashore in 1222. Legend has it that a priest preserved its bones. He believed the creature had come from the legendary palace of a dragon god at the bottom of the ocean. The bones have been displayed for nearly 800 years, and water used to soak the bones was said to prevent diseases. Today only a few of the bones remain, and those are on display at Ryuguji Temple.

No laboratory tests have ever been allowed on the bones, so their exact nature remains unknown.

On a side note, there is a mermaid mummy purported to be over 1,400 years old in one of the oldest-known mermaid shrines in Japan at Fujinomiya, near Mount Fuji. Legend has it that the mermaid was once a fisherman, and according to local mythology, he was transformed into a beast because he deigned to fish in protected waters. The punishment made the mermaid see the error of its ways, and it asked a prince to display its remains to serve as a warning to others.

China's Jiaoren

According to Chinese legend, the Jiaoren weren't just beautiful mermaids. They were very skilled craftspeople who could weave beautiful white cloth called "dragon yarn" that could never get wet. They said that if a mermaid cried, her tears turned into pearls. During the Jin Dynasty, one account told the story of a mermaid who emerged from the water and decided to sell dragon yarn to humans. If anyone were kind to her and gave her a place to stay, she would thank them by crying into a jar, filling it with precious pearls.

Throughout history, there are several accounts of high-society people claiming that they owned cloth made from a mermaid's dragon yarn.

Africa's Mami Wata

The "water spirit" Mami Wata is sometimes described as a mermaid, sometimes as a snake charmer, and occasionally as a combination of both. Found in many African folk stories, the legend of Mami Wata made its way to the Americas during the Atlantic slave trade. Although she can sometimes take human form, she is never fully human. She is closely associated with healing, fertility, and sex.

In conclusion to the chapter, we are discovering new animals and fish in our oceans and seas. There are some rivers like the Amazon that, even today, have not been fully explored. I've shown you but a few of the legendary creatures that continue to be seen by witnesses. Cryptozoology continues to grow in popularity as more and more people are going out and investigating these cryptids.

With our planet's surface covered mostly with water, it is hard to say what is lurking in the deepest parts of the oceans. There are lakes with depths that go beyond what man is used to exploring. There are still new aquatic animals being discovered every day from the bottom of the ocean to the Amazon River basin.

Author Peter Benchley wrote, "You could start now, and spend another forty years learning about the sea without running out of new things to know."

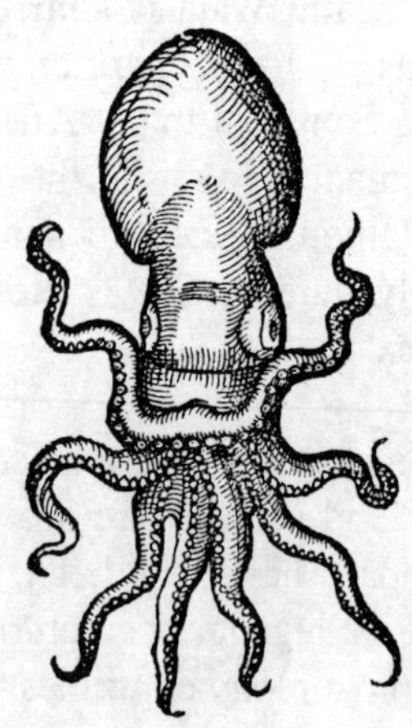

Chapter 6

Monster Hunt: Aquatic Cryptids

I went on my first aquatic cryptid legend trip back in 1975. My interest in these waterway creatures started with my mother, who was born and raised in Scotland. While growing up, she would tell me stories about the Loch Ness monster. When we finally visited Loch Ness in 1975, I walked the shores for hours looking for the legendary lake beast. Unfortunately, the weather turned bad, and we had to leave. I remember that there weren't a lot of Nessie souvenirs to purchase back then, and I remember seeing a team from *National Geographic* magazine out there looking for the creature. It was an exciting trip and something I will never forget.

When I returned to the United States, I remember thinking that I wished there were lake monsters in North America. As luck would have it, I was watching the popular television show *In Search Of*, and the episode was about a lake monster in Canada called OgooPogoo. I went to the library and found some books on the unexplained and found that Lake Champlain in New York has a legendary lake monster called Champ. I continued my research and found that there were numerous other lake and river monsters in the continental United States. Legends of these aquatic cryptids date back to the time of the Native Americans before the European settlers showed up.

If you plan on embarking on a legend trip to investigate a lake monster, you need to know where you are going to look for this cryptid and pack the right equipment. As I said earlier, I like to have everything planned out before leaving on a legend trip. Being that this is an aquatic beast, my list of equipment is going to be different, with items added like a canoe or boat. With a boat comes a lot of different things you need to plan for and have on your packing list. I've compiled a quick list of equipment you'll need at the end of this chapter and a more detailed list of equipment in Chapter 16.

There are differences to consider when looking for aquatic cryptids versus land-based cryptids, such as the difference in the number of sightings between the two. When it comes to lake or river monsters, there are not a lot of sightings compared to other cryptids like land-based ones. Some lake monster sightings are months apart, sometimes years apart. Most sightings are of strange humps moving up and down a river or in the middle of a lake. Most witnesses don't get a perfect look at what the creature is. Some sightings are misidentification of known animals (manatees and sturgeons) or rogue waves that look like humps. But some of these humps are too large to be from a known animal and can't be explained.

Unlike land cryptids, which are primarily nocturnal, aquatic cryptids are seen both in the daytime and nighttime. Evidence suggests that lake/river cryptids are fish-eaters and more active at night. Based on that assumption, you should try to look when the sun is coming up and going down because fish are very active and near the surface at these times.

When the water surface is calm, and the sun is out, there is less mixing of the waters from the different thermal layers, and oxygen in the upper layers is less depleted. The fish will come closer to the surface to get their oxygen from the water. The oxygen is near the surface (which is absorbing oxygen from the air). Presumably, these cryptids are following the fish into the upper layers of the water, which may explain why there are so many sightings in calm, sunny weather.

Sighting in the daytime are usually during the warmer parts of the year. There are more people to make the sightings while enjoying recreational activities going on around the lakeside, i.e., canoeing, swimming, skiing, and scuba diving. Like land-based cryptids, these animals seem to avoid human contact. In other words, when approached, these aquatic beasts submerge into the depths. Noise from boat engines also seems to scare them.

Every animal on earth has a behavior pattern. Reptiles down to fish have some kind of pattern to the way they live. When you read about past sightings, you can see a general profile that these animals seem to be displaying. Usually, these cryptids are observed at a particular time of the year and in specific places. Some animals stay in one area and that is due to low human contact.

When I hear of an aquatic cryptid sighting, like all cryptid sightings, I first check a map of where the sighting happened. If it's in a moving body of water like a river, I look for where the river goes (i.e., lake or the ocean). I also check the feasibility of getting to the sighting location. Will I need a boat, or can I walk along the banks to look for it? I look at the details of the sighting to see which direction the animal went. I consider the time of the year and try to make an educated guess on where the animal is or where it might make another appearance. If you research past sightings in the area, you might be able to pinpoint where it will appear next.

Cryptozoologists do their aquatic monster hunts during the day, primarily due to visibility of the creature (you can't see these animals at night), and that is when the animal seems to like to come to the surface and bathe in the sun. There are also safety considerations to being on a boat or watercraft at night,

As with all legend trips, you need to take into consideration the time of year you want to look for this creature. Summer is the ideal time for hunting, as this is when most sightings occur. You can also plan other things around this legend trip, like water recreation fun, when you're not looking for the creature. If you are taking your family, I highly encourage you to do this.

If you are SCUBA qualified, you might want to do some diving in the sighting location. If you do this, NEVER dive alone. Also, if scuba diving in lakes, you will need the proper diving attire, i.e., dry suit as the water in the depths of some of these lakes can reach freezing levels. Make sure your air tanks are full before arriving. Some lakes do not have places to reload your air tanks. Also, you will need the proper underwater casing for your cameras, and they are not cheap. Some of the housings will only allow you to go down to a certain depth, so carefully check your equipment parameters.

When you arrive at the lake or river, the first thing you need to do is decide where you are going to set up your base of operations. I find campgrounds that are close to the area of the sightings. Loch Ness in Scotland not only has campsites on its shore, but there is also a walking trail that goes around the entire lake. Also, a campground situated in a beautiful location makes the trip much more enjoyable, even if you don't see the monster. Again, I also want to say, never go rucking or hiking by yourself. If you can't find anybody to go with you, then wait until someone is available. I cannot stress this point enough, even if you are simply walking a trail around a lake. You won't have to worry about hunters as hunting is illegal near lakes or rivers on public land.

For scoutmasters and venturing crew guides, you need to see if there is a Boy Scout or Girl Scout camp near the lake and maybe incorporate a lake cryptid legend trip into your weekend outing. It adds to the excitement and gives you and your troop something to look for when they are hiking by the lake.

Setting up a base camp is pretty much the same as making a land-based cryptid legend trip. I always make a checklist to make sure I set up everything we need. Again, you can do it the way you want, because everybody is different. This checklist has worked for me, and I've been doing this for years.

I like to pick an area for my base camp that is close to the lake or river. I have gone to areas that turned out to be full of boats, so you need a plan for multiple locations in case this happens. As I stated earlier, motorboats scare these creatures away. Also, if the area is full of campers, it might be a good idea not to tell everybody you are cryptid lake monster hunting. Additionally, you should locate the nearest hospital, just in case. It doesn't hurt to be proactive, especially with your family or young children.

When you arrive at your actual campsite, the first thing to do is unload your camp gear and get your base camp set up. Put your boat or canoe in a secure location with some way of securing it like a lock and chain to prevent theft. If your boat has an engine, cover it with a tarp, just in case it rains when you are unloading your gear. Also, be careful about what tree you put your boat/canoe under. Some trees have branches that fall and can destroy whatever is under it. Most campsites have secured areas to put your boat/canoe. Keep the life vests and oars in your vehicle. Fuel cans need to go in your boat or car and not in camp where you have a campfire going. Also, always secure SCUBA gear in your vehicle, when you are not using it.

If you are leading this adventure, make sure everybody gets the camp set up before it gets dark. It is vital to get all your gear set up, especially your tents. Around lakes in the summer, insects are a nuisance. Make sure you have the insect repellent ready, and when the sun goes down, you need to have the insect repellent candles. Rivers are different. Mosquitoes do not like flowing water, and fish eat them.

Setting up a campsite is the same as for a land-based cryptid hunt, so please review that chapter for explicit details and advice.

Now that you've got your base camp set up, it is time to scout around the area and see what's out there. In the military, this is called reconnaissance, or "recon" for short. If you have a big enough group, break the members into teams and look in multiple areas. Using a map, with the team members, plot where you want to watch. Look for the location of past sightings and decide based on that. If there is enough time you should take all the teams with you when you go to the area you intend to search. It's easier than going back and explaining it on a map. Something can get lost in the translation. Make sure everybody knows what they should look for and point out where the sightings happened. If it's later in the evening and it's getting dark, wait until the next day to leave the camp, especially if you are looking for river cryptids.

Somebody will need to stay at base camp and monitor the radio. Assign the teams what I call AORs (Areas of Responsibility). These are areas that the team is to investigate and set up static posts, scan the lake or river, and then proceed to the rally point. You can get almost a hundred percent scan of the lake or waterway with multiple teams. These AORs should be marked on the map so the base camp can keep track of them. You should try to have a team on the water with a boat or canoe. It is best to have them where sightings have occurred. If there is a lot of boat traffic, move them to an area where it is quieter and more secluded.

If you are lucky enough to have access to boats, then your boat team needs to stay in a specific area, so if another team sees something strange from the shore, you can give directions to where the team is. Two functional pieces of equipment to have with the boat team is a hydrophone and fish finder. Make sure you have already acquainted yourself and team members with this equipment before the actual hunt.

The hydrophone is a waterproof microphone designed to be used for recording or listening to underwater sound. If you do use this equipment, be aware that any sounds recorded should be checked against previous recordings of known fish/aquatic animals. Hydrophones can be expensive unless you want to purchase a used one

A fish finder (sonar) is an instrument used to locate fish underwater by detecting reflected pulses of sound energy. Sonar is prone to ambiguities and artifacts, and experts should check sonar graphs for interpretation in that field. There are expensive fish finders, and there are cheap ones. It all depends on how much you want to spend on one.

Each team needs to have a working radio with fresh or extra batteries or a cellphone. Place the cellphone in a waterproof bag with a lanyard. I have the teams do radio checks before they move out to their AORs. I've gone over with the teams to always return to base camp if they can't get reception on the radios. In other words, if they can't pick up anybody on the radio, they should turn around and come back. Also, if they see panther or bear tracks, then they are to call it in and return to the rally point. I go over all of this with everybody, before each team moves out to their AOR .

If the lake or river covers a large area, you might consider having the teams use vehicles to go to their AORs. It's easier and quicker. Have a dependable 4x4 vehicle back at base camp in case a car breaks down, or something goes wrong. If another vehicle breaks down, you may have to tow it with yours. That is the reason I own a 4x4 vehicle.

There are occasional land sightings, so looking for drag traces is a good idea. There are fossilized drag traces of animals on prehistoric beaches and waterbeds that may have been left by plesiosaurs/sea turtles. These very much resemble the trails left by elephant seals and sea turtles. First and foremost, look for tracks. Look for loose soil or muddy areas where tracks are easy to see. You'll find these tracks along the banks of the lakes or rivers. You also need to look to see if there is evidence that something substantial came out to the water, like torn-down branches.

If you are conducting your legend trip along a river with

swamplands next to it, you need to watch out for everything around you. For example, in the swamps, there are cypress trees, and their roots grow to the side and up. Swamps flood and the roots grow up above the waterline. These roots, called knees, look like stalagmites and can be sharp and are especially dangerous after dark. Hunters and campers fall and become impaled on them. Have the teams stay on the dirt roads at night. Also, there may be sinkholes, which you can't see, and you can't tell how deep they are, creating a dangerous situation. Make sure you brief your team of all this before you enter the area.

During the recon, designate a rallying point, which is an area to meet after the hunt. It should be on the opposite side of the lake or a certain distance down the river. Have the teams decide where to set up observation points (OPs) where a team can get a good look at the lake or river and where to place the trail cameras. Use trail markers or orange 550 cord to mark your OP (trail markers work best because you can see them at night).

Trail (game) cameras should be facing toward the lake or river. Unlike land-based cryptids, aquatic ones are not shy about having

The author and a friend canoeing in a Florida swamp.

their picture taken. Set them up during the day in secure areas where the creature was sighted. Make sure you remember where you put them. I have found game cameras out in the boonies that were left by owners who forgot where they placed them. Make sure you put a lock on it. Be prepared to leave your camera out for a while unless you are just making a weekend legend trip. Set up some kind of trail marker close by so you can find them to retrieve them.

After you finish the recon, head back to camp. You need to go over the teams AORs and what their plan is. Make sure you answer all questions before going out. Do this now and not in the morning when the teams are hiding out. Make sure everyone knows the plan for the investigation. Reiterate safety procedures to everyone. Finish the evening with dinner and make sure everybody helps with the camp chores and cleans up.

At daybreak, when it is time to move out, get the teams ready, load up the boat/canoe(s), and send the members out to their AORs. Before you head out, always double-check the radios, cameras, and gear. Have all teams keep their video cameras on and recording. Again, teams should stay on their paths or dirt roads. When it comes to rivers, there might be quicksand along the shoreline. It is better to stay on dirt paths and trails to ensure nobody will get lost, and it is easier to backtrack to the rally point. Each team will move to its AOR, wait, and listen.

If, after a couple of hours, nothing has happened, I usually call the teams in and reassign AORs. That way, they don't get bored looking at the same thing all day. Call them in when the sun goes down, and it gets dark. An exception to the rule is when a team starts to see or hear things. If you or one of your teams sees something, then have everybody proceed to that AOR or see what they can observe from their own AOR. Remember, always keep the video camera in record mode and keep a running commentary explaining where you are and what time it is.

When you get all the teams back, inventory all gear. If you and your team will be getting back to base camp late, as a safety measure, call on the radio and let the base know you have stopped and are looking for something. Give them your location as well. It only takes a couple of seconds to do this. If a team does not show up at the prescribed time, don't panic. First, call them on the radio and see what their location is. If they don't answer (radio/cellphone) and it has been a while, then send out only one team with a member who knows the area.

Now, if you want to do some nighttime operations and see if the creature comes out, you need to make sure every team knows what to do in case they get lost or are running late. Ensure each team is equipped with a thermal viewer and nightvision goggles.

On a side note, I don't recommend having a boat team if you are doing night ops.

A thermal imager is a great tool to use when looking for all kinds of cryptids, including aquatic ones. These expensive devices will scan an area and pick up heat signatures. In other words, if there is something alive and giving off heat, this device will pick it up. It works during the daytime as well as at night. Thermal imagers come in a variety of designs, but they are all expensive. Production companies rent thermal imagers on monster hunting and paranormal shows. As I said, they are great for legend tripping, but they are costly.

Night vision scopes/cameras magnify any kind of light source, and you can see for quite a distance. They go through batteries rapidly, so make sure there are extra batteries on hand. Most are not waterproof, so you might not want scopes assigned to the boat team unless it is a large boat.

If you have done your briefing right and every team stayed in their assigned zone or road, then you will reasonably know the general location of each team. If you lose radio contact due to equipment failure, call out and see if the missing team can hear you. Sound travels better at night. Make sure only one team is calling out to them because if all the teams do this, then you won't be able to hear the lost team when they reply. If you are doing your legend trip on a river and the boat team has not arrived back, you need to make sure they know to call when they are running late or stuck for some reason.

If the worst happens and you can't find them, call the police. A Search and Rescue team will come out, and they often have helicopters equipped with thermal heat-detecting devices and will be able to find the lost members. When the police arrive, give them the location where the team is supposed to be, which will provide them with an area to start their search. In the whole time, I have been legend tripping, I have not lost a team. I always ensure each team has an experienced person with them, stays on the road, and has a working radio.

When all the teams are back at the rally point, do a quick debriefing to find out what all the teams saw or heard. Make sure they know where it was they heard the noise or saw the object. That way, you can return to the location and do a more thorough search of the area to find evidence.

Once back at base camp, get everyone together and go over the day's events and talk about what you saw and heard. Review all pictures and video/audio recordings. If you do have something on the image, you or a team will need to reexamine the area and make sure that what you have in the picture is not a log or floating debris. If you get a video or photo of the aquatic beast, my hat's off to you. You can repeat this procedure depending on how many days you decide to stay out there.

Here is a quick packing list for your legend trip.

Aquatic Cryptid Legend Trip Equipment List:

- Camping gear, including tent(s), sleeping bag(s), and cooking stove

- Outdoor clothing, including snake boots
- Sunglasses
- Rain gear—GORE-TEX is great because it also keeps you warm
- Bug spray/sunblock
- Water and items to clean water
- Food
- Trash bags
- Canteens
- Knife/machete/shovel
- Flashlights/headlights/light sticks
- Batteries for all equipment
- Camera—one that is waterproof or waterproof camera shells
- Camera—one that has IR capabilities
- Camera stands and pods
- Temperature detector
- Binoculars/telescope with stand
- Evidence kit including footprint casting material
- Map of the area/GPS—this is good to use so you can mark your location
- Canoe with oars and life vests

Here is what to carry in the backpacks for day trips:

- Camera (with night vision if overnight)
- Survival kit
- First-aid kit—include poison ivy cream, moleskin for blisters
- Foot powder (cold weather)
- Petroleum jelly (hot weather and swamps)
- Extra socks
- Canteen with cup
- Flashlight (two)—always carry a headlamp and an extra flashlight
- GPS (with extra batteries)/ Map of the area

- Compass—in case the GPS stops working
- Poncho (for use in bad weather or as a shelter)
- Rain gear
- Back-up knife
- Water purifier pump
- Plaster casting kit if expecting footprints
- Binoculars
- Trail camera
- 550 parachute cord
- Marking kit
- Bear mace
- Machete
- Food (beef jerky, trail mix, peanut butter crackers, and an MRE)
- Solar wrap used to recharge a cell phone or GPS
- Toilet paper/baby wipes (you will need them)
- Sunscreen/bug spray

Boat crew

- Life vest
- Radio/Cellphone
- Dry bag
- Waterproof flashlight
- Waterproof housing for the camera
- Waterproof bag(s) for radio or cellphone
- Sunscreen
- Sunglasses
- Headgear
- Fish finder
- Hydrophone
- Map in a waterproof bag
- Binoculars

Since people started going camping for recreation, the most popular spots were next to a lake or river. It is one of the best things to wake up and see the lake when you exit your tent or camper. I love sitting down by the lake in the morning, sipping a cup of coffee. Watching the sun come up over the trees is, to me, one of the most relaxing and beautiful things to see.

While there are plenty of lake monsters to investigate, don't forget to enjoy your surroundings and the journey itself.

Chapter 7

Haunted Places Around the World

Ghosts, specters, and apparitions of the undead are legends known the world over. These linked supernatural terms encapsulate an area of interest that fascinates and horrifies at the same time. From ghostly graveyards to spooky prisons, countries all over the world have haunted places. Remember listening to ghost stories as a child, then covering yourself up with your blanket in bed, wondering what ghost lurked in your closet or under your bed? Some ghost stories are steeped purely in folklore and legend, while some carry more weight.

The next legend tripping category I want to go into is the paranormal research field. Today "ghost hunting" has gained popularity as a result of formulaic paranormal television shows. I was surprised to see just how many haunted sites there are throughout the world. In fact, in this chapter I cover just a fraction of them, and it is the biggest chapter on legends.

A ghost hunt or paranormal investigation is a scary and exciting legend trip. Another great thing about this category of legend trip is there are countless places to go ghost hunting; the hard part is finding a location where a paranormal investigation hasn't already been conducted. There are places where paranormal incidents continue to happen, but be prepared to travel to find haunted places suitable for doing an investigation. The following list is just a kind of a highlights list of the famous haunted places around the world. Most of them do offer tours, and some have nighttime ghost tours. I listed the ones on my bucket list.

Some countries frown upon ghost hunts due to their culture. China does not allow ghost hunting. They believe that ghosts are relatives that have returned to survivors and they are treated with respect in Chinese culture. Because of this, Shangai Disneyland does not have a haunted mansion attraction.

On a side note, just because a building is abandoned, it doesn't mean it's haunted. You can be charged with trespassing for entering a structure without permission. In some countries, you will get expelled for intrusion.

1. The Tower of London, London, England
https://www.hauntedrooms.co.uk/the-tower-of-london-ghosts

Many famous people have called the Tower of London their final resting place. Though the former fortress is now flooded with tourists daily, it is still one of the bloodiest places in Europe. Built by William the Conqueror in 1070, the sprawling fortress is most famously known for the number of royal deaths that have occurred there. Tragedy has steeped this infamous fortress for over 900 years and it is home to many ghostly sightings of English royalty, including Anne Boleyn, whose headless apparition is said to haunt the hallowed halls of the tower and Mary, Queen of Scots**.** One of London's most notable historic sites, this former palace, was long used as the city's most notorious prison. It was the site of many executions—including two of Henry VIII's wives.

Other full-bodied apparitions have also been seen, including Lady Jane Grey, who was spotted by a guardsman in 1957. In the White Tower, the White Lady has been seen, often standing at the window, where she once stood waving to her children on the other side of the building.

Perhaps the most spine-chilling of all reports involves the mysterious appearance of two children. Stories include that these

The Tower of London as seen from the River Thames.

specters roam throughout the castle and have been spotted playing on the battlements. They appear to be in their nightgowns, holding hands with a look of terror on their faces. Some researchers believe that they are two former princes who were sent to the Tower after they were deemed illegitimate by Parliament. They vanished one day, and legend has it that their uncle, the Duke of Gloucester, ordered them murdered.

In 1674, a wooden box containing two small skeletons was found beneath a staircase in the White Tower. To this day, visitors report sightings of numerous spirits continuing to inhabit the Tower's halls.

2. The Langham Hotel, London, England
https://www.hauntedrooms.co.uk/product/the-langham-hotel-london

Legend has it that the ghosts are so active at this 153-year-old hotel that they drove out several English national team cricket players back in 2014, who cited sudden heat and lights, and an unexplained presence during the night. Paranormal researchers believe that it houses some elite spirits such as former resident Emperor Louis Napoleon III and a German prince who jumped to his death from his upper-level window.

3. Wychwood Forest, Oxfordshire, England
http://www.wychwoodproject.org/cms/content/history-wychwood-forest

This forest's air of mystery stems from the story of Amy Robsart, the wife of the Earl of Leicester. Amy mysteriously broke her neck and died in 1560; years later, her husband encountered her ghost in Wychwood while on a hunting trip. Her spirit told the Earl that he would join her in the afterlife in just a few days. As promised, he fell ill shortly after the encounter and quickly died. Local legend says that anyone who encounters the ghost of Amy in Wychwood Forest will have the same fate as the dearly departed Earl of Leicester befall them.

The haunted Wychwood Forest near Oxford.

Raynham Hall in Norfolk, England, where the Brown Lady resides.

4. Dering Woods, Smarden, England
https://theghosthuntuk.com/uks-haunted-screaming-woods/

The Dering Woods, also referred to as "the Screaming Woods," have a long history of paranormal activity and are a popular place for ghost hunters. Visitors exploring the woods have reported bloodcurdling screams coming from the forest's depths at night as well as footsteps and whispers on foggy days. Legend has it that the screams are from a ghostly highwayman, who was captured and killed by villagers in the 18th century, and whose ghost still holds quite the grudge. Others believe the hauntings are the result of a 1948 massacre, where 20 people were supposedly found dead in the forest on the morning of November 1. Residents reported seeing strange lights emanating from the woods that Halloween night and autopsies of the bodies couldn't determine a cause of death.

5. Raynham Hall, Norfolk, England
https://www.spookyisles.com/the-brown-lady-of-raynham-hall-a-hoax-or-a-haunting/

Completed in 1637, Raynham Hall is considered one of the

most beautiful English country homes of its time. This gorgeous country home also has a dark past. The estate has garnered an infamous reputation thanks to the Brown Lady of Raynham Hall. Believed to be the spirit of the adulterous Lady Dorothy Walpole, the Brown Lady caused an uproar when a photograph purporting to have captured her essence was published in the December 1936 edition of *Country Life* magazine.

6. Ancient Ram Inn, Wotton-Under-Edge, England
https://www.travelawaits.com/2480927/england-haunted-ancient-ram-inn/

This 12th-century inn is one of the oldest in the Western world. Legend has it that it was once a pagan burial ground and that more than 20 spirits haunt the inn. With ghostly children, a high priestess, and even an incubus wandering the halls, guests have reportedly leaped from the windows in a frenzy to escape.

7. Highgate Cemetery, England
https://www.hauntedrooms.co.uk/highgate-cemetery-london

The highlight of this Egyptian-influenced Victorian cemetery remains the overgrown West Cemetery—only accessible by guided tour—where a maze of paths leads to a circular ring of tombs topped by an imposing cedar tree. In this cemetery you can encounter a ghostly phantom of a woman searching for her kids, a floating ghost of a nun, people vanishing in thin air, and several other crazy things can happen around you!

8. Ruthin Castle, Wales
http://www.ghost-story.co.uk/index.php/haunted-buildings/haunted-castles/318-ruthin-castle-hotel-denbighshire-wales

Behind the red sandstone façade of this gorgeous medieval castle lies a gruesome history that, supposedly, still haunts the estate today. The Grey Lady is the most active ghost that haunts the

Ruthin Castle in Wales.

premises. This mysterious woman is said to be Lady Grey, wife of Reginald de Grey, who was excuted for murdering a peasant girl who she suspected to be having an affair with her husband.

9. Edinburgh Castle, Scotland
https://amyscrypt.com/edinburgh-castle-scotland-haunted-ghosts/

Nestled at the head of Edinburgh's Old Town, this 12th-century fortress was, for many years, an active military base. If its stone walls could talk, they would tell grim tales, including that of a piper who entered the castle's tunnels never to be seen—or heard from—again. Many visitors and staff of this now tourist destination, have experienced many things over the years.

Experiences include shadowy figures, strange lights, sudden drops in temperature, unexplained mists, unusual sounds, the feeling of being watched, and unexpected intense feelings of dread, sadness, and despair.

The most common is the feeling of being touched and pulled, as well as the sighting of apparitions. Spirits that have been witnessed include an old man wearing an apron, a headless drummer boy, and the piper who mysteriously lost his life after getting lost in the tunnels below the castle.

10. Mary King's Close, Edinburgh, Scotland
https://www.scotsman.com/whats-on/arts-and-entertainment/ghosts-mary-kings-close-2463961

This spooky area of the city is an underground warren of streets and dwellings. It was once a thriving trade area where Edinburgh's tradesmen used to live and work; however, in 1645, the close was believed to have been abandoned after an outbreak of the plague. Those that were infected stayed behind in isolation.

Since the 17th century, there have been reports of paranormal goings-on in the close. Today many ghost hunters consider it the most haunted place in Scotland. The Coltheart family who lived

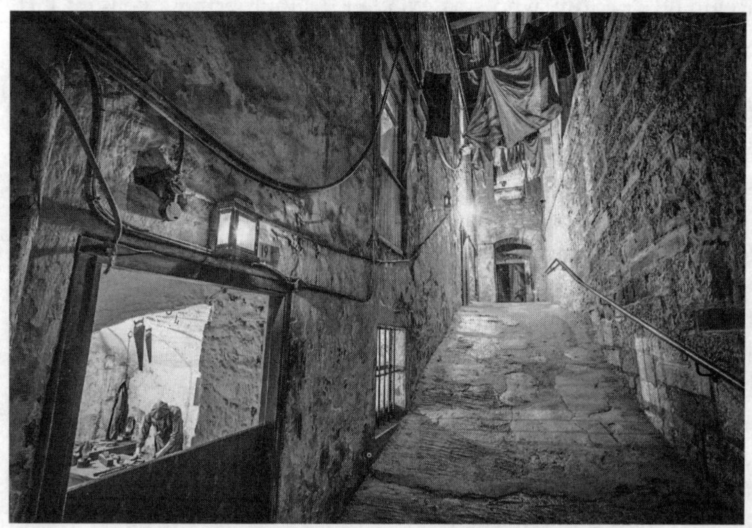

The haunted Mary King's Close in Edinburgh.

there in 1685 where the first ones to report something paranormal. Soon after they moved in after the outbreak of the plague, they began to see ghostly figures, and were left terrified after seeing phantom disembodied limbs, and experiencing very vivid nightmares.

Today, it is now a popular tourist destination, running daily tours for people interested in learning about the history and the legends associated with the close. Staff and visitors have reported seeing the ghost of a 'worried woman,' a woman in black, and a little girl named Annie. The spirit of Annie will interact with people who leave her gifts in one of the rooms.

Other reports include sounds, such as scratching, the sounds of a party or tavern, and footsteps that seem to follow you around. Throughout the area, particularly in Mr. Chesney's house, stones have been thrown, and intense EVPs (electronic voice phenomena) have been captured.

11. The Palace of Holyroodhouse, Edinburgh, Scotland https://www.ancient-origins.net/ancient-places-europe/dark-history-hangs-over-royal-residence-haunted-halls-holyrood-palace-007463

Best known as the home of Mary, Queen of Scots, the palace was the setting for many dramatic episodes in her short reign. Also known as Holyrood Palace, it is located in Edinburgh, Scotland, and is immersed in stories and legends of crimes committed, and victims that remain restless souls, within the palace walls. One such soul is a witch named Agnes Sampson, whose ghost has scared many visitors who visit the ancient residence.

Despite being centuries old, wooden planks in one corner of a room still contain a blood stain from where the private secretary of Queen Mary was brutally murdered. According to accounts of visitors, the sound of crying can be heard emanating from the basement of Holyrood Palace.

12. Charleville Castle, County Offaly, Ireland
http://www.charlevillecastle.ie/

This destination's stunning architecture belies its true nature. Charleville Castle was built in 1798 for Earl of Charleville William Bury and his family. It remained in the family until 1963 when Charles Bury suddenly dropped dead. Widely believed to be one of the most haunted locations in Europe, many apparitions are said to reside within its walls—most notably the spirit of a young girl named Harriet. She met a tragic end in an accident on one of the castle's main staircases.

Today, people report hearing disembodied voices and classical music throughout the property. Visitors have claimed that sounds of children playing fill the air in the room that was once a nursery, and the apparition of Harriet can be seen in the stairwell.

Legend has it that the castle was built on ancient land where religious leaders once convened. The current owners of the property say they've seen hooded figures walking around on the castle grounds.

13. Leap Castle, Roscrea, Ireland
https://www.kinnitty.com/places-to-visit/leap-castle/

This Irish castle was built between the 13th and late 15th century and has seen more gruesome deaths than any other castle. The bloody legend of Leap Castle dates back to its construction in the late 13th century. Having been inhabited by several destructive Irish clans throughout history, many violent deaths have taken place within these storied walls, trapping the victims' souls for eternity.

Legend says that during a struggle for power within the O'Carroll clan (which had a fondness for poisoning dinner guests), one member plunged a sword into his brother—a priest—as he was holding mass in the castle's chapel. The room is now called "The Bloody Chapel," and the priest is said to haunt the

The haunted Leap Castle with its Bloody Chapel.

church at night. The horror doesn't end there. During renovations in the early 1900s, workers found a secret dungeon in the Bloody Chapel with so many human skeletons, they filled three cartloads when hauled away. The dungeon had a trap door so that prisoners would fall and have their lungs punctured by wooden spikes on the ground, and die a slow, horrific death within earshot of the sinister clan members above. The Red Lady, seen holding a dagger, is the most commonly sighted ghost on the grounds.

14. Ross Castle, County Meath, Ireland
https://www.ross-castle.com/history/ghosts

Built by English Lord Richard Nugent, a famously cruel aristocrat, Ross Castle located in County Meath is now a five-bedroom B&B. It is said to be haunted by Lord Nugent's daughter, Sabina. The legend goes that Sabina had fallen in love with the son of an enemy Irish chieftain and eloped. Fate doomed the newlyweds as they were caught in a storm as they rowed across Lake Sheelin and Sabina's husband died.

Sabina secluded herself in her room in deep depression and

was unwilling to eat or drink. She soon died, as well. Both Sabina and the Lord's ghostly apparitions are seen at night on the property. Guests have reported hearing voices and doors shutting on their own, sometimes with a startling bang.

15. Paris Catacombs, Paris, France
https://thetourguy.com/travel-blog/most-bone-chilling-paris-catacombs-legends-and-stories/

Created to alleviate the burden of the city's overflowing cemeteries, the bones of more than six million people now lie in the cavernous tunnels beneath the French capital. Many of these bones are stacked into elaborate patterns throughout the catacombs, visible to travelers wishing to explore the Parisian underworld.

Cataphiles and Catacombs folklore tellers say that every November 3rd, the ghost of Philibert Aspairt haunts the labyrinth of the Catacombs. Aspairt was a doorman at the Val-de-Grâce hospital during the French Revolution. During one of his trips down to the dark cellar to fetch a specific liqueur, Philibert, in the pitch, found himself incredibly lost and confused. His body was found 11 years later by a group of cataphiles.

In the early 1990s, a group of cataphiles (people who study and explore the Paris Catacombs regularly) were walking through the dark chambers and discovered a video camera on the ground.

The video in the camera shows a man who got himself lost in the catacombs and ends abruptly with the man dropping his camera on the ground. To this day, no one knows who this man was, or if he came out alive.

16. Chateau de Brissac, Brissac-Quince, France
https://great-castles.com/brissacghost.php

This beautiful towering building is notoriously known as the place where Charlotte of France was killed. According to the legend, Charlotte, the illegitimate daughter of King Charles VII,

The Chateau de Brissac in Brittany.

was killed by her husband after discovering her affair. Visitors claim to have seen a "Green Lady," because of the color of her dress, roaming the halls.

The current residents (the current Duke of Brissac and his family) have become accustomed to her roaming the rooms, but she has scared many a guest. She is often seen in the tower room of the chapel, wearing her green dress. What's terrifying, however, is her face. If she looks at you, you'll see that her face has gaping holes were her eyes and nose should be, resembling what a corpse would look like. As well as her sightings, her moans are also often heard throughout the castle in the early hours.

17. Château de Trécesson, Brittany, France
https://tourisme-broceliande.bzh/en/lieu/chateau-de-trecesson/

The legend goes that a thief had been lurking around the Château de Trécesson and spotted two people digging a hole.

Then, the two people dragged a young woman, dressed in a bridal gown, and threw her into the pit.

The thief ran home and told his wife about what he'd seen, claiming that he'd overheard the two people saying they'd buried the young woman alive because she had "dishonored" her family. His wife told him to run back and save the young woman, but once he returned, the young bride was already dead.

18. Poveglia Island, Venice Italy
https://www.thevintagenews.com/2019/05/08/poveglia/

A short trip from Venice, the beautiful island of Poveglia has scars from being a quarantine zone for people suffering from the plague. Used for over a century to quarantine victims of plague and other illnesses, Poveglia was later home to a psychiatric hospital or insane asylum.

Since its closure in 1968, the Italian island has remained uninhabited—save for the alleged ghosts of the tormented souls who once called it home.

Today many locals dare not step foot on the abandoned island for fear of being cursed. Fishermen also refuse to fish in the area for fear of dragging up human remains. Ghost hunters claim this spot is a hotbed of paranormal activity.

The ghosts of the patients and victims of disease are said to haunt the island and its buildings. Voices and screams are often heard, with EVPs often captured. Dark, fleeting shadows are seen. There have been reports of people becoming possessed by a supernatural force. On the television show *Ghost Adventures* host Zak Bagans was possessed during the crew's visit a few years ago. On the show Zak suddenly became overcome by rage. Visitors coming on the island have reported feeling an oppressive evil feeling and they often depart in absolute terror.

19. Capuchin Catacomb, Italy
https://www.lifeinitaly.com/travel-destinations/the-capuchin-crypt-of-palermo

Outside the city of Palermo, mummies of more than 2,000 individuals lie within the catacombs of this Sicilian monastery, many dressed to reflect the station they held in life. When entering the catacomb one may be reminded of Dante's inscription above the gates of Hell: "Abandon all hope, ye who enter here." It is not to Hell you walk, however. It is, in the end, a serene place of rest, albeit creepy for most.

Initially reserved exclusively for the burial of religious officials, it was later expanded to include noblemen and the families of wealthy benefactors—like the young Rosalia Lombardo, called the "Sleeping Beauty" for her impeccably-preserved remains.

Though denied by the monks that take care of he caracombs. It is rumored to be haunted.

Taking photos and videos are strictly prohibited in the catacombs.

20. Castello di Montebello, Torriana, Italy
http://www.castellodimontebello.com

The region of Emilia-Romagna is renowned for its beautiful landscapes and excellent food. Located here is a 14th-century hilltop tower. Like many castles that populate the Italian countryside, this stone structure has a dark history. The ghostly tale of Azzurrina has made this location one of the most haunted in Italy.

In 1375 this castle was the the home of an albino girl, Guendalina, who was kept under guard in the tower. The story goes that on the 21st of June, 1375 she ran down the basement stairs to retrieve a dropped ball—never to be seen again. The day of the summer solstice is when people still report hearing her cries. There have been many investigations into these sounds, and paranormal researchers have visited on several occasions.

Today the castle is a popular tourist attraction and is open for tours.

21. Palacio de Linares, Madrid, Spain
http://www.madridtourist.info/linares_palace.html

Formerly the home of the Marquis and Marchioness of Linares, the Palace of Linares was built for Don José Murga and his wife, Raimunda Osorio. It's one of Madrid's most emblematic palaces and is known for its beautiful architecture and exquisite interior.

Hidden beneath its opulent exterior are trap doors, disappearing staircases and, legend has it, the ghost of Don José and Raimunda's daughter. There are reports of the singing and crying of an unseen young girl heard in the palace from time to time when there are no more visitors in the building.

22. Davelis Cave, Mount Penteli, Attica, Greece
https://theculturetrip.com/europe/greece/articles/the-story-behind-greeces-haunted-davelis-cave/

This cave, Attica's second-highest, has a long history of otherworldly activity—in antiquity, it was a place of worship for Pan and other mythical beings, a role that evolved in the Middle Ages into a Christian religion of the extremist kind, with ascetic hermits setting up camp at its entrance. More recently, it has allegedly been used as a place of occultism and satanic activity.

Davelis cave has a long history of ghostly phenomena such as glowing orbs and vague forms of human figures consisting of mists and shadows. There have even been a few reports of strange creatures resembling sheep that disappear when approached.

There are stories of cave explorers who have become severely disoriented and unsure of where they are or how long they were in the cave. Some people who have gone into the cave have never

The haunted Davelis Cave on Mount Penteli, Attica, Greece.

been seen again. Researchers suspect that they got lost in the maze of tunnels.

Unsurprisingly, people claim to have seen apparitions and felt inexplicable dread in its vicinity; there have even been reported sightings of UFOs.

The real history of this cave and its current paranormal reputation has not been fully investigated.

23. Babenhausen Barracks, Hesse, Germany
https://ghostwatch.net/paranormal-reports/haunted-locations/report/31-babenhausen-barracks

The barracks are located on Babenhausen Kaserne, near Hesse, Germany. A Kaserne is a military base for military units. It has a long history of being used during multiple wars to house soldiers for combat. It has been home to soldiers, both German and American, over time.

Babenhausen Kaserne's history actually goes back to the year 1891, when three squadrons of the Red Dragoons made its home in the Babenhausen castle from 1869 until the group left in 1891. After those, numerous German units occupied the Kaserne.

During World War II, it was home to a development detachment of the German air force (Luftwaffe). The Luftwaffe stationed several fighter units at the nearby Babenhausen airfield.

The Kaserne was also used as a POW camp for 400 soldiers until the United States Army's 3rd Infantry Division liberated it on 25 March 1945.

After the war, from 1947 to 2006, various US Army units occupied the Kaserne. There are stories of soldiers who have picked up a telephone and have reported hearing a woman talking backward; it's not clear whether it's in English or German.

On 29 June 2007, after 56 years, the US officially returned the Babenhausen Kaserne to the German government. The former military base, as well as the barracks, fell into years of disuse.

There have been numerous reports of paranormal activity within the barracks, including reports of the ghosts of World War II German soldiers walking the barracks hallway at night. Lights are known to turn on and off by themselves. US Army military police have investigated strange ghostly voices coming from the basement. At night, disembodied footsteps and German commands echoed through the barracks with no one there.

Later a German company, Meltedgum, turned a section of the barracks into a museum. Ghost hunters from all over the world have journeyed there to conduct paranormal investigations.

On a side note, there is another legend of a witch who was burned at the stake. Her ghost is said to have seduced and killed several German soldiers.

24. The Black Forest, Germany
https://www.roughguides.com/destinations/europe/germany/the-black-forest/

In the state of Baden-Württemberg in southwest Germany

is one of the country's most picturesque and extensive, forested mountain ranges. It is known in Germany as the Schwarzwald meaning "Black Forest," for its impenetrable darkness. Hardly any sunlight breaks through the dense fir trees of the dark wooded area. The Black Forest reaches to the south, where it borders the beautiful Rhine river, and to the north is the Feldberg, the highest mountain in the Black Forest.

Is it any wonder the Brothers Grimm set so many of their fairy tales here? The Black Forest is the site of some of the scariest fairy tales the brothers ever wrote. For centuries, there have been tales of prowling werewolves, a headless specter riding on a magnificent white steed, a king who kidnaps women to take them to his underwater lair, witches waiting for lost travelers, and the devil himself.

There is even a tale of a Slender Man-like figure called der Grossmann. Described as being a tall, horribly disfigured man with bulging eyes and many arms, he attempts to lure young children into the Black Forest never to emerge again. Indeed, a tale made up to scare children but it heightens the forest's sense of spooky mysticism.

The Black Forest is also the subject of a 1974 gothic novel by Ludwig Flammenberg (which is a pseudonym for Carl Friedrich Kahlert) called *The Necromancer; or, The Tale of the Black Forest.*

Today the Black Forest is a popular tourist area known for cuckoo clocks and world-renowned thermal spas—and the Grimm Brothers' fairy tales.

25. Burg Wolfsegg, Wolfsegg, Germany
https://amyscrypt.com/wolfsegg-castle-germany/

This 800-year-old castle in the municipality of Wolfsegg, Germany, is haunted by a "White Woman" who scares off any visitors who pass. Legend has it that the ghost is Klara von Helfenstein, who was reportedly murdered by her jealous husband.

The haunted castle of Burg Wolfsegg, Wolfsegg, Germany.

Researchers later discovered that Klara outlived her husband and wasn't victim to murder at his hands. Whatever the truth may be about her death, many visitors, who have seen her ghost, believe that it is her spirit remaining at the castle.

There is also the legend of the hole that exists not too far from the castle within part of the forest that surrounds it. Large amounts of bones have been found in this deep crevice within many of its chambers. Many people have gone missing under mysterious circumstances within the forest. Legend has it that there is a monster that lives in the hole. No one has been able to describe the beast, but even today, strange noises emanate from the forest and the area around the hole.

26. Castle Frankenstein, Odenwald, Germany
https://the-line-up.com/frankenstein-castle

Two hundred years ago, Mary Shelley had a "waking dream"

that would become one of the most famous horror novels of all time, *Frankenstein*.

Lord Conrad II Reiz of Breuberg constructed the castle in 1250. He christened the structure "Frankenstein Castle" and afterward adopted the name "von und zu Frankenstein." The term "Frank" refers to the ancient Germanic tribe, while "stein" means stone. "Frankenstein" means "Stone of the Franks."

One of its most famous inhabitants was Johann Konrad Dippel, whose studies led him to try to bring the dead back to life, a practice that involved exhuming corpses and experimenting on them. Dippel and his subjects are said to still roam the castle, which now lies in ruins. Some say that the castle's dark legend made its way to a young Mary Shelley and provided inspiration for her great novel, but the real history is almost as colorful.

Today during the Halloween season, the castle is set up as a haunted attraction getting hundreds of visitors from all over the world.

27. Borgvattnet Haunted Vicarage, Ragunda, Sweden https://coolinterestingstuff.com/borgvattnet-the-haunted-vicarage-sweden

Nestled in the foothills of Sweden is an old clergy house, originally built in 1876. There have been reports of weird happenings in this parsonage since the 1960s. The gray wooden structure now serves as bed and breakfast in a rural area featuring snowmobiling, fishing, and not a lot more. Guests at Borgvattnet have claimed to hear footsteps, music, and the sound of three crying ladies coming from the inn—and the proprietors will reward you with a certificate that says you stayed through the night.

The first ghost ever documented at the vicarage came in 1927 when the chaplain Nils Hedlund resided there. He reported many strange happenings, including one particular encounter with something paranormal. He was on his way up to the attic to gather his laundry when he witnessed his laundry being torn down from the line by an unseen force.

Rudolf Tangden, a priest who lived at the vicarage during the 1930s, saw an elderly woman dressed in grey appear in a room. He followed her as she walked away, but she vanished in front of his eyes. In the 1940s Tangden's successor, Otto Lindgren, and his wife said they had several paranormal experiences, including unexplained sounds and moving objects.

One story tells of a woman who was staying in the guestroom and was awoken in the middle of the night to see three women sitting there staring at her. She quickly turned on the light, and they were still looking at her; however, they now appeared blurry.

In 1945 the chaplain Erick Lindgren moved into the vicarage, and he began a journal recording many of his own experiences in the house. He reported being thrown out of his chair regularly by an unseen force.

The current building is serving as a restaurant/cafe, as well as a guest house. If you dare to stay the entire night, you'll receive an overnight-stay certificate to prove it!

28. Akershus Fortress, Norway
https://www.sofn.com/blog/a-mysterious-fortress-on-the-oslo-fjord/

Many in Norway consider Akershus Castle to be the most haunted place in the country. Akershus Fortress was built in the late 1290s and served as a defensive stronghold for the city of Oslo. It was the ultimate defense against foreign attacks and was instrumental in the Seven Years' War. The most famous legend is of the demon dog named Malcanisen that's said to guard the gates to the castle. Legend says that anyone who is approached by Malcanisen will have a horrible death sometime in the following three months.

It served as a prison during the 18th and 19th centuries,

with many prisoners dying during their imprisonment. Nazis also occupied the castle during World War II, carrying out many executions on the site.

The ghost of a woman called Mantelgeisten is often seen within the castle, walking back towards her chamber. She appears from the darkness wearing a long robe and has no facial features.

Today the sprawling fortress is used for some royal functions and can be toured by the public; however, locals say its war-torn past has yet to leave, noting that some have seen the ghosts of soldiers roaming the halls.

29. Finnish National Theater, Helsinki, Finland https://explorehelsinki.wordpress.com/2016/10/30/ghosts-behind-the-stage/

First established in 1872, this theater has gained a reputation for being one of the most haunted places in Helsinki. Legend has it that this building has the ghosts of at least three former actors still treading the boards here. One is an unnamed "Grey Lady," another is Aarne Leppänen, who died in 1937. The third apparition, Urho Somersalmi, is well known in the world of Finnish actors. One night he took an axe, which he had been presented with by his country's Actors' Union, and murdered his wife. He then hanged himself. Workers claim that they often see him wandering in the corridors carrying that exact axe.

30.Hoͥfði House, Reykjavik, Iceland https://visitreykjavik.is/hofdi-house

Overlooking Reykjavik's waterfront, the Hoͥfði House is most famous for hosting a meeting between Ronald Regan and Michael Gorbachev in 1986, a historic moment during the end of the Cold War. The building has housed many other famous figures over the years, including Queen Elizabeth, Winston Churchill, and Marlene Dietrich, plus a handful of British ambassadors.

It was one such ambassador who first experienced "The White Lady," a ghost who many believe to be a victim of suicide. The phantom lady caused so much panic and distress, the ambassador persuaded the British foreign office to sell the house immediately.

31. Corvin Castle, Romania
http://romaniatourism.com/castles-fortresses-romania-corvin-castle-hunedoara.html

These dark, brooding castle ruins sitting up in the Carpathian mountains are known the world over. Corvin Castle is most famous for being where Vlad the Impaler was held prisoner by John Hunyadi, Hungary's military leader, and regent during the King's minority. Vlad III's despicable acts of cruel torture inspired Bram Stoker's novel *Dracula*. Also known as Hunyadi Castle or Hunedoara Castle, this awe-inspiring Renaissance Gothic–style castle is said to be haunted by the spirits of the lives taken within these castle walls. Several paranormal researchers and documentarians have investigated the estate.

Featured in numerous paranormal television shows and movies, the castle, today it is one of Romania's most popular tourist destinations, with thousands of visitors coming each year.

32. Bran Castle, Romania
http://www.bran-castle.com/

Count Dracula first appeared in the novel *Dracula,* published in 1897, by the Irish writer Bram Stoker. The famous vampire is a Transylvanian count with a castle located high above a valley, perched on a rock with a flowing river below in the Principality of Transylvania.

Bram Stoker never visited Romania but, based upon a description of the castle that was available to him in turn-of-the-century Britain, he depicted it as being the home of his vampire character.

The famous Castle Bran in Transylvania.

Nestled high on a hill in Transylvania, the castle rises above the trees in the Carpathian Mountains with its burnt-orange-tiled turrets and steeples.

It was built between 1377 and 1388 as a strategic site overlooking a heavily trafficked mountain pass between Transylvania and Wallachia. Researchers have concluded that although the Vlad might have passed several times near Bran, there is no historical document attesting that he ever visited it.

This doesn't stop hundreds of visitors from all over the world who descend on the Transylvania castle to experience the eerie atmosphere of the area.

Bran Castle was a favorite residence of Romania's Queen Marie, whose ghost is said to walk the hallways at night.

Today, the castle is open as a museum. It is a popular location for Halloween events, like the 2016 competition to win the chance to stay in the castle Halloween night, retracing the steps of Jonathan Harker from the opening pages of Bram Stoker's novel.

33. The Island of Daksa, Croatia
https://balkanist.net/haunted-croatian-island-one-will-buy/

The island of Daksa's legend is so frightening that no one will buy the place, despite being prime for-sale real estate just off the coast of Dubrovnik. The deserted island was the site of a massacre of 48 Nazi sympathizers, including the mayor, after Dubrovnik's liberation. Legend has it that the bodies were left unburied, decaying for decades. Passerbys have reported on stormy nights, moaning coming from the island.

34. Čachtice Castle, Slovakia
https://slovakia.travel/en/the-castle-of-cachtice

High up in the Karpaty mountains are the ruins of the "mysterious castle in the mountains." It towers above the village Čachtice in western Slovakia. It is famous for once being the residence of the bloody countess Elizabeth Báthory. Perhaps the world's most prolific female serial killer.

Legend has it that the countess killed over 600 young girls and bathed in their blood to stay forever young and beautiful. The gadget used by the countess to obtain blood was a kind of iron maiden with knives incorporated in its lid. When the unfortunate victim was placed into the iron maiden and the lid closed, the blades would pierce her chest, and the blood flooded down into a prepared tub.

Between 1602 and 1604, rumors began to spread of Countess Báthory's atrocities. In 1610, King Matthias II assigned Thurzó, the Palatine of Hungary, to investigate. As a result of the investigations, the countess was arrested, along with four of her servants, for these crimes. Her sentence was that she be locked in a tower at Čachtice Castle, for the rest of her life.

The castle was burnt during the Rebellion of Estates by the soldiers of Francis II Rákoczi and fell into decay.

Today it is a popular site where visitors can hike up to the ruins and take in the panoramic view. There are reports of Countess Bathory's ghost walking the ruins at night. It was also one of the locations used in the classic horror film *Nosferatu*, but this castle's haunted history extends beyond the big screen.

35. Hoia-Baciu Forest, Romania
https://www.travelawaits.com/2478360/hoia-baciu-forest-bermuda-triangle-romania/

Located just west of Cluj-Napoca, this eerie wooded area consists of 729 acres. In 1968, this mysterious forest gained instant fame when a military technician captured a photograph of a "UFO" hovering over the forest. Hoia-Baciu has gained paranormal notoriety around the world, with some believing it to be a portal that causes visitors to disappear. The history of the forest is shrouded in mystery.

Those who have passed through the woods without being zapped have reported experiencing rashes, nausea, and feelings of anxiety. Known as the "Bermuda Triangle of Transylvania," the spooky curved trees that populate the forest just add to the eerie atmosphere. There is the story of a young girl who vanished into the woods, only to return five years later with no recollection of what had happened. Another tale involves a shepherd and a herd of sheep disappearing in the forest without a trace.

Today, several local companies offer guided tours of the forest where you'll get a one-of-a-kind experience filled with history, folklore, and mystery. There are marked hiking and bike trails for recreational purposes.

More recently, the Travel Channel television show *Ghost Adventures* filmed an investigation there.

36. The Kremlin, Moscow, Russia
https://gulfnews.com/world/europe/the-ghosts-in-the-kremlin-1.1923489

The 1930s-era Kremlin, located in St Peter's Square, is said to be haunted by Soviet leaders Lenin, Trotsky, and other former tzars. Surrounded by the Kremlin Wall and Kremlin towers, this massive complex has four palaces, a bell tower, and four cathedrals. It has endured for over five centuries as the cradle of Russian power and is the official residence of the president of the Russian Federation.

Security guards have reported seeing the ghost of Josef Stalin, preceded by an icy chill. Apparitions of Nicholas the Second are said to foreshadow impending disaster. Ivan the Terrible still lurks about too. He died of a stroke during a game of chess, and his ghost is occasionally spotted on the bell tower, and people have reported that they have heard his footsteps.

Today the Kremlin is a popular site for visitors from around the world, with guided tours of the vast complex. Unfortunately, the government does not permit paranormal investigations of any of the buildings and structures of the Kremlin.

37. Taj Mahal Palace Hotel, Mumbai, India
https://amyscrypt.com/taj-mahal-palace-hotel-haunted-mumbai-india/

The five-star Taj Mahal Palace is a waterfront hotel, located right in the heart of Mumbai. Dubbed one of the best hotels in India, it features fantastic views and interiors fit for a royal.

This luxury hotel opened its doors in 1903 and has since attracted many well-known guests ranging from movie stars to world leaders. It served as a hospital during World War II. In 2008 the hotel made the headlines when terrorists stormed the building and held several guests hostage. In the end, 137 people died, with 31 of these deaths occurring within the Taj Mahal Palace Hotel.

One of the hotel's more macabre claims to fame is its aura of mystery. According to legend, the building's architect, W.A. Chambers, upon discovering the hotel was facing the wrong

The famous Taj Mahal Hotel in Mumbai, India.

direction, jumped to his death from the fifth floor. His spirit now roams the halls, running into guests in the hallways and walking around the roof. There is one story of Chambers' ghost knocking a staff member unconscious who was attempting to steal precious silverware.

This hotel has the reputation of being not only the most haunted in India but also the world.

38. Morgan House, India
https://timesofindia.indiatimes.com/travel/destinations/a-haunted-boutique-hotel-in-kalimpong-frequented-by-bollywood-stars/as66183093.cms

Kalimpong is a beautiful hill station in West Bengal, India, known for its educational institutions, established during the British colonial period.

Here in this beautiful town lies The Morgan House. It was

built in the 1930s by English jute baron George Morgan and his wife, who lived on the property shortly after getting married.

The legend states that Mr. Morgan used to torture his wife, causing her to fall into a state of sorrow and unhappiness. Eventually, Mrs. Morgan died, and Mr. Morgan abandoned the property. A trust took ownership of the house after its abandonment.

For decades, the home sat on the hill in a state of disrepair until, after India attained independence, the government took control of the property.

Now, the Morgan House is a boutique hotel, though people still report hearing the tapping of Mrs. Morgan's heels in the hallways. The hotel offers a beautiful view of the Kanchenjunga mountain range.

39. Dow Hill Forest, India
https://www.nativeplanet.com/travel-guide/dow-hill-of-kurseong-the-most-haunted-place-in-india-002542.html

Located in the West Bengal town of Kurseong, the Dow Hill Victoria Boys' School is known as one of the most haunted places in India. Witnesses claim to hear footsteps echoing through the halls when the school is closed from December to March.

It is the surrounding forest that garners the most paranormal attention. Kurseong is a hill station in West Bengal studded with picturesque landscapes, wooded mountains, and green tea plantations. Nicknamed "The Land of Orchids," this area has a dark side to it!

Legend has it that the wooded area is the site of several murders, and woodsmen have reported seeing a headless boy wandering among the trees, and along the path between the school and forest appropriately named "Death Road." Witnesses have reported a feeling of being watched and followed. Also, there have been reports of mysterious red eyes glaring from the dark woods and the ghost of a woman with gray clothing wandering the area at night.

40. Monte Cristo Homestead, New South Wales, Australia
https://www.montecristo.com.au/

This historic homestead in Junee, New South Wales, is regarded as the most haunted location in Australia. Its reputation stems from several tragic events that have occurred since 1885 when it was first built. From the time of its construction up to 1948, the Crawley family owned and resided in the property. During this time, the family was beset by many deaths. A young child died when he fell down the stairs. A maid to the family fell from the balcony, and a stable boy burned to death on the property.

Legend has it that the caretaker kept his mentally ill son, named Harold, chained up in the cottage for 40 years. Later, the police found Harold curled up next to the body of his dead mother. He died shortly after in a mental institute.

The tragedy doesn't end with the Crawleys. When a group of caretakers took over the home in 1961, a caretaker was shot and killed in the caretaker's cottage.

There have been apparitions, strange orbs seen, and poltergeist incidents along with strange phantom noises heard by witnesses.

The property is currently operating as a bed and breakfast and runs ghost tours.

41. Port Arthur, Australia
https://portarthur.org.au/tour/paranormal-investigation/

Port Arthur is a former convict settlement on the Tasman Peninsula, which is connected to the mainland by an isthmus just 30 meters wide. Between 1833 and 1853, it was the destination for the hardest of convicted British criminals. During those decades, the settlement—touted as "inescapable"—focused on correcting the inmates' morality, using methods like solitary confinement and mandatory church services. During its 47 years as a penal settlement, more than 1,000 people died.

Closed in 1877 as a prison, Port Arthur sits on the scenic Tasman Peninsula with a chapel, guard tower, and mass graves of former felons serving as reminders of the country's dark past as a British Empire prison colony.

There have been more than 2,000 reports of unexplained activity at this location, making this place one of the most haunted in Australia. There have been numerous reports of doors opening and closing by themselves, phantom footsteps and unearthly noises, and dark figures appearing.

Today ghost tours are available of the ruins and open-air museum, as well as the nearby Isle of the Dead, an island housing the bodies of deceased convicts in unmarked graves.

42. Hotel Kurrajong, Canberra, Australia
https://hotelkurrajong.com.au/

This four-star hotel has a long list of ghosts roaming its halls. One of the entities seen is the ghost of former Prime Minister Ben Chifley, who died on the night of June 13, 1951 after suffering a heart attack in room 214. His gray-suited ghost is known to appear in that same room from time to time, writes *The Canberra Times*. And then there's the Old Parliament House itself, where security guards and cleaning staff have reported hearing their names whispered in the night.

43. Aradale Hospital, Australia
https://www.eerietours.com.au/

Known as "Mad-Man's Hill," this hosptial is said to be the location of over 130,000 deaths during its 150-year history. Australia's most haunted asylum was constructed in 1860, to accommodate the growing number of "lunatics" in the colony of Victoria. It opened its doors for patients in 1865. It was closed as an asylum in 1993. The facility is now abandoned and is one of

Victoria's creepiest sites.

With over 60 buildings and 100 acres, and countless reports of paranormal activity, Aradale has become popular with ghost hunters.

The best-known ghost to roam the halls of this abandoned hospital is that of Nurse Kerry. Witnesses have seen her continuing her nursing duties, making her rounds of her former patients in the afterlife.

On Aradale's old men's wings, where it secured its most dangerous patients, people have claimed to have been bitten, scratched, and violently pushed.

Visitors have reported experiencing unexpected fainting, nausea, and pains while walking through individual rooms.

Even though the building is not in use, there are Ghost tours and paranormal investigations events.

44. Manly Quarantine Station, Australia
https://www.qstation.com.au/ghost-tours.html

The quarantine station was built in Sydney's harbor in the 1830s to hold settlers who came off the ships suspected of having diseases. Since being open, 600 people died out of the 26,000 who stayed there till its closure in the 1980s. The unfortunate souls died from deadly diseases like the bubonic plague, smallpox, cholera, tuberculosis, typhoid fever, and Spanish influenza.

Unlike other haunted locations, every building and space across the station has had reports of apparitions or ghostly figures. With hundreds of ghost incidents, the station is one of Australia's most haunted sites.

Some guests heard voices repeating the same thing over and over, even though they weren't standing near anyone. Some visitors claimed to have captured images of spirits while at the station.

Today there is a hotel on the compound, which offers

incredible views across Sydney and out to sea. In the evening, the hotel offers ghost tours to its guests and visitors.

45. Larnach Castle, New Zealand
https://hauntedauckland.com/site/larnach-castle-dunedin/

Located outside of the city of Dunedin, situated on the picturesque Otago Peninsula, is the only castle in New Zealand. Larnach Castle was built between 1871 and 1887 to serve as the residence of William Larnach, a prominent local politician. It is famous for its 3,000-square-foot ballroom, which Larnach had built as a 21st birthday present for his favorite daughter, Kate. Unfortunately, she later died of typhoid at age 26.

After William Larnach died in 1907, it was sold and used for many things, including a lunatic asylum, a hospital for shell-shocked soldiers and a nuns' retreat.

Later is was purchased in 1967 by Barry and Margaret Baker, who restored the castle to its original splendor, restoring all the original furniture.

Legend has it that Larnach's daughter Kate haunts the ballroom to this very day. In 2008 it was reported that there had been more than 30 reported sightings. The witnesses reported being touched and pushed by an unseen force and other occurrences at the castle.

Today the castle is one of New Zealands popular tourist attractions, complete with a nighttime ghost hunt. Paranormal investigators investigated the castle's hauntings on the hit television show *Ghost Hunters International*.

46. Halifax Citadel, Fort George, Canada
https://www.pc.gc.ca/en/lhn-nhs/ns/halifax/activ/visite-hante-ghost-tour

Situated on the summit of Citadel Hill is Canada's most haunted historic site. This star-shaped fort located in the town of Halifax, Nova Scotia, is almost 300 years old, with the original foundations built in 1749, and reconstructed in 1856.

To date, there have been hundreds of ghostly sightings and incidents at the fort. A lot of visitors have reported disembodied voices, unexplained bangs and knocks, and the feeling of being watched. Some people have reported an unseen presence pushing them.

Staff and visitors have reported apparitions of a man in a red cloak, and a lady who shows herself in mirrors. There is even the ghost of a soldier in uniform seen walking into one of the rooms in the old prison area and simply vanishing.

Today the fort is a National Historic site and offers tours that include ghost tours. On a side note, there is a ghost of a little girl that follows the groups on the ghost tours, with the guests often experiencing her holding their hands.

47. Casa Loma, Toronto, Canada
https://www.toronto.com/news-story/4180181-ghost-stories-abound-at-casa-loma/

Businessman Sir Henry Pellatt built this castle in 1914 for his wife, Lady Mary Pellatt. In this Gothic Revival-style house are corridors and secret passageways. There are tunnels underneath the property.

The castle during World War II had a top secret mission, which even today is not fully known. It is one of the supposed sites for the ultra-secret Station M.

The castle is said to be haunted by several ghosts, one of which is Henry glaring out of the windows on the second floor. The spirit of Mary will turn off the cameras of those who have tried to capture a snapshot of her. In the tunnels, guests have reported speaking to and otherwise interacting with an unseen presence.

A ghost frequently reported is known as the White Lady, and she has been observed roaming the corridors at night.

Now a historic house museum and landmark, staff workers

at the castle have reported seeing apparitions, being touched by unseen figures, and even hearing disembodied voices around the property.

During the Halloween season, the castle becomes a haunted attraction called Legends of Horror at Casa Loma.

48. The Fairmont Banff Springs Hotel, Calgary, Alberta https://www.hauntedrooms.com/canada/haunted-places/haunted-hotels/banff-springs-hotel-alberta

Set in Banff National Park, this grand hotel lies within 1.8 km of Bow Falls and the Whyte Museum of the Canadian Rockies. The hotel has seven restaurants and two bars. There's also a spa, indoor and outdoor pools, and a golf course, and 76,000 sq. ft. of meeting space. It is nicknamed "Castle in the Rockies."

There have been paranormal incidents at this hotel throughout its history, since it opened for business in 1888. One of the most famous legends is of the Ghost Bride. The story of the Ghost Bride dates back to the late 1920s. The story goes that on a young couple's wedding day, the bride, decked out in her wedding gown, descended one of the hotel's marble staircases. Something startled her, causing her to slip and fall. Some say she caught her heel in the hem of her dress. The bride fell to her death on those steps.

Today hotel staff and guests alike have reported seeing a veiled figure in a wedding dress moving up and down the stairs and dancing in the ballroom.

Then there is the legend of Room 873. The story goes that a man murdered his wife and young daughter before committing suicide in Room 873. Maids charged with cleaning the room were unable to remove bloody fingerprints from the bathroom mirror.

The guests who stayed in Room 873 claimed that horrible disembodied screams plagued them through the night. Paranormal incidents got so bad that the hotel sealed off the room with bricks. Despite the hotel's best efforts, the ghosts are still very much in residence at Banff Springs with reports of a young daughter seen standing outside her room, as if lost.

The hotel staff asserts that the murder-suicide is merely a ghost story and that no murder-suicide occurred in the hotel. But, if you go to the 8th floor, you will see that Room 873 is missing, and on the wall where the room door should be is a sign not to knock on the wall.

On a side note, author Steven King heard of the murder and used it in his best-selling book *The Shining.*

49. Carl Beck House, Ontario, Canada
https://www.hauntedplaces.org/item/carl-beck-house/

Built by lumber magnate Carl Beck in the late 1800s, this house in Penetanguishene is known as one of the most haunted houses in Ontario. All the homes that Beck had built have a signature tower-like structure on one corner.

According to legend, Beck and his family lived in the house together. When his wife passed away, Mary, the eldest daughter, was put in charge of raising the nine younger siblings. When Carl died, he left Mary only one dollar in his will. Today, a figure of an angry woman in a dark blouse and skirt, presumably Mary, is said to appear in the upstairs windows.

Today the Beck House is apartments, and you can rent part of the Carl Beck House starting at $95 per night. But it is your responsibility to acquire appropriate permissions before investigating any location listed on this site. It is private property, and many “ghost hunters” have been arrested because they failed to contact property owners and local authorities ahead of time. There is a waiting list to rent at this residence.

50. Island of Dolls, Mexico
http://www.isladelasmunecas.com/

South of Mexico City, between the canals of Lake Xochimilco,

The haunted Island of the Dolls in Mexico.

you will find a small island called Isla de las Muñecas. On the island, you will find hundreds of discarded dolls in various stages of deterioration hanging from trees.

The story goes that Don Julian Santana Barrera, the island's sole resident, found the body of a young girl floating in the water who had died from drowning. Shortly after that, Julian saw a doll floating near the canals. Most probably, the doll belonged to the girl. Julian took the doll and strung it high in a tree to pay homage to the girl's spirit.

Over the years, Julian has placed more dolls on the trees throughout the island. Julian, and some visitors, claim that the dolls are possessed by the spirits of girls who passed too soon, reporting that the dolls would move independently and even speak to passersby. Today, tourists to the island often speak of the doll's eyes following them. Others have also reported that the mutilated dolls whisper to them, especially at night.

In 2001, after 50 years of collecting dolls and hanging them on the island, Julian drowned in the same spot where the girl died. Julian's ghost is said to remain on the island, along with the young girls'.

Featured on Travel Channel's *Destination Unknown* show, the dolls have since become a popular attraction for travelers brave enough to make the journey.

51.Teatro Tapia, San Juan, Puerto Rico
https://www.laconcharesort.com/haunted-places-to-visit-in-puerto-rico/

Puerto Rico is known for its natural beauty and rich history. One of the most famous spooky sites on the island is Teatro Tapia, a theater known for its plays, concerts, and paranormal activity. Named after Alejandro Tapia y Rivera, it is the oldest freestanding drama stage building located in San Juan.

According to legend, an actress fell to her death while performing at the theater. Some visitors claim to have seen her ghost wandering the theater grounds, while others report mysterious footsteps, doors swinging open and shut, and an unseen choir of voices coming from the stage.

The television show *Ghost Hunters International* conducted a paranormal investigation of the theater.

Today, the theater still holds many ballet and music performances, so purchase a ticket to see some local acts—and maybe a local ghost while you are at it.

52. Casa de la Poesia, Bogota, Colombia
https://www.casadepoesiasilva.com/

The Silva Poetry House was once home to poet Jose Asuncion Silva. Tragically, he shot himself through the heart and died on the property in 1896.

Now a museum, it is owned by the Colombian historical-cultural organization. Visitors to the museum have reported feeling an overwhelming sense of sadness upon entering, as well as hearing whispers and moans at dusk and dawn. People passing the property have reported hearing cries and whispering coming

The haunted Casa de Poesia Silva is the house in the foreground.

from within.

53. La Recoleta Cemetery, Buenos Aires, Argentina
https://wander-argentina.com/haunted-buenos-aires-ghost-stories-of-the-city-landmarks/

The La Recoleta Cemetery features thousands of statues, mausoleums, fairytale grottoes, and intricate tombstones, as well as the remains of Argentina's most iconic figure, Eva Perón.

The stone walkways and labyrinth of mausoleums are as beautiful as they are eerie, and Recoleta has a couple of haunted legends of its own. One of the most famous stories involves David Alleno, a former gravedigger and caretaker who worked at the cemetery for 30 years before killing himself. Today, visitors to the cemetery report hearing Alleno's keys jingling as his ghost walks the pathways at dawn.

Another story is that of the socialite, Rufina Cambaceres, who died while preparing to see a show at the Colón Theater. She was transported to the cemetery by horse-drawn carriage on a rainy day after her death in 1902.

Due to the weather, workers left her casket in the cemetery's chapel to be interred later. The next day, the caretakers found the coffin disturbed, and the lid was out of place.

The authorities, thinking there had been a grave robbing, opened the casket and discovered that Rufina still had her jewelry in place, and to their horror, found scratch marks on the inside of the coffin. Her body was bruised and bloody. She had been put in the coffin and tried to scratch her way out of the casket in a panic. She died of a heart attack due to a lack of air and panic.

Later it was discovered that Rufina had suffered from a rare medical condition leaving her in an unconscious state, fooling doctors into believing she had died.

There is a life-size Art Nouveau statue of Rufina with her hand on the door to her mausoleum, a family tribute to 'the girl who died twice.' Visitors have reported seeing her ghost by her tomb.

The La Recoleta Cemetery is today one of the most visited tourist attractions within Buenos Aires. It is free to enter and open during the day, all week long, plus there are nighttime ghost tours.

54. Xunantunich, Belize
https://www.mybelize.net/xunantunich-belize/

Xunantunich are ancient Mayan ruins that lie deep in the jungles of Belize, less than a mile from the Guatemala border. The site has sat abandoned for the past millennium. Xunantunich in Maya means "Stone Woman" or "Maiden of the Rock."

An earthquake caused the original civilization to crumble, but the complex was rediscovered by explorers in the 1890s. Since then, Xunantunich has served as an important archaeological site.

The ancient city's famous ghost is a black-haired female with red, glowing eyes. She was first spotted by a local hunter in the 1800s. She has been seen many times since then. No one knows precisely who the "Stone Lady" is, but many speculate that she may have been a human sacrifice. According to research, death rituals took place on the top of the El Castillo pyramid.

It doesn't attract significant scores of tourists because of its remote location, but the view from El Castillo of the surrounding landscape is truly breathtaking.

There are tours offered to the ruins, but because it is an active archaeological site, there are currently no nighttime tours available.

55. Aokigahara Forest, Japan
http://www.aokigaharaforest.com/Aokigahara-the-haunted-forest.html

Known as the "Sea of Trees," this seemingly serene forest at the foot of Mount Fuji has a tormented past. It is 13.5 miles of sprawling forest that has a long history of paranormal incidents in Japanese literature and folklore.

In recent years this forest, growing over hardened lava, became known as "the suicide forest." Some blame this trend on the forest's association with demons in Japanese mythology. Others point towards large underground deposits of iron, which interfere with compasses and make it easy to get lost. Police records show that 247 people made suicide attempts in the forest in 2010, 54 of them successfully.

On an interesting note, when the forest guardians (rangers) find a dead body, it will be taken to a special room designed for corpses found in the forest. The corpse being placed on a bed, the guard will sleep in the same room with the body. Legend has it that if the corpse is left alone in the room, its yurei (spirit) will move all night in the dormitories screaming and being deranged.

Signs at some trailheads now advertise help line information to hikers. Many hikers will mark their path with tape or string to make it easier to find their way back out again.

Legend has it that the yurei of those who have perished in the forest are now vengeful spirits dedicated to tormenting visitors and luring those that are sad and lost off the path.

The police have installed security cameras at the entrance of the Suicide Forest and increased patrols in an attempt to reduce the number of suicides.

The police have recommended that you do not hike by yourself here.

56. Kiyotaki Tunnel, Arashiyama, Japan
https://www.hidingfromjapaneseghosts.com/kiyotakitunnel.html

One of the most famous haunted places in Japan is not a castle or home. It is a tunnel that has gained international fame for its paranormal incidents. The tunnel connects Asrashiyama to the town of Sagakiyotaki.

At roughly 500 meters long, supernatural occurrences have plagued this tunnel since it was constructed in 1927 as part of the railroad.

People have reported having a ghostly phantom passenger when they enter the tunnel, and it then disappears when they exit it. There are road mirrors outside on each side of the tunnel, and visitors have reported seeing ghostly apparitions in them. In Japanese culture, that is a prelude to death.

The ghostly sightings occur largely at night, and many people urge against visiting at night unless completely necessary.

There are two legends about the haunted tunnel; one is that the ghosts of the slave workers who died making the tunnel still roam there. The other is that the hauntings and strange occurrences are caused by an ancient warrior who died in battle and cursed the ground.

Whatever the case, people in the area avoid the tunnel at night and caution any visitors from visiting it during the twilight hour.

57. Chaonei No. 81, or "Chaonei Church," Bejing, China https://www.thevintagenews.com/2016/03/28/this-abandoned-chaonei-no-81-house-in-china-is-described-as-beijings-most-celebrated-haunted-house/

Known as the Chaonei Church, this Baroque-style house in the Chaoyangmen neighborhood is best known as "Beijing's most celebrated haunted house."

The building is part of a more significant property with a concrete wall that surrounds it, and it has a metal gate entrance from the street. There are three buildings, and Chanoei No. 81 is the main house.

There are no historical records about its structure, but it has seen a lot of history. It wasused as a Chinese language school to train foreign missionaries and then as government offices for the People's Republic of China. It was occupied for a short time by

The haunted Chaonei Church in Beijing.

the Red Guards during the Cultural Revolution in the 1960s. It sat abandoned after that.

There are numerous ghost legends about this Chanoei No 81. One legend is that of a British priest who built the house to be a church, but vanished before construction was completed.

The most famous tale is about the mistress of a government official who left her during the Communist war. She later hung herself and is said to now haunt the property.

There is also the tale of three drunk construction workers who disappeared on the property. According to the story, the three men were in the building next door when they decided to break through the wall which separated their building from the Chaonei home. They disappeared and were reportedly never seen again.

The house was the subject of the 2014 3D horror movie *The House That Never Dies*.

Today, the house is owned by Beijing's Roman Catholic Archdiocese. There are plans to make it the Vatican embassy. In 2016 it was restored and since 2017 is opened for renting.

58. The Forbidden City, Beijing, China
http://english.visitbeijing.com.cn/

No trip to Beijing is complete without a visit to the famous Forbidden City, China's former imperial palace that now serves as a museum. But you might not know that the popular tourist destination has quite a reputation among supernatural enthusiasts.

The Forbidden City was the home of the emperors of the Ming and Qing dynasties between 1420 and 1912 when China's last emperor abdicated

During its 600-year tenure as a palace, the complex had its fair share of murders, whether by jealous concubines poisoning one another or executions performed at the emperor's behest. There have been many reports of strange phenomena since the palace opened to the public in the 1940s.

The most common story involves a woman dressed in white (as most good ghost stories do) strolling around the grounds and sobbing.

The City is only really accessible during the day, and there are parts of the Imperial Palace that are entirely off-limits to tourists. Recently the government started opening up more parts which include a haunted garden.

59. The Old Changi Hospital, Changi, Singapore.
https://the-line-up.com/old-changi-hospital-haunted

Originally built back in 1935, the now abandoned Old Changi Hospital was as part of the old Changi military base that served the British Royal Air Force, during which time it was called the RAF Hospital.

During the occupation by the Japanese in WWII, the compound was used as a prison and torture camp for British soldiers and their allies by the notorious Kempeitai (the Japenese secret police). Legend has it that the Kempeitai would torture the prisoners to death and then impale the severed heads of executed prisoners on iron stakes outside of public buildings during the occupation.

After the end of World War II, the building was again a British military hospital. During this time ghostly sightings began to be reported by the staff.

In 1965, the hospital was renamed the ANZUK Hospital and served members of the Commonwealth armed forces of Australia, New Zealand, and the United Kingdom. The Singapore Armed Forces took it over in 1975. It was replaced in 1997 by the Changi General Hospital and has stood derelict and decaying ever since.

Cursed by its notorious past, the old hospital is considered one of the most haunted places in Singapore. There are reports of loud bangs, unexplained screams, and ghostly apparitions walking down the corridors. The spirits of children are known to haunt the old children's ward. Some people have even reported seeing bloodied Japanese soldiers.

While filming a horror movie on the hospital grounds, the film crew reported odd occurrences, including sudden loud noises, ghostly voices, and a woman with a "black aura."

Today the old abandoned structure sits empty at the end of Halton Road, surrounded by a wealthy neighborhood of chalets, villas, and a seaside resort.

The hospital is now closed off with a metal fence and "do not enter" signs. The Singapore Ghost Club does, however, organize paranormal investigations at the hospital.

60. Kellie's Castle, Batu Gajah, Malaysia
https://www.malaysia.travel/en/ay/places/states-of-malaysia/perak/kellies-castle

Believe it or not, there is a haunted Scottish castle in Malaysia. It is called Kellie's Castle. William Kellie Smith, a rubber plantation owner, wanted a castle for his family, and construction began in 1915. Smith returned to Great Britain and, unfortunately, caught pneumonia while he was on his way to Lisbon to pick up his elevator. He died at the age of 56 in 1926. Smith's family did not return to Malaysia to continue building the castle, and soon after, it was sold off, and fell into a state of disrepair.

A portion of the structure sustained damage due to bombing during World War II. Legend has it that Japanese soldiers executed prisoners of war on the castle grounds, leaving an eerie, unsettling vibe as one enters the property.

In the 1960s, three secret tunnels were discovered under the castle. Inside one of them, a car was found parked. Nothing was ever found or verified as to who the car's owner was. Researchers believe that there are more tunnels on the property.

Today, overlooking the picturesque view of Batu Gajah, Perak, the castle ruins are a tourist attraction and have a reputation for being one of the most haunted places in Malaysia. The ghost of

Kellie's Castle at Batu Gajah, Malaysia.

Kellie is said to haunt the second floor of the stone structure, and a young girl, believed to be his daughter, has also supposedly been seen around the property.

61. Lawang Sewu, Semarang, Indonesia
https://www.indonesia.travel/us/en/destinations/java/semarang/lawang-sewu

Built in the early 20th century by Dutch colonialists, Lawang Sewu (or "Thousand Doors") served as the head office for the Dutch East Indian Railway Company.

During World War II, the Japanese invaded Indonesia and used the building as a military headquarters. There are reports that the Japanese used the basement as a prison, and many harsh interrogations, tortures, and violent executions occurred within the building's walls—all of which contribute to its current status as one of Indonesia's most haunted sites.

The most popular ghostly apparition, a Dutch woman believed

to have committed suicide, is seen when roaming around the property. A TV crew caught the female specter on film during the production of a TV program.

Legend has it that a kuntilanak (a female vampiric ghost) prowls the basement in B building, and there are headless spirits that wander its corridors and grounds.

In 2011, First Lady Ani Yudhoyono had the buildings renovated to make it a tourist attraction.

Today, there are tours of Building B, and it's basement, perhaps to confirm whether the many circulating ghost stories tied to Lawang Sewu have any truth to them.

62. Tao Dan Park, Vietnam
http://www.thanhniennews.com/society/vietnam-park-haunted-by-dead-young-man-933.html

In the center of Ho Chi Minh City, visitors can enjoy a nice walk through this beautiful and tranquil park. What makes the sprawling area one of the most haunted places in the world? At night, a ghostly apparition has been seen by many lurking in the shadows of the park's trees. Locals believe that it is the ghost of a young man, killed in an attack during the Vietnam War, returning to the park every night searching for his lost love.

Park authorities denied allegations that the ghost of a young man is prowling the park.

Visitors are welcome, since it is a park and has security guards on duty around the clock.

63. Castle of Good Hope, South Africa
https://www.castleofgoodhope.co.za/

Built by the Dutch East India Company in the 17th century, it is the oldest building in South Africa. It was used as a replenishment station for ships passing through the treacherous waters near the cape. The castle's moat fills with water at high tide. Today a popular tourist attraction, this castle has a curse on it.

It contains an infamous dungeon known as the "dark hole" or Danker Gat that has seen gruesome punishments and executions, prompting many reports of ghost sightings today.

Once the seat of government and military operations, the bastion-style fort is now a historical monument in Cape Town and a local hotbed for paranormal activity.

Legend has it that the ghost of Governor Pieter Gijsbert van Noodt haunts the castle. The story goes that the violent ruling governor died of a heart attack while ordering a hanging. The story goes on to say that one of the men doomed to the noose cursed the governor before being executed, sealing his soul to the castle forever.

There is the Lady in Grey, who is seen wringing her hands and crying as she runs through the castle. During excavation, workers unearthed a female skeleton at the old sally gates. Paranormal

The entrance to the Castle of Good Hope in Cape Town.

researchers believe these remains are connected to this ghost.

Another story is of the bell inside the bell tower ringing on its own. On certain nights the bell will ring. What makes it strange is that the bell tower has been sealed off for years. Legend has it that it the restless soul of a soldier who hung himself from the bell's rope centuries back.

Today the Castle of Good Hope is a museum. Because it houses the William Fehr collection of Africana, it does not offer any nighttime ghost tours. On a side note, soldiers who are responsible for guarding the Castle, to this day, will walk around the outside of the building at night, instead of passing through the castle's archways for fear of these unrested ghosts.

64. Jazirat Al Hamra, United Arab Emirates

You'll find the nearly-abandoned town of Jazirat Al Hamra about 14 miles southwest of Ras Al Khaimah in northern UAE—located between a large mall and a huge waterpark.

This ancient city was established in the 14th century and grew into a thriving pearl fishing village in the 1830s. Then in 1868, it was abandoned. The town now consists of dirt roads, 13 mosques, and more than 300 coral-and-mud houses.

People claim that visitors are bound to experience strange noises and chilling apparitions, usually djinns (genies) in the form of animals.

In 2016 three KT journalists spent the night in the village to see if any paranormal incidents would happen. While they did hear strange noises, they didn't see any apparitions or ghosts.

Today the town is now called Al Hamra Heritage Village, and there is renovation in the works. The nearby hotels do offer daytime tours.

In conclusion to this chapter, I will repeat that I have shown you but a few of the haunted places around the world. There are a whole lot more that I did not mention. I could have written a whole book on haunted places around the world.

When you do visit another country, check out the haunted places. Find out if they do nighttime ghost walks. Contact the local paranormal groups and see when they are going out on a ghost hunt. Have a great time, but be cognizant of the laws in that country when you go out legend tripping.

The ghost town of Jazirat Al Hamra in the United Arab Emirates.

Chapter 8:

Ghost Hunt

Time: Just after midnight
Place: Fountains Abbey

The moon casts its shadow through the large open windows as you slowly walk around the extensive stone ruins of what was once a large church. The cold night air shoots through you that night, but you're thankful that you had the common sense to dress warmly for the night. You look around; you can't help but think about what this place was like centuries ago. You look down at the only light coming from your EKG meter. You watch the dial closely in case it moves for any kind of noise. You have come here to these old ruins in England to conduct a ghost hunt.

Fountains Abbey is one of the largest and best-preserved ruined Cistercian monasteries in England. The abbey was founded in 1132, and operated for 407 years, becoming one of the wealthiest monasteries in England. It was closed in 1539 under the order of Henry VIII.

The abbey precinct covered 70 acres (28 ha) surrounded by an 11-foot (3.4 meter) wall built in the 13th century, some parts of which are visible to the south and west of the abbey. The area consists of three zones cut by the River Skell flowing from west to east across the site.

The church and claustral buildings stand at the center of the precinct north of the Skell, the inner court containing the domestic buildings stretches down to the river and the outer court housing the industrial and agricultural buildings lies on the river's south bank. The early abbey buildings were added to and altered over time, causing deviations from the strict Cistercian style. Outside the walls were the abbey's granges.

Located approximately 3 miles (5 kilometers) southwest of Ripon in North Yorkshire, near the village of Aldfield, these stone ruins are all that's left of a magnificent church with a long history for being haunted.

The owners have allowed you and your team to stay the night and see if the stories are true. Suddenly you hear a noise. You look back out the door, and down the hall, you see a shadow move from one side to the other. A shiver runs down your spine. Welcome to paranormal legend trips!

Paranormal legend trips, usually referred to as ghost hunts, are much different from cryptid monster hunts. To begin with, you have to approach ghosting with an entirely different attitude. You're looking for something that might not be visible to the cynical eye. You have to learn to be extremely quiet and patient.

Paranormal research dates back to the 18th century in England

Fountains Abbey.

with organizations such as the Society for Psychical Research. It was the first organization of its kind in the world. The Society for Psychical Research (SPR) originated from a discussion between journalist Edmund Rogers and the physicist William F. Barrett in autumn 1881. At a conference on 5 and 6 January of 1882 at the headquarters of the British National Association of Spiritualists, the foundation of the Society was proposed.

In the 1930s, spiritualists became distraught when they discovered that the SPR was not accepting outside testimony as proof, and the Society accused some prominent mediums of fraud. Noted author Arthur Conan Doyle, who was very active with spiritualists, resigned from the SPR to protest what he regarded as the SPR's overly restrictive standards of proof.

One of the first paranormal investigators, Harry Price, published his *Confessions of a Ghost-Hunter* in 1936. Price was a British parapsychologist, psychic researcher, and author who gained public prominence for his investigations into psychical phenomena and his exposure of fraudulent spiritualist mediums. He is best known for his paranormal investigation of one of the most haunted places in Great Britain, Borley Rectory in Essex, England. Price is also credited with coming up with the basic formula for conducting a paranormal investigation.

The oldest paranormal investigative organization is the Ghost Club, founded in London. The club has its roots in Cambridge in 1855, where fellows at Trinity College began to discuss ghosts and psychic phenomena, but it was officially launched in London in 1862. Members included famous authors of the time, Charles Dickens and Sir Arthur Conan Doyle.

The club is still around today and continues to meet monthly at the Victory Services Club near Marble Arch in London. Several investigations are performed in England and Scotland every year.

Now ghost hunting in some countries is not at the top of list of popular things to do at night. People in some countries view the whole idea of ghosts differently from people in the United States.

In Malaysia, there is a type of supernatural being called toyols, which are dead fetuses or stillborn babies reanimated by black magic. They are described as tiny green-skinned goblins with glowing red eyes. Legend has it that the owners/masters keep the toyols in jars, feeding them milk and candy and sometimes blood. The masters will let the toyols out of the jars to steal and commit crimes for them. The background on this legend may have originated in pre-Islamic Mecca, where infanticide was common.

In India, there are stories of headless ghosts of people decapitated in train accidents called skondhokatas. They are said to haunt the places where they died. These specters are known to be violent and dangerous, but easy to outwit because they have no heads.

There is a type of ghost in Russia called strigoi. They are said to be the ghosts of people who lived or died under unhappy circumstances: suicides, the illegitimate, the unbaptized. Unlike most paranormal entities, these strigoi like to live on human blood, like vampires. They are said to have red hair and bluish-purple eyes. There is a custom of burying a person with a bottle of whiskey to prevent them from returning as a strigoi. Vampire legends go back as far as the Mesopotamian civilizations and have always been part of supernatural legends.

China also has a vampire type ghost called a Jiang Shi ("Stiff Corpse"). These spirits are of people who died by suicide or violence. Jiang Shi have greenish skin, wear the robes of the Qing Dynasty, and move by hopping or bouncing, which is why they are sometimes called "Chinese hopping vampires." They feed off the qi (life essence) of living humans. However, more modern legends describe them as sucking blood, likely due to the influence of Western vampire myths.

When it comes to ghost hunting in China, the idea of exploring a haunted place is not considered entertaining. At the Disney parks in China, they don't have any haunted attractions. You won't find any ghost storybooks on children's bookshelves in China. The Chinese, especially the elders, believe in ghosts. Except for the Jiang Shi, spirits are treated with respect. These ghosts are of relatives, who come back to help survivors.

In Norway, there is a ghost called a gjenganger, and they are said to be able to kill a person with a pinch. Legend has it that they are the ghosts of murdered people, murderers and those who committed suicide. Unlike most ghosts, gjenganger look like ordinary living people, which makes them difficult to spot. The pinched skin will turn blue and cause a wasting disease, which will eventually travel to the victim's heart.

Despite this scary legend, ghost hunting has a strong following in Norway. Today a lot of highly secular modern countries that are otherwise seen as leading Europe's inexorable, science-led march away from superstition and religion are embracing paranormal investigations and the unexplained.

So, when planning a ghost hunt, be cognizant of the country that you are visiting and their beliefs in the supernatural.

A ghost, also known as a specter or phantom, is a paranormal entity that makes its presence known to a person or place. An apparition is how the ghost manifests itself to the living.

When conducting a ghost hunt it is good to know the different kinds of ghosts and apparitions you might encounter. Following is a list that I have complied from many different paranormal websites.

Ghosts or entities can manifest themselves in several different ways. Here is a list of the different types of ghosts.

Full Body Apparition

Describes the entity visibly appearing as a complete image or solid form. In Charles Dickens 1843 book *A Christmas Carol* the ghost of Bob Marley appeared as a full body apparition to

Ebenezer Scrooge.

Entities may also appear as a partial body—appearing as just a part of a person such as a head, an arm, or the torso. In the movie *Ghostbusters*, the ghost in the library was described as a full torso apparition.

The Poltergeist

Also known as 'noisy ghosts,' these invisible entities manipulate the physical environment and can move objects or furniture.

The Interactive Personality

These are the most common ghosts that humans encounter. These entities are believed to be loved ones returning to bring comfort or to convey important information.

Orbs

This is probably the most common type of photographic evidence that ghost hunters believe supports the existence of ghosts. They are either blue or white translucent balls of light that appear hovering over the ground in pictures. Most skeptics believe they are nothing more than dust particles or insects.

Funnel Ghosts

These entities are believed to be loved ones returning to visit. Mostly encountered in old historical buildings or inside private homes where they once lived, funnel ghosts cause cold spots and when they are visibly seen they look like a swirling funnel

Ectoplasm / Ectomist

These entities can appear several feet off the ground. They can also be caught in photographs as a swirling mass of mist in either white, grey, or black. Ectoplasm was made popular in the *Ghostbusters* movies.

Inanimate Ghosts

These ghosts are embodied by objects rather than people. They can take the form of ships, cars, trains, or even lamps. These ghosts create residual hauntings, which means there is no interaction between you and the ghost.

Animal Ghosts

They can appear as a full body apparitions but are commonly heard rather than seen. One of the most popular of these entities is that of that of a giant cat that appears at the United States Capital building in Washington, DC.

Shadow People

A lot of people spot these ghosts out of the corner of their eye, but when they turn to look at them, the entity vanishes.

Doppelgänger

In German it means "double doer" and is a non-biologically-related look-alike or double of a living person. In the paranormal field, these entities can mimic the look of someone who is still living and are harbingers of bad luck. They are also known to project themselves in multiple places at once so that there are multiple beings seen that look the same.

The next two types of ghosts, I don't deal with when I am ghost hunting. They are considered dangerous and should be left to professionals in the paranormal field.

Demons

These dark entities can invade homes, attach themselves to objects, and inflict mental and physical torture. They can morph into any shape but are usually witnessed as black masses. These entities should never be challenged because they are extremely dangerous and can kill.

Demon Possessed Humans

When an evil spirit infiltrates a living person, it controls their conscious energy. They can hurt and kill as they please. They are as dangerous as demons. The movie *The Exorcist* was about a possessed girl. As a youth, this movie left an imprint on me about the paranormal.

Here is a list of the different apparitions that ghost hunters encounter that I recently found at anomalien.com.

Atmospheric Apparition

This type of ghost sighting is a visual "imprint" that got left behind in the environment from a past event. These events are typically, but are not limited to, violent and tragic events.

Historical Apparitions

These apparitions are one step up from the atmospheric apparition. They typically haunt older homes and appear as a full body appriition acting natural. They are always dressed in period clothing and do not speak, communicate or acknowledge the presence of the living.

Recurring Apparitions

Recurring apparitions are ghosts that occur in regular cycles over a period, usually once annually. This type of ghost sighting is one of the most popular. The date of manifestation usually occurs on an anniversary date or a day of special importance.

Modern Apparitions

Modern ghosts are the spirits of present-day ghosts. Not all ghosts are from ancient haunted places or of two-hundred-year-old dead people. These ghosts are relatively new, looking and sounding like modern people.

Crisis or Deathbed Apparitions

These apparitions appear to family members or close friends just before or soon after a person's death. My wife experienced this apparition of her grandfather.

Family Apparitions

These spirits attach themselves to a family member(s). They can haunt every member of the family through each generation until the family line comes to an end.

Haunted Objects and Object Apparitions

This supernatural phenomenon is one of the strangest, most puzzling enigmas of all the hauntings. Most ghost hunters do not believe that an object can be haunted; rather they believe that an entity can attached itself to objects that usually have some significance to the deceased. Haunted objects can also be referred to as cursed.

Modes of Transportation

These are the manifestations of vehicles such as cars, trucks, bicycles, carriages, trains, airplanes and ships. There are almost always associated in some way with a violently tragic demise.

Photographic Apparitions

These are ghosts that are not seen visually but can be photographed. Most people are unaware that they have taken a picture of a ghost until they develop the film.

Out-Of-Body Apparitions

The strange occurrences of out-of-body apparitions are when

people report seeing the ghost of someone who is still alive and could not have been nearby at the time of the sighting.

Natural and Fraudulent Apparitions

This simply means that there is a logical and natural explanation for the occurrences being mistaken for something supernatural.

If you have your heart set on doing paranormal research, contact a local paranormal investigation group in your destination country and ask if you can accompany them on their next ghost hunt. A lot of countries have ghost hunting clubs, and they usually have a website and are regularly looking for new members. They typically welcome an outsider if you are serious about it.

Good paranormal groups take the investigation seriously, and you can learn a lot from them. Plus, they know where the local haunted sites are. Tell them you want to see how a paranormal investigation is done by professionals. That will boost their egos. Ghost hunters love to show off what they do. While most paranormal groups are in it for the science and curiosity, some keep their finds private and will ask you to commit to their club rules.

Now, if you don't want to deal with these paranormal groups and want to do a ghost hunt on your own, then I will show you how to conduct one. Some places that are reputed to be haunted will charge a fee for groups to conduct an investigation. For some people, it is all about the money. It is becoming increasingly hard to find a haunting local somebody hasn't already investigated, especially a lighthouse. Most lighthouses will make you pay to do an investigation, but I will say this: we have a great time when we go to lighthouses.

Also, on a side note, my wife has a policy that she will not allow young children on a paranormal investigation. This kind of thing can really scare a child who can develop lasting fears. You never know what you are going to see in a supposedly haunted house, and there have been cases where a child becomes the center of the paranormal activity. I saw a TV show in which a woman took her younger son with her on a ghost hunt. He supposedly got possessed by the ghost or evil spirit. This can happen to young family members if you bring them on paranormal investigations. Monster hunts are different because when you leave the woods, the monsters stay in the woods. Ghosts can supposedly follow you home.

The best place to start is a graveyard or cemetery. Most paranormal groups like to stake out cemeteries if they can't find another place to investigate. There is nothing wrong with this, and it can be fun and a lot less dangerous than a building. Just remember, not every graveyard or cemetery is haunted. If you are just starting and you want to do investigations with just your family, then a cemetery is the best place to start. There is always a cemetery in the area.

If you decide to take this course of action, you need to contact the local law enforcement officers and notify them you and your family will be out there, so you don't get in trouble. Most people don't know you have to ask permission to go into a cemetery after hours, and in some states, it is illegal to be in a cemetery after dark, so check your local ordinances. There have been some cases of vandalism, so the police are very cautious when they see people roaming around a graveyard at night.

Also, some satanic religious groups have been known to do their rituals at night in cemeteries. Most law enforcement agencies will allow you to do a ghost hunt if it is a county cemetery; they just want to be told who is out there. Privately-owned cemeteries will not allow you to do an investigation because it is an insurance liability. If you do go there at night, you can and will be charged with trespassing.

Some law enforcement agencies do not pass the word of your nightly adventure, and you will have some patrol car roll up on you and ask what you are doing. If this happens, just explain to them what you are doing and relay that you have permission to be out there. The patrol will radio it in, and all will be well. In some countries, the police are corrupt, and you might have to pay them off. I always keep my money in a different location than my wallet, in case this happens. Don't let this faze or deter you. Whenever you are investigating the unknown, you are always going to run into obstacles. It happens all the time with my family and me.

When you find a cemetery to investigate, and you get permission, you need to do a daytime reconnaissance of the location. Check it out and look for where you want to set up and walk around. Most cemeteries have small paths for visitors to drive, so it won't be hard to pick different routes for the teams. If a headstone is a towering figure, it does not necessarily mean there is a ghost or entity around it. It just means the dearly departed's family is wealthy. My wife likes to look for the really old tombstones. She feels this is where you will get the most activity. Make a sketch with references to the areas where you want to conduct your ghost hunt. Sometimes extensive cemeteries will have maps they give out, which you can mark and use.

Once you have planned out which area you want to hit that night, go home and sit down with the group and decide who is going to go where. Again, I don't recommend this kind of legend trip for some children. If you choose to go this avenue, I recommend you keep the children at base camp and let them run the primary radio, or if you set up a camera, let them keep an eye on it. You also want to find an area away from the main streets. Car lights and noise can affect your cameras and listening devices. Like doing a monster hunt, you need to check out the cemetery/building in the daytime and plan where you want to conduct the investigation and find what you think will be "hot spots." Hot spots are areas where you think there will be or have been told there is paranormal activity. Most cemeteries are not big, so it shouldn't be challenging to do. Mark the area with some kind of marking. With it being a cemetery, make sure the marking is not permanent.

If you are doing a paranormal investigation in a residence, a high-powered laser is a great tool to have. This device emits a grid of green dots useful for detecting shadows or general visual disturbances. If you have a hot spot in a room, set a running camera in front of it to catch potential evidence.

When it comes to a paranormal investigation, you want to try to get video proof. You do this by placing cameras at strategic points in the area of the residence where you are conducting your investigation. To be thorough, you will need more than one camera, possibly three, depending on the size of the place. You need to set them up in areas where nobody else can disturb them, other than the ghost(s). Some professional investigators set up night vision cameras, which are all tied into a central computer recording all cameras at once. This is great if you can afford these systems, and you are serious.

Most investigators carry a camera with them when they do a walk-through of the place. It is probably the most exciting part of the investigation. You are walking around an area in complete darkness, other than the light from the camera, knowing some unknown entity haunts this location. You should also place audio recorders around different locations. Paranormal investigators have gotten some of their best proof with these.

After the investigation is over, retrieve the cameras and load the recordings into the computer and listen. It is exhilarating to hear a faint voice and then bring up the volume to hear what the voice is saying. Just be careful to rule out any outside source before you present your evidence. Some old, abandoned residences make great homes for stray cats, and they are often the culprits in paranormal recordings.

Like a monster hunt where you can break up into teams, you can either break into groups or stay as one big group. Just make sure you go over what the game plan is with each team member. It makes everybody feel a little safer if something should happen. Also, assign a specific piece of equipment to each team member, so you don't carry it all yourself and end up forgetting something. It makes everybody feel part of the team and the investigation. Have one member be responsible for carrying and setting up the video cameras while another will carry and use the EVP monitor. I usually take the night vision device. Because my wife knows what to look for, I have her lead the investigations and choose who's carrying what piece of equipment. My wife takes the investigations seriously, and every team member enjoys each outing.

When you start your ghost hunt, it is good to walk around and wait till you get a hit on your EVP. Then have one person, and one person only, attempt to talk to the ghost during what is called the contact session. My wife usually does this because she knows what to say. Be careful when letting the younger kids do this. They might think its silly and start asking stupid questions. If there is an entity or ghost, it might not like what is being said. This is why Tracy insists she does all the talking. It's crucial nobody talks during the contact session. Whoever is holding the listening device needs to ensure the device is turned on. Always bring extra batteries. You can mount your camera on a stand or tripod, but it is a lot better just to carry it around. Both of my cameras have night vision capabilities.

If you do not get any EVP readings, then walk to another area you want to investigate. First, look around and take in your surroundings. Then have one person conduct the contact session and listen. This person has to be serious about it. If they don't believe in what they are doing, then nothing is going to happen. If nothing happens—and it usually does—first of all, do not get disappointed, but just move on to another location. You can leave a listening device or a trail camera in the area, but don't forget where you have left it. These devices can be expensive. Mark it on your sketch and move on to the next location. When you get a hit, the excitement begins. Be prepared to see something, and if you do or your family does, don't get scared and run. You need to talk to your family and make a plan in case something does happen. Most of the time, you won't hear anything except squirrels, raccoons, and armadillos.

When teams make their walk-around, it is good to have what are called "trigger objects." Ghost hunters use trigger objects to draw or lure spirits out. A trigger object just gives the spirit a way to show it is there, by making the trigger object move. To lure spirit children, a ball can be put down for them to play with. Some paranormal investigators do not like balls as trigger objects because they easily move on their own. They do, however, attract spirit children. It is best not to use an object which might fall over easily, such as a stuffed animal. The consensus is, once you

A photograph of some of the equipment used on a ghost hunt.

have an object that won't move on its own, place it within a circle or on a piece of paper and draw a line next to it. A variation on this method is to place an object on a layer of flour. Then put it somewhere your group will not disturb it and aim a camera at it. Also, place a meter next to it and see if your camera picks up any fluctuations on the meter when the object moves. It is best to use small trigger objects, but not too small to see on a camera.

When you have made it to your last hot spot and you are finished, you need to turn around and go back and retrieve your listening devices and trail cameras. Don't leave them overnight in a cemetery; a building is one thing, but out in the open is another. You can do another sweep of the hot spot if you want, and again see if anything happens. Some people believe nothing will happen till after midnight. I don't know why they think this, but you can give it a try. If you have young teenagers, they will get tired by then. Again, try to keep everybody excited and motivated; this way, they don't become disappointed if nothing happens.

When you finish, you've retrieved all your listening devices and cameras, then it is time to head home and go over the videos and sounds. This takes time, and I recommend you do it after a good night's sleep. You need to get the whole family or team involved in going over the evidence. Each person receives a sound device to listen to or a video to watch. This is the boring part of the investigation, yet one of the most essential elements as this is where your investigation pays off. If you find yourself falling asleep while you are watching the video or listening to the recording, turn off the recording device and take a break. You could miss something important if you were to fall asleep.

If you do see something odd or paranormal, you need to watch it a couple of times. You need to say to yourself, "What could this normally be?" If you see an object move, ask yourself if somebody off-camera made it move. I hate to say it, but ninety percent of the time, a person accidentally moved a table or rug, causing the object in question to move. A popular television show was questioned on the integrity of an object seen moving on the show. A lot of people think it was hoaxed in the interest of ratings. Think about it: how many people are going to watch a show where the ghost investigators never find anything? If you even suspect the object moving was an accident, then let it go and move on to another. If an object moves by paranormal means, then it will most likely move again.

If you see something which looks like an apparition, again, look at what else it could be. A car driving by can cast weird lights on a wall. Also, look and see where everybody else in the investigation was during the apparition sighting. I'm not trying to discourage you from seeing things. It is just you need to know you have considered every possible explanation for the apparition before concluding a haunting. If you say it is a ghost, and it turns out to have a logical explanation, you will lose some credibility as a paranormal investigator. I go into every investigation with an open mind, but I also keep a rational thought as well. Being a military policeman for more than twenty-one years taught me that.

With that being said, if you find something nobody can explain, then you have had a successful investigation. If you are ghost hunting in a building, you have to get your proof together and present it to the owners or the people in charge of the building. I have found most of them already believe they have a haunting, so when you tell them you didn't find anything, they might not take the conclusion very well. Others might be thankful for not having a haunted residence. If you have proof, or what you believe to be proof, give the owners the privilege of deciding how or if they want the results shown to the public as they may not want them to be shared. It probably won't happen, but you have to provide them the courtesy.

Many paranormal groups have a website, which is where they like to show their investigation results and videos. As I have stated before, I do not expect to become a wealthy person with ghost pictures. To date, all photographs have come under scrutiny, and most people think they are hoaxes. If you go ghost hunting and you get some outstanding evidence, then enjoy it and show it off, but don't expect some big television company will want to have you on a show. I have seen many good supposed ghost photos, and the people who took them believed in their hearts the photos were genuine, and they left it at that. They don't care what anybody thinks. If you are ghost hunting to enjoy it with your family and you get some really good evidence, then enjoy it as a family. Some people like the idea of ghosts because if there are ghosts then there is life after death, which means there is a heaven and hell. They believe ghosts are stuck in purgatory.

Ghost hunting offers hours of excitement and a lifetime of stories to be told from generation to generation. On the flip side, it can also be boring. It is rare something happens right away during an investigation. Unfortunately, there are times when nothing happens at all. You need to stress to your family ghosts do not just appear at the drop of a dime. There are different kinds of hauntings, and some only happen during a particular part of the year. You may set up your equipment in the wrong room or location. It is important during an investigation you don't just sit around and wait. You need to be mobile and walk around, which is when you find the cold spots and feel something touch you. I'm not saying you can't sit around at all; just don't stay there all night as you will end up falling asleep. If your team falls asleep, they will lose interest in ghost hunting.

I encourage you to allow all team members to use some of the equipment. Encourage them to use all the equipment at different points during your investigation. It will stop them from getting bored. Young team members love using the Bionic Ear. It also keeps them interested in the investigation. I wish I had more than one because all of them want to use it. Just remind them they will hear everything, including small animals roaming around the property. If they hear or see something, do not be quick to doubt them; remember, the location is supposed to be haunted. Listen to what they say and ask questions, but in the end, don't say, "It was probably a stray cat." Ask them what they think it might be. When my kids say they heard something, I ask where and we see what made the noise.

Unfortunately, when it comes to ghost hunting, usually nothing happens. I'm not trying to be cynical, just realistic. You, as the team leader, need to encourage your team and keep them motivated. Stress to your team that if you continue to ghost hunt, it will eventually pay off. You have to be positive when you are looking for something like cryptids and ghosts. People gravitate to a person with a positive attitude.

When you end the ghost hunt, your group needs to retrieve your equipment. If you make a mess, be sure to clean it up. A rule of thumb in the military is to give it back better than the way you got it, and this includes a home. If the home is trashed at the beginning, do not conduct the ghost hunt. You don't want your family getting sick. We have had this happen before. We made an excuse we couldn't conduct the investigation for some reason, and we left. If a witness is serious about having an investigation done, then they will have a clean house. Also, it might be a good idea to conduct a walk-through with a member of the home and make sure everything is good with both parties.

If it is late when you finish, have your team get some rest, including yourself. When you get up in the morning, assign each member a listening or viewing device to review possible evidence. For example, one member could view one of the videos, another member could view the other video, and another could listen to the recordings. Have them do this for maybe thirty minutes, and then change over. What happens is, you get tired of watching the screen, and you end up falling asleep, and the same thing happens with listening devices. Also, have them take breaks on their own. You or somebody needs to keep an eye on them and make sure they don't fall asleep. They might miss seeing something on the video or audio.

Here is a list of items to take with you for ghost hunting. In Chapter 17 on equipment, there are more items you can add.

Ghost Legend Trip

- Camera—one that has IR capabilities
- Camera stands and pods
- EVP (electronic voice phenomenon) detector
- Temperature detector
- Flashlights/headlights/light sticks
- Batteries for all equipment devices
- Game cameras—it is better to have more than one, so you can put them in multiple places
- Cold weather clothes
- Sound recorder

Chapter 9

Mysterious Places of Legend Around the Word

Mysteries abound where we seek for answers.
—Ray Bradbury.

There are places around the world where the unexplained happens. There are places where strange lights appear in the sky. There are locations where people mysteriously disappear and are never seen again. Around the world are areas where the laws of gravity are in chaos. There are places that, legend has it, have a curse on them, and bad things happen to those who don't heed the curse. Strange stairs and other things are found out in the middle of the woods with no explanation as to why they are there. This chapter will look at these mysterious places and their history.

You may notice that this chapter is longer than the other ones about legends. The reason is, when I got to researching mysterious places, I go could not believe how many there are, and I wanted to include as many as I could, from the famous to the lesser-known ones.

Anyone who knows about UFOs and extraterrestrials knows about the crashed UFO at Roswell, New Mexico. Many UFO enthusiast have journeyed to this hot and dry place. Being one of those UFO enthusiasts, I visited this historic site in 1986.

When it comes to extraterrestrial beings and UFOs, there

have been sightings of alien-like creatures in almost every part of the world. Some of these supposed UFO landing sites, you can still visit. When it comes to UFO sightings, they occur almost daily. The US is considered the hotbed of UFO sightings, with South America following close behind. The Mutual UFO Network (MUFON) keeps an up-to-date database of UFO sightings all over the world.

UFO Sites

Sometimes referred to as "Britain's Roswell," the UK's most well-known UFO sightings were reported in late 1980 on a Royal Air Force military base near England's east coast. On December 26 of that year, the first sighting occurred when two United States Air Force members reported seeing lights falling to Earth over nearby Rendlesham Forest at around 3 am. According to an official Air Force memo that later documented the incident, the servicemen entered the forest to investigate and saw a metallic object giving off lights and moving around. When local police arrived, they reportedly didn't see any lights other than the bright beacon of a nearby lighthouse, but later discovered markings near the site.

A few days later, more service members went to investigate the forest site and reported seeing three bright lights in the sky that shone for hours. Astronomers and researchers have disputed the sightings as bright stars and the site markings as indentations made by animals. However, the lieutenant who wrote the memo and a few witnesses maintain what they reported in December 1980 is correct.

The longest-lasting series of reported UFO sightings in Belgium began in November 1989 and ended the following April. Around 13,500 people claimed to witness large, triangular flying objects hovering low in the sky. In the spring of 1990, military fighter pilots investigated and pursued some of the unidentifiable objects, but the objects flew out of range before the pilots could observe anything further. Written off as a harmless mystery, it has remained one of the most significant alleged UFO sightings in history.

Wycliffe Well, Australia
https://www.amusingplanet.com/2015/07/wycliffe-well-ufo-capital-of-australia.html

Wycliffe Well, located in the Northern Territory in Australia, is the self-proclaimed UFO capital of Australia. And for good reason: sightings are "guaranteed" every few days. Wycliffe Well Holiday Park, which has various accommodation options from £8 for campers, is pretty much the only place to stay. It doesn't miss out on the extraterrestrial marketing opportunities, with plenty of life-sized alien models dotted around, plus a "UFO loading pad." The general store also offers up a range of extraterrestrial souvenirs, with the walls covered in newspaper clippings of UFO sightings.

Warminster, England

Warminster, on the edge of Salisbury Plain in the English county of Wiltshire, has been a supposed hotbed of UFO activity since the 17th century. Cley Hill, a 240m Iron Age hillfort, has become an unofficial UFO observatory where spotters head, hoping for a glimpse of the pulsating lights that have characterized many previous sightings. For those lucky enough to see one, Warminster has its very own designated National Reporting Centre for UFOs.

Chile
https://chile.travel/en/ufologia-en-chile-los-mejores-destinos-para-el-avistamiento-de-ovnis

This South American nation is said to have had the highest number of UFO sightings, thanks to its clear skies and steep ridges and plateaus. In 2008, the Chilean tourist board even launched an official UFO trail in San Clemente in the Maule region to capitalize on the hundreds of sightings. Spanning 19 miles through the Andes, top attractions include the mineral-rich Colbun lake and El Enladrillado, a large flat area created by 200 volcanic blocks that some believe to be an alien landing pad.

M-Triangle, Russia
https://www.huffpost.com/entry/m-triangle_n_3551983

The M-Triangle, a remote area near the Ural Mountains and 600 miles east of Moscow, is said to be Russia's answer to Area 51. Locals have reported seeing a whole range of phenomena over the past hundred years, including hovering lights, translucent beings, and strange symbols written across the sky. There have even been bizarre rumors that people who've visited the area develop enhanced intelligence or superhuman powers.

The M-Triangle sits opposite the village of Molyobka in the Beryozovsky District, and the region is gearing up to cater to UFO enthusiasts, with plans afoot for a UFO park, hotels, and observatories.

A statue of an alien near the Russian town of Molyobka.

Famous Mysterious Places

There places on this Earth that the mere mention of brings on a sense of mystery and intrigue. Even today, there are still unanswered questions that leave scientists puzzled about these sites. The great thing is that you can visit them.

Dragon's Triangle

https://www.marineinsight.com/maritime-history/unexplained-mystery-the-devils-sea-the-dragons-triangle/

A lot of people have heard of the Bermuda Triangle, where numerous ships and planes have mysteriously disappeared without a trace. But there is another area where this happens. Known as the Dragons Triangle or Devil's Sea, it is situated in the Philippine Sea between Japan, the Philippines, and Guam. Geographically, the triangle is situated around Miyake, which is the Japanese island that lies around a hundred kilometers south of Tokyo. The Japanese refer to the area as "Ma-No Umi," which means the Sea of the Devil.

Legends surrounding this area go back to 1000 BCE. The Chinese believe that there is a giant dragon lurking in the depths of the sea.

In 1281 AD conqueror Kublai Khan, the fifth Great Khan of the Mongol Empire, lost his vessels and 40,000 crew members aboard in this triangular area, reportedly due to typhoons.

A large number of fishing vessels and over five military ships disappeared in the Devil's Sea in the 1940s and 1950s. The exact number of disappearances is unknown.

One disappearance that made international news was in 1953, when the Kaiyo-Maru No. 5, a Japanese research vessel sent on a mission to study the area, disappeared with all hands.

Famed cryptozoologist and paranormal enthusiast Ivan T. Sanderson explained that the mysterious disappearances occur in vile vortices, where the Earth's electromagnetic waves are purportedly stronger than anywhere else. The Dragon's Triangle is in one of these vortices.

The Burle Triangle
https://www.atlasobscura.com/places/burle-triangle

Europe has its triangle area where strange and inexplicable things happen. Located in France, the Burle Triangle (or "le Triangle de la Burle) is named after the frosty wind blowing in the area, which causes frequent snowstorms. It holds the French record for unexplained aircraft accidents. The points of the triangle are Mount Pilat, Mount Mézenc, and the small town of Le Puy.

In 1982, *l'Eveil* ("The Awakening"), a local newspaper of Le Puy-en-Velay city, spoke of a "Triangle of Death" where more than 60 victims died in mysterious plane crashes.

Also known for many UFO sightings, some investigators attribute their interference to the many planes that have crashed there. One, in particular, happened in November 1943, when a Halifax bomber plane crashed. The one sole survivor reported that the aircraft was "surrounded by a multitude of small multicolored lights." The Halifax bomber was navigating with all lights off, as was appropriate for the nighttime mission.

Another weird incident occurred in 1965 over Mount Mézenc, where two F-104 planes went down. Witnesses in the area claimed to have seen six spheres, pink in color, surrounding the impact site.

Whatever was happening over the skies of the Burle Triangle?Were there extraterrestrial ships stopping aircraft from flying there? Some UFO enthusiasts believe that there is a portal for UFOs to enter and exit. Or is it something more hiding in the mountains of France? Whatever was happening at the Burle Triangle, it remains a mystery to this day.

Stonehenge
http://www.stonehenge.co.uk/

Located on the outskirts of Wiltshire, England, about two miles (3 km) west of Amesbury lies one of the most iconic sites in the world consisting of a ring of thirty gigantic standing stones. Each of the stone monoliths is about 13 feet high, seven feet (2.1 m) wide, and weighs around 25 tons. Stonehenge is one of the most mysterious sites in Europe.

The prehistoric monument from more than 5,000 years ago is such a famous landmark that people might not think of it as mysterious anymore. But how and why these massive stones in England were made and arranged over 1,500 years has captivated researchers, historians, and curious visitors for years. What a lot of people don't know, until they visit the site, is that there are also 115 prehistoric ax-head carvings on the stones that date from around 1800–1700 BC. They were only recently discovered in 2011, using a 3D laser scan.

I got to visit this mysterious place back in 1975. For an eleven-year-old, it was neat for about five minutes. I remember thinking how huge the rocks were and wondering how they could have moved them back then, but we weren't allowed to run around the monoliths and climb on them. The only thing I remember that caught my attention was that there were mysterious lights seen at night near Stonehenge. Also, the parking area back then was quite a walk from the site.

Today Stonehenge is a major tourist attraction in England. Not only have they built a visitor's center, but there is also a recreation of a Neolithic village with five structures that were created based on archaeological evidence of houses found at Durrington Walls. Stonehenge is open every day, except for Christmas Eve and Christmas Day. To guarantee entrance at the time and day of your choosing, you must book your entrance ticket in advance.

Located north of Stonehenge is the Westbury White Horse.

Located on the edge of Bratton Downs and lying just below an Iron Age hill fort is a giant figure of a horse. It can be seen from miles and is the oldest of several white horses carved in Wiltshire. Standing at 180 feet tall by 170 feet wide, it is uncertain who carved the figure or what it represents. Some researchers believe it is to commemorate the victory of King Alfred at the Battle of Ethandun, which took place nearby in 878 AD. It is free to see this hillside attraction.

Skellig Michael, Ireland
https://skelligislands.com/

This mystical island, which sits 8 miles off the coast of Ireland, was named a UNESCO World Heritage Site in 1996. There are several Celtic and Christian legends about the rocky island, which rises 715 feet out of the water. A group of monks settled there and built a settlement in the sixth century that still stands today. Fans of *Star Wars* might recognize the island as Luke Skywalker's home in the most recent *Star Wars* films.

The Skellig Michael Landing Tour departs daily from Portmagee marina between 8:30 and 9:30; this is due to allocated landing time slots at Skellig Michael. It takes approximately 1 hour to reach Skellig Michael. You are allowed 2.5 hours on the island to climb the 640 steps to the top and explore the island. You can book the tour at https://www.skelligmichaelcruises.com/

Easter Island
https://www.nationalgeographic.com/travel/world-heritage/easter-island/

This world-famous island is located in the southeastern Pacific Ocean, at the southeasternmost point of the Polynesian Triangle in Oceania. It is famous for its nearly 1,000 extant monumental statues, called moai, created by the early Rapa Nui people. In 1995, UNESCO named Easter Island a World Heritage Site, with much

Skellig Michael off the coast of Ireland.

of the island protected within Rapa Nui National Park. There are flights to the island, one of the remotest in the world, from either Tahiti or Santiago, Chile. Easter Island is politically part of Chile and imports most of its food from Santiago.

Angkor Wat, Cambodia
https://www.nationalgeographic.com/travel/world-heritage/angkor/

Right outside of Siem Reap, in Cambodia, is the largest religious monument in the world. This Hindu-Buddhist temple complex measures 402 acres (162.6 hectares). Angkor Wat, translated from Khmer (the official language of Cambodia), literally means "City Temple." It was initially constructed in the 12th century as a Hindu temple dedicated to the god Vishnu, who is one of the three principal gods in the Hindu pantheon (Shiva and Brahma are the others). Later, toward the end of the 12th century, it is was transformed into a Buddhist temple.

Teotihuacan, Mexico
https://teotihuacanguide.com/

Situated fifty km northeast of Mexico City is the mysterious city of Teotihuacan. While its origins are still a mystery, what is known is that it was built between the 1st and 7th centuries AD. Archeologists believe the city collapsed, but from what no one knows. Some theorize that there was an invasion or that famine set in. The Aztecs know it as the place where the gods were created.

Archeologists are not sure who built this remarkable city, but evidence shows that it hosted a patchwork of cultures, including the Maya, Mixtec, and Zapotec.

Today a significant tourist attraction, thousands of visitors come each year to marvel at the ancient city. The ancient city consists of the following structures:

Pyramid of the Sun—The largest pyramid in the Western Hemisphere, it is also the third-largest pyramid in the world (the pyramid of Cholula is also sometimes said to be the largest

The Pyramid of the Sun and the Avenue of the Dead at Teotihuacan.

pyramid in the Western Hemisphere).

Pyramid of the Moon—The second-largest pyramid on site, used to conduct ceremonies in honor of the goddess of water, fertility, and the Earth.

Temple of the Feathered Serpent—The third largest pyramid, Teotihuacán, takes its name from the iconic carved heads that adorn the eastern side.

Palace of Quetzlpapalotl—It has ornately carved pillars and beautiful murals, all centered around a beautiful courtyard.

The Avenue of the Dead—This main path is a wide avenue, possibly a canal, between the various pyramids and structures at Teotihuacán.

Machu Picchu, Peru
https://www.machupicchu.gob.pe/inicio?request_locale=ES

At a height of 7,972 feet above sea level, this UNESCO World Heritege site is probably the highest of mysterious places on Earth. This Incan citadel is set high in the Andes Mountains in Peru, above the Urubamba River valley.

The exact use of this stone fortress remains a mystery to this day. Archeologists have determined that it was built in the 15th century and abandoned a century later at the time of the Spanish conquest. Some of the construction there, though, is megalithic and identical to that at much older sites. It was first brought to the world's attention in 1911 by American historian Hiram Bingham. It is still unknown what happened to the inhabitants, but they may have all died from smallpox introduced by travelers from Europe.

Renowned amongst ancient alien theorists for its sophisticated dry stone walls, with huge blocks fused without the use of mortar, it also has intriguing buildings that play on astronomical alignments and panoramic views. Today this impressive sight is a popular tourist attraction in Peru. Hundreds of tourists every year trek up the sheer cliffs to reach the top of this plateau.

To visit this mysterious fortress in the mountains, you must first make your way to Cusco, either by plane or bus from Lima. The bus ride is twenty-two hours, but it does help you get acclimated to the altitude. Once you have adequately acclimated to Cusco, you should have no serious problems with the altitude at Machu Picchu, since it is lower.

You will need to be in pretty good physical shape walk up the numerous stone steps to the site. If you are afraid of heights, you may not want to go. The cliffs and stairs along the path to the site are high and have no safety features. Also, the Dirección Regional de Cultura Cusco (DRC) limits visitors per day to Machu Picchu to 2,500.

Nazca Lines
http://www.discover-peru.org/the-nazca-lines/

Covering an area of nearly 1,000 sq. kilometers in southern Peru are hundreds of different pre-Columbian geoglyphs etched into desert sands, depicting different figures, including animals and plants. The ancient Nazca people of Peru created them by digging trenches in the desert's reddish-brown Earth, revealing a light-colored clay underneath.

More than 2,000 years ago, some of them were as large as 30 miles across. The designs have withstood time, in large part due to their isolated location in a windless and stable desert climate.

The geoglyphs range from simple straight lines to geometric shapes to more complicated animals like a hummingbird, spider, and monkey. There's also a human-like figure.

They are best viewed from the air, although surrounding foothills offer ideal vantage points for some of the designs. Despite being studied by scientists for almost 100 years, their function is still unknown. Ancient alien theorists believe that the Nazca people were either communicating with their gods or extraterrestrial visitors. There are several small airplane companies

Some of the lines and the hummingbird glyph at Nazca, Peru.

in Nazca that fly out of the local airport over the lines every day and offer reasonable prices for flights ranging from 45 minutes to two hours.

La Zona del Silencio (Zone of Silence)
https://random-times.com/2018/07/02/zona-del-silencio-the-urban-legend-magnet-for-curious/

There is an odd thirty square-mile area in northern Mexico, where things are just unexplainable. Located near the Bolsón de Mapimí in Durango, Mexico, overlapping the Mapimí Biosphere Reserve, the Zone contains dozens of flora and fauna endemic to the area and is rich in uranium and magnetite. The name appears on Mexican maps of the region and is well known to the local government.

Strange things happen here, like radio signals and electronic equipment being lost or going haywire. In 1970 a radioactive US military test rocket sent into space crashed in the Zone some 500 miles away from its reentry destination. The rocket went off course, it was carrying two small containers of cobalt 57, a radioactive element. Local farmers found the crash in the northeast corner of the State of Durango. Later the US military transported the missile wreckage and a small amount of contaminated topsoil back to the US. It was never explained why the missile went off-target.

The nickname of this mysterious place was given in 1966 when Pemex, the national oil company, sent an expedition to explore the area. The leader, Augusto Harry de la Peña, was frustrated by the problems he was having with his radio. He christened it the Zone of Silence.

Many have observed strange lights and UFOs in the vicinity. The area is sometimes compared to the Bermuda Triangle, as both are between parallels 26 and 28.

A ranching family in the area has spoken of frequent visits from two men and one woman, all Spanish-speaking with long blonde hair, who simply request to fill their canteens with fresh water and then leave. One time they reportedly told an interested family member they come "from above." A researcher who ended up lost in the Zone said a trio of similar-looking people led him back to his camp, then disappeared.

A couple whose vehicle got trapped in a torrential storm, meanwhile, was helped by two unusually tall men wearing baseball caps and yellow raincoats, who pushed their truck to safety. When the couple got out of their vehicle to give thanks, the mysterious good Samaritans were gone.

Gravity Hills

These weird areas are where the laws of gravity have gone haywire. They are found all over the world and are popular roadside attractions. And the best part is that they are free to experience. You set your car into neutral at the base of the hill and wait for it to creep up the hill mysteriously. Such hills have long had roadside attraction appeal, and everything from ghosts to aliens to magnetic forces have been attributed as the cause of the phenomenon.

There are many possible explanations for what could make an object break one of the sacred laws of science. Mysterious magnetic sources beneath the Earth's surface could be slowly pulling you towards them. A glitch in space-time could cause the laws of physics to unravel into backward chaos. An army of angry ghosts could be muscling your car to the top of the hill with nothing but their bare ghost hands.

Other explanations are a deviation in gravity, magnetic effects caused by underground metal deposits, and in some cases, volcanic activity in ancient times. There is, however, maybe only one real cause, one which only affects those with sight. The effect is caused by the peculiar series of uphill and downhill stretches in which gravity hills are located. There is no proper point of reference or no view of the horizon. If one lays a level on the hill, it often shows that things are going downhill indeed.

All the gravity hills have a legendary paranormal story to explain the unexplained occurrence. There are a number of them located in the United States, but here are some located around the world.

Electric Brae Gravity Hill Illusion, South Ayrshire, Scotland http://www.eureka4you.com/magnetichillworldwide/Ayrshire-UK.htm

Known locally as Croy Br, this gravity hill runs the quarter mile from the bend overlooking Croy railway viaduct in the west (286 feet Above Ordnance Datum) to the wooded Craigencroy Glen (303 feet AOD) to the east. The slope is 1 in 86 upwards from the bend to the Glen. The configuration of the land on either side of the road provides an optical illusion making it look as if the slope is going the other way. Therefore, a stationary car on the road with the brakes off will appear to move slowly uphill.

During WW II, General Eisenhower would bring guests to marvel at this phenomenon.

Today, people are still amazed as their cars seemingly freewheel up the hill. Others stop and put a ball in the middle of the road and watch it roll uphill.

Rua do Amendoim (Peanut Street), Belo Horizonte, Brazil
https://cityseeker.com/belo-horizonte/822653-rua-do-amendoim-peanut-street

The pretty residential street of Rua Professor Otávio Coelho de Magalhães, or "Rua do Amendoim" (Peanut Street) as it is known to locals, will always have ample parking.

Like a lot of gravity hills, this one is an optical illusion. Though the street appears to be on a steep incline, there is a slight dip in the road. Though cars seem to be rolling uphill, they're rolling down. That doesn't stop people from recording hundreds of videos capturing the strange sight of cars making their way uphill, though.

Even today, it attracts thousands of visitors every month who want to witness its curious optical illusion.

The road is accessible from Praça do Papa at the junction with Rua Junventino Dias. A sign that reads "Rua do Amendoim—Curiosity" can be seen at the intersection.

Black Rock Magnetic Hill, Australia
https://www.atlasobscura.com/places/magnetic-hill

This attraction is located on Black Rock Road near the townships of Pekina and Peterborough in rural South Australia, several hours drive northeast of Adelaide.

A drive along the road will reveal a strange sculpture of a giant magnet and rusty bicycle. Looking forward, as the road winds its way upwards into a small nest of hills, you would expect a car in

A sign at Black Rock Magnetic Hill, Australia.

neutral to roll back down the hill. But in some strange confluence of topographic anomalies, a car set in neutral will begin to (or appears to) roll uphill.

To find this gravity hill, you need to take the road from Peterborough to Orroroo. Around 25 km from Peterborough, you will come to a T-Junction—left to Jamestown and right to Orroroo. Turn left and travel approximately 1 km, where you cross over a railway crossing. Around 400 meters from that crossing and on the right-hand side of the road, there is a gravel road with a sign that says Magnetic Hill 8 km. Just follow the signs.

The Uphill-Downhill Road of Ariccia, Albano Laziale, Italy
https://www.atlasobscura.com/places/the-uphill-downhill-road-of-ariccia-albano-laziale-italy

This curious spot is popular in Italy, and Italian national TV reported about it. As with other 'anti-gravity hills,' It looks like an ordinary street in the woods with a gentle slope, but if you pour water or put a ball on the pavement, it seems to go uphill! When one walks on the hill, one "can feel that going uphill is much easier than going downhill."

On a side note, according to Google, things are indeed going uphill in defiance of gravity.

Cursed Islands

Are there islands around the world that are cursed? Legend has it that there are. From the Hawaiian islands to the tropics of Malaysia, to Europe and beyond, these sunny island paradises have dark secrets. Local and native superstitions and actual reports tell of those afflicted by a curse. Are these simply stories created to scare off visitors? Are supernatural forces actually to blame?One of the most famous cursed places in the world is Oak Island in Nova Scotia. The reason I decided to put it in my chapter on lost treasures is that the curse is only a small part of the legend.

Gaiola Island, Italy
https://theculturetrip.com/europe/italy/articles/the-story-behind-italys-cursed-gaiola-island/

Isold Della Gaiola is a small but beautifully formed island just off the Gulf of Naples, where emerald waters are clear enough for glimpses of the submerged ancient ruins below. There's even a private villa from which to enjoy the spectacular panoramic views. The island takes its name from the cavities that dot the coast of Posillipo, originating from the Latin word "cavea," meaning "little cave," and then morphing through the dialect to "Cavio-la."

Yet the island remains abandoned, and many locals refuse to go near it for fear of becoming the next victim of the island's curse. Everyone who has owned this island has soon died after acquiring it, starting with Captain Gaspare Albenga, who was piloting his ship around the island, crashed into rocks and drowned in 1911. All the island's owners have either died or had some family member die; sometimes they just lost their family fortune.

In the 1920s, a Swiss man named Hans Bran purchased the island and was murdered and later found wrapped in a rug. The next owner, Otto Grunback from Germany, died of a heart attack while on the island. The next owner was Gianni Agnelli, the head of Fiat, whose only son committed suicide. The last owner, Gianpasquale Grappone, was sent to prison when his insurance company failed.

Today the island is part of the Gaiola Underwater Park, a protected marine area owned by the region of Campania. Those who are brave enough to ignore the curse can reach Isola Della Gaiola with a short swim from the mainland.

Peche Island, Canada
https://www.citywindsor.ca/residents/parksandforestry/City-Parks/Pages/Peche-Island-.aspx

This little island lies just off shore in the Detroit River about two kilometers east of Belle Isle. The island was formed from a peninsula of the Canadian coast by the action of the Detroit River.

This uninhabited wilderness has a legend that keeps anyone from wanting to own it. The native Anishinaabe people of this region have legends about Peche Island that go back before recorded time, tales that come to us only by the passing of sacred stories from mouth to ear.

For almost 100 years, the Laforest family settled the island, and according to the descendants, there is a curse on it. The story behind the curse goes like this.

In 1882, Leon and his wife Rosalie Laforest and their twelve children had a twenty-five-acre farm when Canadian whiskey baron Hiram Walker purchased the island. Leon Laforest died in September of that year, leaving his widow and children to fend for themselves. Walker sent a gang from his distillery to the island to coerce Rosalie Laforest and the children to leave the island by spring. Rosalie refused to leave.

The authorities intervened and removed the family from the island. Before getting on the boat, Rosalie dropped to her knees and said, "No one will ever do anything with the island!" She had put a curse on not only the island but the Walker family.

Hiram Walker constructed a mansion on Peche Island, which consisted of over 40 rooms. The whiskey baron spent considerable amounts of money on the estate, which also had a greenhouse, orchards, stables, a carriage house, ice house, golf course, and a generator house for electric lighting.

The mansion was intended to be a resort for the rich and the high society of Detroit. Oddly enough, no pictures exist of it or the house. Everything was going great for Walker at this point.

Soon after Hiram Walker began developing his Peche Island paradise, Willis Walker, the lawyer who had handled the purchase of it from the Hall estate, suddenly died. He was only 28. Hiram himself became very ill around the same time and eventually suffered a minor stroke. He fell sick and transferred the title of the land in June 1895 to his daughter Elizabeth, with the house barely complete. Regardless, Hiram died soon after, in 1899. He never got to enjoy the fruits of his labor.

Elizabeth got rid of the doomed property in 1907, selling it to Walter E. Campbell, president of the Detroit, Belle Isle, & Windsor Ferry Company, which also owned Boblo Island Park. Less than a year later, he suddenly died there. With no one living there, the mansion fell into serious disrepair, and development plans ceased.

In 1929, a massive fire consumed the decaying mansion started by what some people thinkwas, a lightning bolt. It burned to the ground, eerily lighting up the night like a Viking pyre. Peche remained under the ownership of the Detroit, Belle Isle, & Windsor Ferry Company, who shunned the island and mostly let it go back to nature.

The City of Windsor acquired the land from the Province of Ontario in 1999. It is now a naturalized park with walking trails, and you can access it by boat.

Palmyra Atoll

https://www.fws.gov/refuge/palmyra_atoll/

This a small island located roughly 1,000 miles south of Hawaii, that has no permanent human population. But over the years, this island has experienced several disturbing paranormal occurrences that have led many to believe that it is cursed.

The atoll consists of a ring-shaped scattering of small islets made up of coral, much of which is overgrown with dense rainforest vegetation. White beaches, tranquil waters, and colorful marine life in the reef makes this place a diver's paradise. It does not seem like a place that would be haunted or plagued.

The first recorded sighting of Palmyra was in 1798. American sailor Edmund Fanning was en route to Asia, aboard his ship *The Betsy*, but failed to report it.

Later in 1802, the *Palmyra* (from which the island takes its name) failed to see the atoll's rocky reef and wrecked upon its coral.

In 1870, the ship *The Angel* crashed reef on the edge of the lagoon. The crew made it ashore. Later they were found murdered on the atoll. To this day, who killed the *Angel* sailors remains a mystery.

Legend has it that there is buried treasure on the atoll. In 1816, a Spanish pirate ship named *Esperanza*, loaded with plundered Inca treasure from Peru, became marooned. The crew buried the cache, and made two rafts in an effort to escape. One raft was picked up by a passing ship with one survivor. He related the story of the treasure and then died. They never found the second raft. Today the atoll is also said to be haunted by the ghosts of dead

An aerial photo of Palmyra Atoll.

sailors.

During the Second World War, the US Navy occupied the island—though their presence did little to ward off whatever evil spirits seemed to reside there. A patrol plane quite literally dropped out of the sky as it was passing over the island. Rescue teams were not able to recover any trace of an aircraft, nor a single crew member. Another story tells of a plane that flew off course after having just taken off from the atoll and simply disappeared off the radar, never to be seen again.

In 1974 Palmyra Atoll made the headlines worldwide as the location of a disappearance and murder that would later be the subject of a best-selling book and television movie. Malcolm Graham III and his wife Eleanor, or "Muff," on August 30, 1974, camped on Palmyra as they were yachting around the Pacific, in their yacht, the *Sea Wind*. They planned on staying at sea for about a year.

In 1981 a couple visiting the atoll—Sharon and Robert

Jordan from South Africa—discovered a human skull washed up on a beach. The authorities identified it as belonging to Eleanor Graham. Later her bones were discovered inside an aluminum box along the coast. Forensic analysis tests suggest that she was beaten over the head, dismembered, and had her face burnt using a welding torch. Her husband, Malcolm, was never recovered.

Ex-convict Buck Duane Walker and his girlfriend Stephanie Stearns were brought in and questioned when they sailed the Grahams' yacht into Honolulu harbor. They claimed that they had met the Grahams on the atoll and were later invited to the Grahams' yacht for dinner. They said that when they arrived, they found the boat empty. Suspecting that the Grahams had met with an accident, they sailed the yacht back to Hawaii.

In 1985, Buck Duane Walker was found guilty of the murder of Muff Graham. Stearns was acquitted due to insufficient evidence. Vincent Bugliosi and Bruce Henderson wrote a book about the murder called *And the Sea Will Tell*, which was then made into a 1991 television movie.

Today if you visit the atoll, you will find a temporary population of "non-occupants," namely scientists employed by various departments of the US government and by The Nature Conservancy. The Palmyra Atoll Research Consortium scholars are also pursuing research.

It's not uncommon to hear Pacific travelers still talk about the "Palmyra curse."

Daksa Island, Croatia
https://balkanist.net/haunted-croatian-island-one-will-buy/

With its pristine woodland, private beaches, and very own monastery, this Mediterranean isle looks like the perfect getaway.

Yet Croatia's Daksa Island has been on the market for five years without a single buyer showing interest—despite the owners slashing the $A3 million asking price in half.

In 1944, forty-eight people were charged with being Nazi sympathizers and executed on the island. Naturally, their ghosts are said to haunt the island, scaring off tourists and potential investors.

Lokrum Island, Croatia
https://www.dubrovnik-travel.net/lokrum-island/

One of a series of beautiful islands off the coast of Croatia. Just 2,000 feet from the port of Dubrovnik, it has long been inhabited, with recorded mentions dating back as early as the 11th century, when Lokrum was the site of a Benedictine abbey and monastery. The monks took advantage of the favorable climate by harvesting exotic fruits on the island. This gave birth to its name, "Lokrum," coming from the Latin "acrumen," meaning sour fruit.

Stories about the island's history vary, though one popular telling has it that widespread fires once struck Lokrum. The locals prayed to Saint Benedict, vowing to build a monastery if their homes were saved. Legend has it that heavy rain appeared and extinguished the fires, and so the abbey and monastery were built.

In 1798, the monks were ordered off the island by the French. As the last Benedictines left in 1808, they held a mass, placing a curse on the island. In 1859, the island was the property of the Habsburgs, and Archduke Maximilian Ferdinand had a regal mansion and botanical gardens constructed on Lokrum. He later became Emperor of Mexico and was executed not long after, and locals were quick to blame it on the curse.

Even today, the people of Dubrovnik are delighted to share tales of fishing boats swallowed by the sea, or of pleasure-seekers who visited Lokrum Island overnight and were never seen again.

Clipperton Island, Tahiti
https://www.qsl.net/clipperton2000/

Ferdinand Magellan discovered this island in 1521. It was

later named after John Clipperton, an English pirate who led a mutiny against William Dampier in 1704.

According to legend, Clipperton hid treasure on the atoll that has never been found.

More than 100 years later, the island was taken over by an American guano (a type of phosphate-rich manure excreted by seabirds and bats) mining companiy.

In 1857, the French disputed America's claim to Clipperton, declaring the island was, in fact, part of Tahiti. In 1897, after several years of no permanent settlement, Mexico moved in and established a military outpost on the island.

In 1906, the British Pacific Island Company annexed Clipperton, building a joint township with the Mexican government to mine guano. A lighthouse was built in the same year. In 1914, about 100 people, both men and women, lived on the island. Every two months, a ship from Acapulco went to the island to bring food. However, with the start of the Mexican civil war, the atoll was no longer reachable by ship, and the people on the island were on their own.

By 1915, most of the inhabitants had died. The last settlers had wanted to leave on the American warship Lexington, which had reached the atoll in late 1915, but the Mexican military governor declared that evacuation was not necessary.

By 1917, all the men on the island had died except the lighthouse keeper, along with 15 women. By July of that year, all but three of the women had died, and they were picked up by the American ship Yorktown.

France and Mexico have disputed the ownership of Clipperton. France approached the Vatican for a decision on who owned the lonely atoll. In 1930, the Vatican gave the rights to the King of Italy, Vikor Emanuel II, who declared one year later that Clipperton was a part of France.

When Clipperton was finally declared as a French possession, the lighthouse was rebuilt, and the French settled a military outpost on the island. The outpost only remained for there seven years, and then the French abandoned it.

It has remained uninhabited ever since.

Lazzaretto Nuovo
https://www.lazzarettonuovo.com/visit-the-island/

This small island sits at the mouth of a lagoon that flows into Venice, Italy, and was originally home to a monastery.

In the 15th century, authorities designated it a quarantine area for ships approaching Venice, to protect the city from the plague. This continued until the 18th century when the quarantine facilities were abandoned and converted into a military base.

The Italian government gave up on the site in 1975, and it suffered years of neglect. Community efforts have since turned it into a cultural museum site, now supported by the Italian Ministry of Arts and Culture. The island is currently open for tourism but remains uninhabited.

The Langkawi Islands, Malaysia
http://www.langkawi-info.com/info/legends.htm

Despite lush, tropical forests that are believed to have existed for as long as 450 million years, Langkawi has only recently become a popular tourist destination with the construction of its first duty free port in the late 1980s.

Before that, these islands were primarily avoided by locals who feared their curse. Legend has it that a beautiful island girl called Mahsuri, married to the warrior known as Wan Darus, had once lived on the island. During the time of the Burmese-Siamese War (towards the end of the 18th century), Wan Darus was called away—and sometime later, Mahsuri offered shelter to a handsome traveler named Deraman.

Though her offer was made out of pure generosity, other

women on the island grew jealous of Mahsuri's handsome visitor, and stories soon spread about an alleged affair. When one day their jealousy grew to a peak, Mahsuri's neighbors attacked her, stabbing the girl to death in a rice field.

According to the story, Mahsuri placed a curse on the island as she lay dying in that field; she vowed that the island would be destroyed, and see no prosperity for a full seven generations. Not long after that, more and more of the superstitious islanders began to leave, and the Langkawi Islands were primarily abandoned for decades. It is only now, more than seven generations after the supposed murder, that locals—and tourists—are returning to the islands once more.

Cook Islands, South Pacific
https://www.tahitilegends.com/south-pacific/cook-islands-about#

The South Pacific has long been home to stories of witch doctors and their spells, but few such stories have had such widespread effect as the "Curse of the Cook Islands."

In 1911, the New Zealander William John Wigmore leased a plot of land from the Cook Islander More Uriatua. More decided later that he wanted his land back, and refused to give his approval to the intended copra plantation. An argument ensued, and Wigmore shot More dead. Wigmore was deported, and in 1913 More's daughter, Metua A More, is said to have placed a curse on the island.

The exact terms of that curse stated that any business venture conducted at the plot of land known as Vaimaanga would be fated to ruin. It seemed to work, too. In the 1950s and 60s, plans to construct a commercial citrus orchard fell flat on their face, as did a proposed herb plantation and a later pineapple growing business.

In the late 1980s the Sheraton hotel chain bought the land, and invested more than $60 million into an intended holiday resort. The project was plagued by setbacks though, dogged by one failure after another, until a point where an estimated $120 million had been pumped into the doomed endeavor.

On May 25, 1990, a full 77 years after the initial curse was placed, Metua's grandson More Rua returned to the spot in order to reinforce the curse. Dressed in the Kakau and Rakei Taunga, the ceremonial dress of a Cook Island high priest, Rua conducted the ritual armed with a war spear.

With the base of his spear, Rua struck a commemorative plaque that celebrated the commencement of the Sheraton hotel project. Supposedly the rock shattered, and the cracks spread deep down into the Earth beneath the building site.

In 1993, the construction came to a final halt. with 80% of the Sheraton project finished. Today the Sheraton resort, a palatial 200-room holiday complex, lies trashed and abandoned in this island paradise.

A Cursed Fort

Bhangarh Fort, India

https://www.thehindu.com/opinion/columns/the-most-haunted-fort-in-india/article20231373.ece

Located at the border of the Sariska Tiger Reserve in the Alwar district of Rajasthan, this abandoned fortress sticks out in the middle of the desert. No one lives in or near this fort because there is a *legend*—a legend that has survived for centuries about this old abandoned fort, making it one of the most cursed places in India.

Bhangarh's ruins include several impressive structures, including several temples, public chambers, and the royal palace. Intricate carvings and sculptures adorn all the temples.

Kachwaha ruler of Amber, Raja Bhagwant Singh, built the fort for his younger son Madho Singh in 1573 AD.

Some legends surround the fort as to why it was mysteriously

The entrance to Bhangarh Fort.

abandoned. The most famous legend tells of a black magician who fell in love with a princess. He attempted to use a love potion to win her affection, but the princess dodged his moves and flung the potion onto a large boulder, dislodging it, causing it to roll down—physically crushing the magician. The legend is that before taking his final breath, he cursed the fort, saying it would end up in a state in which no one could live.

You can visit this completely ruined, haunted fort of Bhangarh, if you can get past the very eerie, negative aura to it, during the daytime. Because of incidents in the fort, the Archaeological Survey of India has posted signs prohibiting visitors between sunset and sunrise.

Mysterious Stairs and Sealed Vaults
https://www.historicmysteries.com/mysterious-stairs-forests-legends-history/

There are hundreds of stories of hikers and campers finding bizarre stuff out in the woods. Everything from crashed planes, concrete safes, and steel cages to human skeletons have been found in the middle of these desolate locations. This kind of thing occurs all around the world.

Imagine that you are hiking through the woods. You've gotten far back there when you come upon a set of stairs sitting alone in the forest, leading to nowhere. Who put them there, and why? I recently discovered this phenomenon on the Internet and started reading more.

Numerous people have been coming forward with reports of isolated stairs in the woods and national parks, and telling some of the creepiest stories about otherworldly experiences when they climbed the mysterious staircase. Oddly enough, there are very few photos of the staircases that were found in the woods, making the phenomenon even more mysterious

The stairs differ wildly in style, age, condition, and design and are located miles from the closest town, without any logical reason for them to be there. Some of the stairs do look like they were part of a settlement or structure. But some of them are new and there for some unknown reason.

While many legends in this book are centuries old, the "stairs in the woods," pheunomenon is a modern tale. There are several theories about what the stairs might be. Some researchers believe that they are simply the foundations of a lost settlement. Others believe that the stairs have a paranormal origin like a gateway to another dimension, or hell. An interesting thing about some of these stories is when the witness(s) comes across one of these stair cases, they can't find it when they go back.

Some researchers believe that the stories about these stairs are fictional, the accounts of the mysterious steps originating on the forum Reddit. On this forum, users post eerie, yet believable, works of fiction. After Reddit posted the "stairs in the woods" story, many readers came forward with their accounts of mysterious steps and where to find them.

Here is a list of mysterious staircases and sealed vaults around the world.

Etruscan Pyramid of Bomarzo, Italy
https://www.atlasobscura.com/places/etruscan-pyramid-bomarzo

In the sleepy little town of Bomarzo is an ancient pyramid. Located in the Viterbo province of Lazio, Italy, this area in 700 BC was part of the broader region of Etruria. During that time, the Etruscans built a structure out of the volcanic rock in a nearby valley. Today it is called the Etruscan Pyramid of Bomarzo by the local people. The rock structure has steep stairs, a number of platforms, rectangular cubicles, and channels running at odd angles decorate the front wall.

For many years local villagers called the large rock with the stairs hewn out Sasso del Predicatore ("Stone of the Preacher") or the "Stone with Steps." Then in 1991 by two local archaeologists named Giovanni Lamoratta and Giuseppe Maiorano discovered

The mysterious Etruscan staircase at Bomarzo.

that that the steps were part of a large pyramid hidden away in the woods.

Archaeologists believe that the Etruscans used the pyramid as an altar for sacrificing animals. Carved in the structure are steps and gutters. The gutters were for the blood of sacrificed animals. The stone structure is positioned toward the northwest, facing the direction of the Etruscan underworld gods.

In 2008, Salvatore Fosci rediscovered a monumental Etruscan pyramid-shaped altar

The surrounding area has Etruscan inscriptions, tombs, medieval ruins, and a mysterious tower of Chia. The tower was owned by the famous writer/director Pier Paolo Pasolini until he died in 1975. According to legend, his ghost haunts the tower.

There are hiking trails that connect the pyramid, the tower, waterfalls, and old watermills of Fosso Castello within a four-hour hike.

Mount Phnom Kulen, Cambodia
https://www.siemreap.net/visit/attractions/sightseeing/phnom-kulen/

Phnom Kulen is Cambodia's most sacred mountain. Kulen mountain means "Mountain of the Lychees." It is the birthplace of the ancient Khmer empire, dating back to 802 AD when Jayavarman II was said to declare himself a devaraja (god-king) at its peak.

Today it is a national park where a large number of Cambodians visit during the weekends, especially during religious festivals. Visitors come to visit Wat Preah Ang Thom, a sacred temple that contains a giant reclining Buddha.

It is a seven-mile trek to climb to the summit or hit the waterfall. The waterfall, featured in the 2001 action-adventure movie *Lara Croft: Tomb Raider*, is considered one of the most beautiful waterfalls in the world. The path to the peak passes the famous River of a Thousand Lingas. There you will find carvings of Hindu gods and symbols, believed to date back to the reign of King Udayadityavarman II. The Wat Preah Ang Thom temple is next to the river.

Natural medicine doctors flock to this place, while some visit to seek blessings from its holy waters, particularly the potent life-giving waters at Kbal Spean. Also located near the waterfall is the Prasat Krau Romeas temple ruins, which date back to the 9th century.

Padmanabhaswamy Temple, Kerala, India
http://www.transindiatravels.com/kerala/trivandrum/padmanabhaswamy-temple/

In Thiruvananthapuram in Kerala, India is one of India's most popular and most sacred temples. The Padmanabhaswamy Temple's history dates back as early as the 6th century in ancient Tamil literature. It takes its name from the word "Padmanabha," which means, "One emerging from the lotus," and this theme is illustrated well on the Sri Padmanabha icon. It has the deity Brahma emerging from Vishnu's navel on a lotus. The entire temple icon is carved out of a massive stone measuring 20 feet high and 2.5 feet thick and covered in gold.

A trust headed by the royal family, established in 1729, runs the shrine. The temple and its assets belonged to Lord Padmanabhaswamy and the Travancore Royal Family.

What makes this temple so mysterious is what lies inside. Six enormous secret vaults house many of the Temple's treasures. The vault doors, made of iron, lack locks, hatches, or any form of openings. The vaults were named Chambers A through F.

Five of the vaults, A, C, D, E, and F, have been opened, and inside were found 22 billion dollars' worth of golden idols, elephants, necklaces, and coins. They also discovered an

An artist's drawing of the Padmanabhaswamy Temple door.

assortment of jewels, ceremonial costumes, and solid gold coconut shells studded with jewels. A small gold idol of Vishnu was found archaeologists and gemologists to value at thirty million dollars.

The only vault door never opened is the mysterious Vault B. To this day, no one knows what lies beyond its gates and it is not part of the documented Temple Treasury. Legend has it that the chamber is holy, as it houses an idol of Sri Padmanabha and many valuables of mystic origins.

The steel door of Chamber B does not have and bolts, latches, or other means of entry. The only thing people have seen is its gates, guarded by two enormous embossed cobras. Legend has it that if any human attempts made to open the door, will unleash unspeakable horrors throughout India, and perhaps the rest of the world.

Today, no vistors are allowed to view the vault and the High Court of India has issued a warning against opening the doors of the chamber. Visitors have to go through numerous metal detectors, security cameras, and more than 200 guards protecting the Temple and its treasures.

The temple is free to visit but you cannot bring in any mobile phones, tablets, laptops, cameras or any other electronic gadgets. There is also a strict dress code where males must wear a doti (a type of sarong that outwardly resembles trousers) and be bare chested; no upper clothing is allowed. Female visitors must wear a saree (a traditional female garment with various styles of draping, varying from five to nine yards length).

Loretto Chapel Staircase, United States

In Santa Fe, New Mexico is a chapel called Loretto Chapel. Each year hundreds come to visit this church, but not to attend mass. In this church is a hundred-year-old mystery. That mystery is a staircase from the floor to the loft. What makes this a mystery is the physics of its construction.

In 1878, with the chapel newly completed, the Sisters of the Chapel discovered that there was no way to access the choir loft twenty-two feet above the main floor. Every carpenter consulted concluded that because of the interior space of the small church, only a ladder could be used.

Legend says that to find a solution to the problem, the Sisters of the Chapel made a novena to St. Joseph, the patron saint of carpenters.

Later, a man appeared at the Chapel with a donkey and a toolbox looking for work. When the elegant circular staircase was finished, the carpenter disappeared without pay or thanks.

After searching for the man (an ad even ran in the local newspaper) and finding no trace of him, some concluded that he was St. Joseph himself, having come in answer to the sisters' prayers.

The stairway's carpenter, whoever he was, built a magnificent structure. The design was innovative for the time, and some of the design considerations still perplex experts today. You can today take a tour of the Chapel and see these remarkable and mysterious stairs.

If you do plan on visiting any of the haunted or mysterious

places I have gone over, I will again reiterate that you should practice situational awareness. You need to be constantly aware of your surroundings. Always look for potential threats and dangerous situations. It is probably the most critical thing about legend tripping. In an ever-changing world, you need to make sure you know everything about the area or country you are visiting. I can't emphasize that enough. But also don't be scared to visit new places.

There are some beautiful places in the world where the unexplained and mysterious still happen. The Dalai Lama said it best, "Once a year, go someplace you've never been before."

The mysterious Loretto Chapel staircase.

Chapter 10:

UFO Hunt

If people sat outside and looked at the stars each night, I'll bet they'd live a lot differently.
—Bill Waterson

When you look up at the night sky, you behold a heavenly sight, peppered with constellations, planets, and occasional meteors. Every so often, something else appears like a bright light, flashing multicolored lights, moving in strange, unfamiliar patterns. Have you ever looked up at the night sky and wondered who else could be out there? Are there races of aliens visiting this planet in strange crafts? Like all legend trips, searching for extraterrestrials is different but just as exciting. With extraterrestrial or UFO legend trips, the primary focus is the sky as you're looking for something to appear in the heavens. With this, you have to learn to be extremely quiet and to exercise patience.

I remember in the '70s, during the UFO craze, I read in the newspaper where Charles Hickson and Calvin Parker claimed they were abducted by aliens while fishing near Pascagoula, Mississippi. Even though the men were questioned heavily by authorities and naysayers, both men passed lie detector tests. This incident later became known as the 1973 Pascagoula Abduction. Their tale had everybody looking at the night sky, searching for something out of the ordinary. I was one of those heading outside at night with my binoculars to look for UFOs. My fascination with UFOs was set when I saw the 1970 movie *Close Encounters of the*

Third Kind.

I refer to this type of excursion as a UFO Legend Trip, which involves spotting UFOs, usually in the night sky, and taking pictures or recordings to capture their activity. With this legend trip, you can either do an all-nighter or make it a day legend trip. For UFO crash sites, I recommend a day legend trip (Chapter 14). There is a list of equipment at the end of this chapter. You can add more equipment or leave some. It's up to you. These are just basic guidelines when you're out looking for UFOs.

The first thing you need to do is to find out where in your area there have been UFO sightings, or better yet a UFO hotspot. UFO hotspots are areas where there is the highest concentration of UFO sightings. These strange aircraft, like bigfoot and ghosts, don't always reappear where they were initially seen. But there are areas where they are seen more than once. Of course, this is no guarantee you'll see a something, but you have to start somewhere. With all legends, persistence will pay off. If there is not a UFO hotspot in your area, find the closest, and plan a legend trip. This is a legend trip that requires you to stay out all night and maybe camp out. You can stay at a hotel, but it can be expensive.

Here in Florida, the most activity used to be in the Gulf Breeze area, but now the activity seems to be all over Florida. A lot of witnesses reported sightings next to NASA near Titusville. Also, military bases seem to attract UFOs.

Several UFO websites have online databases listing sightings by state, date, and shape so you can find out the latest sightings in your area. You can sign up for their newsletters online, which also feature current UFO sightings. You can also learn a lot by reading through others' reports. These UFO sightings groups are:

- National UFO Reporting Center
- MUFON (Mutual UFO Network)
- UFOdb

Once you find a UFO hotspot you want to check out, you need to gather as much up-to-date information as possible. This information will be pertinent to where you will be conducting an exciting legend trip. If you know somebody who saw the UFO, interview him or her. Also, get their permission before contacting others. Try to locate any witnesses who are involved with the location and the sightings, including residents, employees, and owners—whoever might have knowledge of the potential activity.

Also, you have to familiarize yourself with the constellations and planets. If you don't, you're bound to mistake a star for a UFO. You can get an app for your cellphone called Star Gazer that allows you to point your cellphone up in the sky and it will tell you all the stars, constellations, and planets visible in the night sky in your location. This is great to have, and you won't end up getting over excited when you see blue and red lights twinkling in the sky, and shout out to the team an invasion is coming. Also, go to a place that doesn't have a lot of air traffic, so you don't mistake human aircraft for UFOs

After you have all the information on the area or hotspot, it's time to plan the UFO legend trip. If the area is in a different city or state, you'll need to make travel arrangements. You'll need to decide how many vehicles you'll need and what kind of extra equipment you'll need. Make a call out to your friends and invite them to your extraterrestrial adventure. Once you have your team of legend trippers together, move out.

On a side note: If your legend trip takes you to a higher elevation you should always give your body time to acclimate to the different alttitude, or you can get end up with altitude sickness. Symptoms for this are headaches, dizziness, nausea, vomiting, fatigue, shortness of breath, sleep problems, or a decrease in appetite. You will notice these symptoms within 12 to 24 hours. Keeping hydrated will help. Usually, altitude sickness will subside within a day or two as your body adjusts to the change in altitude.

When you arrive at the UFO hotspot, the first thing you need to take into consideration is where to set up your base of operations. I like to find campgrounds close to the area of the sighting. With UFO sightings, this may not be easy to do. You may have to find a campsite close to the area, or you might be able to get permission from the landowners to camp out there. It's good to go to an area beautiful to look at even if you don't see a UFO. If you have to hike a considerable way to the hotspot, never go rucking or hiking by yourself. If you can't find anybody to go with you, then wait until someone is available. I cannot stress this point enough. Some sightings take place over lakes, and there are usually trails around lakes. Some reports, like the ones in Puerto Rico, report UFOs descending into lakes.

For scout masters and venturing crew guides, you need to see if there is a Boy Scout or Girl Scout camp near the lake and maybe incorporate a UFO legend trip into your weekend outing. It

According to the US Air Force this 1951 photo from New Zealand is of a lenicular cloud, rather than a UFO.

adds to the excitement of the journey. It gives you and your troop something to look for when they are hiking.

Setting up a base camp is pretty much the same as doing a Bigfoot legend trip. I always make a checklist to make sure I set up everything we need. Again, you can do it the way you want, because everybody is different. This checklist has worked for me, and I've been doing this for years. Most of the time, I like to go out bigfoot hunting, so this checklist is used for a bigfoot legend trip.

First, I pick an area for my base camp close to the UFO hotspot, if possible. Plan on different locations in case someone is already camped at your chosen spot or if you have a larger team. You also need a plan on coming back to these spots multiple times over months or even years. Furthermore, if your chosen spot is full of campers, it might be a good idea not to tell everybody what you're doing other than camping.

When you arrive at your actual campsite, the first thing to do is unload your camping gear to get base camp set up. If you brought water gear, put your boat or canoe in a secure location. Fuel cans need to go in your vehicle and not in camp where you have a campfire going.

If you are leading this UFO legend trip, assign jobs or assignments and then make sure everybody gets the camp set up before it gets dark. It is important to get all your gear set up, especially your tents. If your camp is near a lake during the summer, mosquitoes or other insects will drive you crazy. Make sure you have the mosquito candles ready. When the sun goes down, you need to have the bug spray ready.

For more in-depth details on creating a safe and secure campsite, please refer to Chapter 3.

Once you have your base camp set up, it is time to scout around the area where you want to do your UFO investigation to see what's out there. If you have a large area to investigate, break into teams, and check out multiple areas. Get your map out and, with the team, show them where the UFO sightings took place and then plot where you want the teams to set up.

If there is enough time, you should take all the teams with you when you identify the area you intend to observe in the sky. It's easier than going back and explaining it on a map. It is best to do this during daylight hours with the team, allowing review and answering questions about what is going to happen. Make sure everybody knows what they should look for and point out where the sightings occurred. It is OK to go to the areas in the evening, but it's easier to do it during the day so that everyone can get familiar with the area and nobody will get lost. You want to find an area that gives you or your team a full panoramic view of the sky, with nothing blocking it like trees or buildings.

Always have somebody stay back at base camp and monitor the radio. After breaking everyone into teams, assign them AORs (Area of Responsibility). These are areas the team is to investigate and set up static posts, scan the sky and the horizon. You can get almost a hundred percent scan of the sky with multiple teams. These AORs should be marked on a map so the base camp can keep track of them. Also, if somebody gets hurt, the person at base camp can call for medical aid and have it come to the base camp. If your area is large, you might consider having the teams use vehicles to go to their AORs, moving easier and quicker. Have a dependable 4x4 vehicle back at base camp in case a vehicle breaks down or something goes wrong. If another vehicle breaks down, you may have to tow it with your vehicle.

Each team needs to have a working radio with fresh or extra batteries or a cellphone. I have the teams do radio checks before they move out to their AORs. If a team loses contact, they should return to base camp immediately and either get a new radio or a member with a working cellphone. If they see a wild animal like a panther or bear tracks, they are to radio it in and return to the rally point or base camp. Go over all of this with everybody before each team moves out to its AORs. Depending on the size of the investigation area, each team should take water and food. Always take a survival kit because they also have first aid items like Band-Aids and antiseptic wipes.

UFOs can be seen day or night. Your regular nighttime UFOs are called nocturnal lights, while daytime UFOs are called daylight discs. Most nocturnal lights are self-illuminating, while most daylight discs are metallic in color. So while you're walking down the street, look up at the clouds. You may just spot a sparkling daylight disc zipping across the sky. There are occasional UFO landings, so be on the lookout for large burn areas where there shouldn't be any, usually in large fields. Thermal imagers are useful for checking out fields as they pick up heat signatures.

If you're conducting your UFO legend trip near water, watch out for everything around you. For example, if a team needs to move through the swamps to get to their AOR, they need to watch out for hidden dangers like cypress trees. Additionally, there are sinkholes, which you can't see, and you can't tell how deep they are, creating a potentially dangerous situation. Make sure you go over all of this with your team before you enter the area.

A photo of a UFO taken in 1967 in Rhode Island.

During the recon, you need to choose a rallying point, especially if using vehicles. A rally point is a designated area for everyone to meet back up again after the investigation, which is usually in the middle of the AORs or could be base camp.

Equipment

Many people have claimed to have seen a UFO while some have even reported being abducted. Unfortunately, no one has been able to provide definitive proof. It's imperative if you are serious about seeing and recording a UFO sighting that you have serious equipment for getting concrete data. When it comes to cameras, have a camera that takes excellent pictures at night. You'll need a special lens to capture the faint lights and patterns created by the UFOs. You should have a camera on a tripod or stand, pointing where the sighting occurred. Also keep the locks on the pod off, in case you need to reposition the camera to a different location. UFOs usually reappear in the same place over and over again. Just be ready to reposition your camera in case the UFO appears in a different location nearby. A video camera is also useful to have. The more ways you have to document the UFOs, the better. Always make sure somebody is with your equipment at all times.

Telescopes are good to have, but they can be challenging to use when you see a UFO. The lens is focused on one small area and can be difficult to move where the UFO is, and if the UFO is moving, it's more challenging to keep track of it with a telescope. I prefer binoculars as they are easy to use, and most are pretty durable and less expensive than a telescope.

A thermal imager is a great tool to use. These expensive devices will scan an area and pick up heat signatures. In other words, if there is something in the sky giving off heat, this device will pick it up. It works great both during the daytime and at night. Thermal imagers come in a variety of designs, but they are all expensive. As I said, they are great for legend tripping, but they are costly and fragile.

Night vision scopes/cameras magnify any kind of light source, and you can see things from quite a distance away. They go through batteries pretty quickly, so make sure you have extras on hand.

After the recon is complete, head back to camp to review with the teams their AORs and what their plan is. This is the question and answer time. Do this now and not when they are out. Make sure everyone knows the plan for the investigation and reiterate safety procedures to everyone. Then finish off the evening with dinner and move the teams out to their AOR.

The person at base camp needs to keep a record of the details of your legend trip and sightings. Each team should have a notebook and writing instrument at all times to jot down all necessary information right when it happens. Voice recorders are also handy devices that allow teams to record their observations without having to stop and write them down. Later, when you get to base camp, record the information in a log on your computer.

Make sure every team knows what to do if they spot a UFO. First, they need to radio it in to base camp. Even if you aren't sure what you saw was indeed a UFO, you need to write down the following information:

- The date and time of the sighting.
- The location of the sighting.
- The shape, size, and color of the UFO.
- Whether there were additional witnesses.

UFO experts will tell you that after you've hunted for UFOs for awhile, you'll start to notice patterns. Things to remember for your UFO hunt:

- Most UFOs don't move in a straight line, but rather up and down or in zigzags. They may not move in regular patterns at all.

- UFO's don't blink as known aircraft would. They may be shaped like discs, triangles, or something else entirely.
- Also, find out whether what you're seeing may have an explanation; for example, if you're looking for UFOs near an Air Force base, you might be seeing human-made aircraft, even if they look unfamiliar.

Before you and the teams head out to your AORs, always double-check the radios, cameras, and gear. Have all teams keep video cameras on and recording, and then send them to their area. You never know when something will happen, and when it does, it happens quickly, and by the time you get your camera up and running, it is gone. If you don't get anything, just erase the recording. Make sure everyone has the right clothing for the expected weather. It might get cold at night, and the weather might take a turn for the worse, and you and your team will need raingear. Each team will move to their AOR and set up and look and listen. It is better to stay on dirt paths and roads so nobody will get lost, and it's easier to backtrack to the rally point or base camp.

After a couple of hours, if nothing has happened I usually call the teams in and reassign AORs. Teams won't get bored looking at the same thing all the time if their locations are moved. Have the teams call base camp when they first get set up and then every couple of hours. They can also call you at a designated time or when they see something. At least one member of the team should always be awake and watching.

An exception to the rule of staying at your designated AOR is when a team starts to see or hear things. If you or one of your teams hears something, then have everybody proceed to their AOR or see if they can see it from their own AOR. Remember, always keep the video camera in record mode. You can talk into the mic and explain where you are and what time it is.

Now you might have the teams staying in their AOR until a certain time. If they are staying all night, they will need to bring a tent and sleeping bag. If that's the case, I recommend you have a roving team who will either walk or drive around to the various teams and check on them.

Once all teams have returned to based camp at the end of the investigation, inventory all gear. Any team unable to make it back to base camp on time should call on the radio/cellphone and let the base know your location and reason for being stopped. It only takes a couple of seconds to do this. If a team does not show up at the prescribed time, don't panic. First, call them on the radio to determine their location. If there is no answer (radio/cellphone) and it has been a while, send only one team who knows the area.

Daytime operations (ops) to see if a UFO appears are pretty much the same as night, except remember teams might want to find shaded areas rather than sit in the hot sun. It is also sometimes harder to see UFOs during sunny days. NEVER aim your binoculars at the sun.

If a team or team member gets lost, first check what AOR they were assigned. If you have communications with them, have them describe where they are and at what point they knew they were lost. If you have done your briefing right and every team stayed in their assigned zone or road, you will pretty much know the area they should be in. The missing team will probably be close to it. Once you get to the lost team's AOR, call out to them and see if they can hear you. Sound travels better at night. Make sure only one team is calling out to them. If all the teams do this, then you won't be able to hear the lost team when they reply.

If the worst happens and you can't find them, call 911. Fish and Wildlife officers will come out, and they often have helicopters equipped with heat-detecting devices and will be able to find the lost team. When they arrive, give them the location where the team is supposed to be, which will provide them with an area to start their search. In the whole time I have been legend tripping I have not lost a team. I always ensure each team has an experienced person with them, stays on the road, and has a working radio.

When all the teams are back at the rally point, do a quick briefing to find out what all the teams saw or heard. Make sure they know where it was they heard the noise or saw the object and return to the location for a more thorough search. The UFO might return. Talk about what was seen and heard. Review all pictures and recordings. If your team took videos or photographs, look them over. If you do have something on an image, you or a team will need to recheck the area and make sure that what you have in the picture is not a plane or balloon. Repeat this procedure depending on how many days you decide to stay out. If you spot a UFO, report it. You'll be contributing to the UFO community at large.

UFO Legend Trip

- Camera—one that has IR capabilities
- Camera stands and pods
- GPS—this is good to use so you can mark your location
- Bionic ear device
- Camping gear including tent(s), sleeping bag(s), lanterns
- Thermal imager
- Water and items to clean water
- Flashlights/headlights/light sticks
- Rain gear—GORE-TEX is great because it also keeps you warm
- Binoculars/telescope with stand
- Evidence kit (including footprint casting material?)
- Cold weather clothes

Chapter 11

Treasure Legends from Around the World

There comes a time in every rightly constructed boy's life when he has a raging desire to go somewhere and look for hidden treasure.
—Mark Twain

As a youth, one of my favorite books was the *Thousand and One Nights*, or as it is known "The Arabian Nights." It is a collection of Middle Eastern folktales featuring genies, dragons, flying carpets, and hidden treasures. These tales were collected over many centuries by various authors, translators, and scholars across West, Central and South Asia, and North Africa. My favorite tale out of all of them was *Ali Baba and the Forty Thieves*. I just imaged Ali Baba saying "Open Sesame," and the large rock door magically opening, revealing enormous caches of gold and diamonds hidden in the cave.

Today there are still numerous undiscovered treasures around the world. Some of the most popular television shows are about lost treasure and the hunt for it. There are treasure hunters examining maps, looking for a vital clue that will lead them to the cache. There are treasures with only riddles to reveal where they lie. These legend trippers continue their relentless search for their goal.

The number one show of the History Channel is one of the greatest treasure hunts of all time. *The Curse of Oak Island* chronicles the adventures of treasure hunters Rick and Marty Lagina as they attempt to find out what lies at the bottom of the infamous money pit. The center of this mystery is a tree-covered island called Oak Island on the south shore of Nova Scotia that legend has it is the hiding place of one of the greatest treasures of all time, but no one has been able to find it for over 200 years.

The show premiered in 2014 and is now over seven seasons. Once a week, viewers watch as the two brothers from Michigan use modern technology and good old American know-how to look for the treasure. Several people have died trying to strike it rich on Oak Island, inspiring the so-called curse. The Laginas hope to avoid the curse long enough to find the treasure before they run out of money or worse.

As children, through literature and pop culture, we saw pirates as buccaneers who traveled the seven seas, plundering treasure ships, then burying their stolen riches on some hidden island. Adventurers later would search for their fortunes by solving vague riddles, and following questionable maps with the elusive "X marks the spot." Today, there are still several legends of buried treasure. These hidden caches of immense wealth are out there, just waiting for someone to find them. Treasure hunters are still out there too, actively tracking each clue and legend. These legendary treasures—pirate gold, Confederate payload, and outlaw loot—are waiting to be recovered.

Throughout history, fantastic treasures from various cultures have been stolen or have otherwise gone missing. Often their theft or disappearance happens during times of war or disaster when they cannot be protected, or when a military force decides to take treasures back home as a trophy. Sometimes these treasures are recovered, but many are still missing.

But to get back to my favorite legend of buried treasure, the Money Pit, legend has it buried on a 57-hectare privately-owned island in Lunenburg County on the south shore of Nova Scotia, Canada, known as Oak Island. Many there have seen the popular television show *Curse of Oak Island.* The island is nicknamed the "Money Pit," because many treasure hunters have spent millions looking for the unknown treasure only to come up empty-handed. Each hunter has a different theory as to what the treasure is. Some treasure investigators have theories that it may be the Holy Grail or the crown jewels of France; some even think it is a pirate treasure. In the late 1600s, the famous pirate Captain Kidd prowled the region, and one legend has it he buried his treasure on Oak Island. But most historical researchers believe Kidd buried it on Gardiners Island, off Long Island, New York, before he was caught and hung.

Today, Oak Island is privately owned, but they do offer tours. The landscape is dotted with mine shafts from previous attempts to find the treasure, which are roped off and off-limits.

There is one road on the island, and there you will also find a small museum. There you can delve into the history of the island. You will also learn about the many efforts made to find the treasure. If you visit this beautiful region of Canada, you may consider the breathtaking landscape as a natural treasure.

The crown jewels of Ireland were stolen in 1907 from Dublin Castle. The gems comprised a jeweled star of the Order of St. Patrick, a diamond brooch, and five gold collars of that order, all Crown property. The Order of St. Patrick was founded in 1783, to reward those in high office in Ireland and Irish peers on whose support the government of the day depended. Britain controlled Ireland at the time.

Sir Arthur Vicars, the Ulster King of Arms, secured the jewels

DUBLIN METROPOLITAN POLICE.

STOLEN

From a Safe in the Office of Arms, Dublin Castle, during the past month, supposed by means of a false key.

GRAND MASTER'S DIAMOND STAR.

For weeks the Dublin Police published this notice on the stolen jewels.

in his office. At the time, a new safe was being built in the clock tower of Dublin Castle. The last confirmed sighting of the jewels was on June 11, 1907, when Vicars showed the regalia to John Hodgson, the librarian of the Duke of Northumberland.

On July 5, 1907, someone entered Vicars's office by unknown means and removed the jewels and the collars of five knights of the Order. The next morning the office safe was found open and empty. The investigation by the police concluded that Vicars failed to secure the jewels properly and they should not have been in his office. He was unable to exercise due vigilance or proper care as the custodian of the regalia." As a result, Vicars resigned, as did all the staff in his employ. Who stole the jewels and what happened to them remains a mystery to this day. While many theories have been put forward, the lost jewels remain missing.

The Treasure of Lima was sent off aboard a ship by the Spanish occupiers of Peru in 1823. It was en route to Mexico and safety when the captain of the ship—William Thompson—

killed the men sent with him by the Spanish to guard the treasure. Thompson was later captured and brought to Cocos Island off the coast of Costa Rica, where he said he buried the treasure. Instead of finding the treasure, authorities lost their prisoner. No one ever saw either again.

Another legendary story of lost treasure is the story of King John's Lost Jewels. According to folklore, King John was an incompetent and evil ruler. In 1216, King John became ill during his travels trying to get away from his enemies. After deciding to take the safe roads home, he sent his belongings and treasure through an area called The Wash.

The Wash is a large bay on the east coast of England that lies between the counties of Lincolnshire and Norfolk. One of the largest estuaries in the United Kingdom, it is fed by the rivers Witham, Welland, Steeping, Nene, and the Great Ouse. Collecting 10% of the water that drains from the country's lands, it is the second-largest intertidal mudflat in Great Britain. This area was only traversable during low tide.

With it being low tide, King John ordered up to three thousand of his entourage, carrying the royal wardrobe and the treasury of the kingdom, to cross. With conditions at the causeway being wet and muddy, the wagons moved too slowly and sank into the mud. The king's soldiers struggled with the trunks, while others pulled at the horses with the wagons. Unfortunately, all the king's belongings and treasure were washed out by the incoming tide.

Legend has it that at Newark Castle, a monk called Brother Simon poisoned an ailing King John and then stole the remaining royal jewels. He made his way out of England with Europe as his destination.

The tale is said to have taken place between the tiny hamlet of Walpole Cross Keys and what we now call Sutton Bridge that crosses the River Nene. More than 800 years later, King John's treasure remains hidden in The Wash. Today the area still lures treasure hunters hoping to find the king's lost treasure.

The Romanov treasure is a famous lost treasure from Russia. This legend is as alive today as it was in the 18th century. In 1613, Mikhail Romanov became the first Romanov czar of Russia, following fifteen years of political upheaval after the fall of Russia's medieval Rurik Dynasty. He took the name Michael. The Romanovs were the last royal family of the Russian Empire. During the Russian Civil War in the early 20th century, the czar was removed from his royal position, and later Bolshevik troops executed him and his entire family.

Most of their possessions were taken, cataloged, and secured, some never to be seen again. The Romanovs tried desperately to hide their valuables up until the day of their executions. They succeeded in hiding a great deal of them, as evidenced by some of them turning up after the fact. No one knows where they hid the rest of their wealth.

The Flor de la Mar was a 400-ton Portuguese carrack. It sank in the Strait of Malacca in 1511 with one of the most significant sunken treasures of maritime history. Most sunken treasures sound a bit like legend, but this could not be further from the truth in this case. The treasure aboard the *Flor de la Mar* is well documented and still missing.

The Honjo Masamune is a sword said to have been created by the swordsmith Gorō Nyūdō Masamune (lived AD 1264 to 1343), who is considered by many to be the greatest sword maker in Japanese history. It is named after one of its owners, Honjo Shigenaga, who took it as a prize after a 16th-century battle. The sword came into the possession of Tokugawa Ieyasu, a leader who became the first shogun of Japan, after winning a series of wars in the 16th century.

The Tokugawa family passed the sword down to family members until the end of World War II. During the occupation of Japan, the American authorities confiscated the sword. They

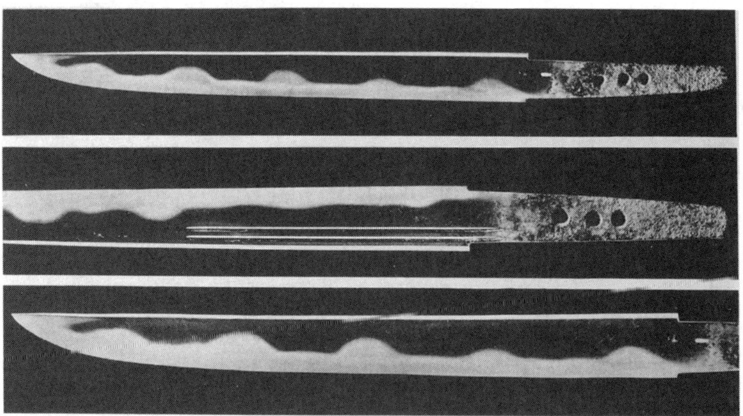

Three photos of the Tanto Hyuga Masamune sword, similar to the Honjo Masamune sword, which has vanished.

were concerned that this sword, and others like it, could be used as weapons against the Americans. The sword never reappeared. Some researchers believe that American soldiers destroyed the sword, along with other captured Japanese weapons. Most researchers believe that an American serviceman took the sword back to the United States as a war trophy.

Genghis Khan's treasure is a famous legend from China. Khan was the first and most legendary ruler of the Mongol Empire. The place of his burial is a mystery, even today. After he died in 1227, his people placed him in a hidden tomb. Legend has it that executioners killed the people who erected the tomb and interred the emperor so its location would remain secret. Though it is uncertain, researchers believe that there are significant riches in his tomb.

There are many legends of lost *Nazi gold*. One of the most popular concerns events that happened in 1945. Legend has it that near the end of World War II, a group of Nazis led by SS officer Ernst Kaltenbrunner demanded water transport from locals near Lake Toplitz in Austria. So, the locals took them to the lake and saw them dump heavy boxes into it. The Nazis presumably filled the boxes with more than 100 million dollars worth of counterfeit pound sterling notes. But some say the Nazi force sunk a vast amount of gold into Lake Toplitz, to keep it from being captured by the invading Allied forces. Since that time, numerous searchers have tried to locate the gold but have met with no success.

It would seem that someone could easily find the cache. However, the bottom half of the lake does not contain oxygen. There is a layer of logs floating just above that level, making it very difficult for divers to search for the treasure.

Constructed in the Catherine Palace in the 18th century in Tsarskoye Selo, near St. Petersburg, the Amber Room contained gold-gilded mosaics, mirrors, and carvings, along with panels constructed out of about 1,000 pounds (450 kilograms) of amber. The Amber Room is or was quite what it sounds like, but also much more. It was highly ornate and decked out in precious and semi-precious jewels. It was 11 feet by 11 feet of glistening treasure that would be worth almost $200 million if anyone knew where it was. Tsarskoe Selo was captured by Germany in 1941, during World War II, and the room's panels and art were disassembled and taken to Germany. After Nazi Germany stole it from the Soviet Union, it disappeared and was never seen again.

Many believe that all the gold panels were destroyed either by the Nazis or by Allied bombing. Russian artisans, with donations from Germany, reconstructed the Amber room. In 2003 the new Amber Room was inaugurated, and it can be seen today in the Catherine Palace.

In 1923, headlines around the world ran the discovery of the Peking Man—fossils of an unknown hominid found in China. The fossils werediscovered in a cave near Beijing between 1929–37 during excavations at Zhoukoudian. Scientists dated the fossils to roughly 750,000 years ago.

The fossils mysteriously disappeared in 1941, during the

Japanese invasion of China. The location of the fossils is unknown. Some researchers have speculated that they were lost at sea; others believe they were transported to the United States; others think they may be found under a parking lot in China.

Have you ever heard of armchair treasure hunts? These are treasure hunts that allow you to research, discover, and solve clues right from your chair in your own home. Then once you think you have solved the clues or riddles, you go in search of and retrieve those lost treasures, or they can be claimed right from your home. While they might not be as exciting as looking for pirate gold, they do provide you with a bounty, which is not legendary but fact.

This treasure hunting subculture started in the UK, with the publication of the 1979 book *Masquerade* by Kit Williams. Masquerade is a short, 32-page picture book that tells the story of a rabbit, Jack Hare, who loses his treasure, and in the end, the reader is encouraged to try to find it. The trick with *Masquerade* was that the treasure was real, an 18-karat jeweled golden hare, hidden somewhere in the UK.

The location was concealed in the drawings by Williams. This led to the treasure being found near the cross-shaped monument to Catherine of Aragon in Ampthill Park. It was at the precise spot touched by the tip of the monument's shadow at noon on the day of either the vernal or autumnal equinox.

On a side note, the first winner, who found the hare in 1982, turned out to have received inside information from Williams' former girlfriend, creating a scandal.

The United States got into the armchair treasure hunt with Michael Stadther's *A Treasure's Trove*, a 2005 fairytale puzzle book that contained clues to fourteen tokens that Stadther hid in parks throughout the United States. When located, the finder could redeem the token for jewels representing characters from the story or for a cash payoff. I participated in this treasure hunt.

Searchers found all the tokens. With the success of the first book/treasure hunt, Michael Stadther wrote a sequel called *Secrets of the Alchemist Dar,* which again contained clues to find one hundred rings. To date none of the rings is known to have been found.

The Oracle: Lost in Time is another book containing a treasure hunt. The book, filled with poems and lavish illustrations, leads to a prize worth at least £5,000. Somewhere in the United Kingdom, the author hid a token in an area accessible to the general public. The reader will take great pleasure in solving the clues that lead to the token. Readers can use the token to visit a website and claim the cash prize.

Somewhere in France, there lies buried a small gold statue of an owl in flight that can be found using the 1992 book *Sur La Trace de La Chouette d'Or (The Hunt for The Golden Owl)*. The author, Max Valentin, secretly hid the owl sculpture at a location in mainland France known only to himself. The location of the treasure remains a mystery nearly 30 years after this book was released.

So you see, there is no shortage of hidden treasure to search for. If you do decide to look for a lost treasure, make sure your legend tripping team knows the story behind it. That makes the whole experience a lot more exciting.

Chapter 12

International Treasure Legend Trip

Ever since I saw the movie *Raiders of the Lost Ark*, I wanted to look for lost treasure. I always dreamed of one day discovering some long lost treasure like the Lost Dutchman's mine. When I was in school, I read an article about the Oak Island Money Pit located off the coast of Nova Scotia. I dreamed of being the one to discover what was buried out there. As a kid, I read a lot of books about buried treasure and found that there is still a lot of undiscovered treasure out there.

There are stories about pirates Lafitte and Gasparilla hiding treasure along the banks of the Suwannee River. Tampa, Florida has a parade and festival to celebrate Gasparilla and the pirate invasion. In November 1953, a hotel operator out of Lakeland, Florida, Bill Sneed, recovered 4,500 gold coins and 3,500 coins of silver when he found a trove chest he located with an "electronic device" in 16 feet of water.

After telling my wife this exciting treasure legend, we decided to go treasure legend tripping on the weekend. When we arrived, after scouting for about an hour, we found a spot on the other side of the river from Fowler's Bluff where legend has it French privateer Jean Lafitte buried his treasure hoard. As the alleged location is on private property, we kept to the public land across the river. The wife and I walked along the banks of the Suwannee for hours with her metal detector, looking for lost treasure. We went in November, so the temperature was pleasant, but unfortunately, the mosquitos were still out, making the trek a little miserable. We combed over two miles of the limited public river's edge, but found nothing of monetary value. We did find some rusty nails and an old butane lighter, but no gold or silver. We did, however, have a great time looking. I brought some food and water, so we stopped at noon and ate lunch by the river. We continued our hunt until the sun started to descend behind the palm trees when we called it a day and headed back to the vehicle. It was exciting thinking we might find something. We stopped at a local restaurant, and the owner entranced us with more stories about Civil War gold also lost in the Suwannee. I asked her, "Just how much gold is supposedly out there?" She didn't hesitate. "$15,000,000," she answered back.

If you want to go treasure hunting in another country you need to find out the laws regarding it. In some countries it is illegal.

In Great Britain, you don't need a licence to use a metal detector, but there are laws about their use. It is illegal to use one on private land without permission from the owner. It is also illegal to use a metal detector on a scheduled ancient monument or in an area of archaeological importance.

Also in Great Britain (but not in Scotland), the Treasure Act of 1996 applies and defines gold or silver finds older than 300 years as treasure and claims them for the Crown. Finds must be reported within 14 days. Scotland's laws are broader: Treasure does not have to be gold or silver and can be less than 300 years old, but in both jurisdictions, a significant find will be offered to museums to bid on.

There are several kinds of treasure hunters. Wreck treasure hunters go looking for treasure in sunken wrecks using expensive gear and equipment. Relic hunters are looking for items with a historical value like the Ark of the Covenant or the Holy Grail. Treasure legend trippers are called cache hunters. A cache hunter is somebody who looks for treasure left behind by different groups such as outlaws, pirates, and the Spanish. In this chapter, I will simply refer to this adventure as treasure legend tripping.

Most people think treasure hunting is searching for treasure on a sunken ship. This is treasure hunting, but it is the most expensive and dangerous kind. The hunts require expensive government permits, and if anything is found, the government gets their share. Sunken treasure hunts can be done without the expensive gear and permits. Shallow waters can easily be searched with an underwater metal detector, and hunters have found valuable objects from the sunken ships pushed closer to shore by storms. This is referred to as beachcombing.

The best time to beachcomb is just hours after the main body of a hurricane has passed through and while it's still raining. Some beachcombers have found silver and gold coins, and even gold jewelry from the old Spanish wrecks sunk in shallow waters just off the US coast.

When it comes to treasure hunting, research and planning are essential. I found this interesting information in an article titled "All Kinds of Buried Treasure," on the website oldandsold.com:

> Check your information, your legends, and your maps as carefully as you can. You cannot do too much research before you dig. Every fact you gain before you start using your spade is getting you much closer to the treasure. Laws are governing the searching for—and the finding of—lost treasure. Know your laws before you dig. Always check with the territorial or state authorities in the area in which you wish to go treasure hunting. There are state laws and federal laws regarding both the finding and keeping of lost treasure.
>
> Information of all types has to be checked. Even maps may have been in your own family for generations that

may need further elucidation. Remember the map you have may be a genuine pirate or lost mine map, but the man who had the treasure or knew where the mine was may not have written down its location. He made the map in the first place because he didn't want anyone else to know where it was. Many times even authentic maps are backward or even in code. "Step ten paces north" may mean step ten paces south. "Pass three rocks" may not mean rocks at all but trees—trees which may have come down since the day the original treasure was buried. But if you have an authentic map and have the determination and the money, you might find treasure. Or you might find it accidentally. It has been done before.

You might find your treasure, provided you have properly checked into the laws of the state in which you're going to search.

Some states, as noted above, have their own regulations concerning the digging for treasure. In Florida, for example, treasure hunters have to have a permit costing around a hundred dollars before they can even begin to hunt for the treasure. They can get it from a land agent in Tallahassee, and after the treasure is located, the state of Florida automatically gets 12 percent of anything found within the territorial jurisdiction of the state. There is also income tax! Yes, folks, you have to pay tax on a found treasure. It is the law. Can you imagine what the income tax would be on Blackbeard's hoards or Jean Lafitte's treasure?

You should research, by either the Internet or correspond to the Chamber of Commerce in the closest city to your treasure spot, to find out the various rules, laws, and regulations concerning both buried treasure and sunken treasure. You need to find out about them before you start to dig or dive. Also, write to the Federal Government in Washington or check out their website on the subject of treasure hunting. (www.oldandsold.com)

Before embarking on a treasure hunt, research the chosen treasure legend thoroughly. Additionally, when going on a treasure hunt, consider the country you are visiting and their laws in regards to treasure hunting.

Here is a list of countries and their laws regarding treasure hunting. I have listed them in alphabetic order. In all European countries, treasure hunting/detecting on any historical ground is illegal. Also if you find any ordinance left over from the Second World War or anything of significance or archaeologically significant related to the War, then you need to stop and immediately contact the local authorities. I did not list any communist countries like China and Cuba, as they do not permit any kind of treasure hunting.

Australia

Detection and prospecting for gold nuggets are both allowed along the beach. Other places you must have a Fossicking License or a Miner's Right permit. National parks are mostly forbidden unless they are covered under your fossicking license. Old goldfields and other mineral exploration areas, ghost towns, historical sites, sports and camping grounds, and piers, are all fair game.

Belgium

Beach search is permitted, but private individuals aren't allowed to look for archaeological artifacts.

Bulgaria

A metal detector must be registered with the Ministry of

Culture (otherwise the owner will be punishable by a fine, or even jail time). Searching for archaeological objects requires permission.

Cambodia

Treasure hunting is not permitted

Canada

There are no laws about using metal detectors; the only restrictions are that you need to get permission from the landowners first on private property. An example would be Oak Island in Nova Scotia, where the treasure still has not been found. The island is owned by a private firm. While they do allow tours of the island, they do not allow you to look for the treasure alone. There are no serious restrictions to explore national and provincial parks as well. Registered archaeological sites are off-limits.

Czech Republic

Metal detecting on beaches is allowed, but to search for archaeological artifacts you will need permission.

Denmark

Metal detecting is allowed. Very large and valuable items found must be turned over to the Danish authorities.

Dominican Republic

Treasure hunting/detecting is allowed and encouraged without any sort of restrictions.

Egypt

Though you can treasure hunt on the beaches, there can be problems getting the detector through customs. Permission will be required in some hotels with private beaches. Archeological sites are strictly forbidden. Stay away from the pyramids with your metal detector.

France

You are allowed to detect but with prior permission. You will need to get permission from the prefecture according to the Article L542-1 in the Code du Patrimoine. Permission is not always given especially to foreign visitors, and due to this, many just go ahead without bothering to get the permit. A word of warning, if you are caught without a permit, you may find yourself with an obligation to pay a fine. All the items that you find need to be declared to the local authorities, especially when it comes to something historically valuable.

You don't need permission and can freely detect on France beaches! However, it is important that you understand that many of them are designated war graves. Therefore, you should check that with the local authorities or police beforehand.

Germany

You can treasure hunt with a permit, but if you find a very large or a very valuable item then you need to turn it over to the state.

If you do get caught without a permit or where you are not supposed to be, they will confiscate all your equipment along with imposing a large fine. Also, US military installations in Germany still belong to the German government.

India

This country has an age-old law known as the Indian Treasure Trove Act from 1878. This Act lays down all the laws that govern buried treasures, defining treasure as 'anything of any value hidden in the soil or anything affixed thereto.' This law is not at all user-friendly and pushes treasure hunters to be professional and hand over all finds to the local government authorities.

Israel

It's forbidden to search for historic artifacts. Illegal treasure hunting is punishable with jail time.

Italy

One of the most beautiful countries in Europe is also one of the best places to go treasure hunting. Again treasure hunting/detecting in any ancient or archaeological site there is strictly forbidden. In places that fall outside of the Italian laws, you still have to get the landowners' permission. You are not allowed to treasure hunt/detect in Sicily, Tuscany, Calabria, or Valle d'Aosta.

Ireland

There are many places that are hiding some exciting and valuable treasures on the Emerald Isle. To treasure hunt/detect there, you need to get permission and approval from the concerned government agencies and the landowners when searching on private land.

With a permit you can go look for gold. In fact, there are many locations in the country where you can find gold. There are many townships and even mountains there that have gold in their names as well. Many ancient places were named for having a presence of gold. The places to look for gold are Coom-an-ore (Hollow of the Gold), Lug-an-ore (Hollow of the Gold), and Glan-an-ore (Glen of the Gold).

Russia

Treasure hunting/detecting is allowed, but it's almost forbidden to search for historic artifacts.

Scotland

To treasure hunt here, you not only need a permit, but you also need to get prior permission from the Archaeology Service.

There is no treasure hunting/detecting allowed within 20 meters of any historical monument. Exploring any historical or archaeological site is treated as a criminal offense and has an associated fine of up to GBP 50,000.

Any finds you come across need to be reported to a museum or the local authorities as almost all finds located in Scotland are subject to the Treasure Trove Law.

Spain

The use of a metal detector for searching for archaeological items in Spain is not allowed without a permit/license. The authorities are quite strict in cracking down on detectorists who are detecting without a license.

The laws vary from region to region, so while in some regions treasure hunting can be completely forbidden, other regions allow it as far as you've got your permit.

As in all countries in Europe treasure hunting in historical or archaeological sites is not allowed. When it comes to beaches in Spain you will need a one-year permit.

Japan

The Land of the Rising Sun is one of the best countries to go treasure hunting/detecting because there is no particular law restricting it. With that being said, all foreign visitors have to turn over anything they find above the ground to the police. Supposedly, you will receive 10 percent of the find.

Buddhist temples, old Shinto shrines, and active castle sites are strictly out of bounds for any kind of treasure hunting/detecting in Japan.

Portugal

Treasure hunting/detecting is officially illegal in Portugal. Beach detection is only allowed for locals, who also need to obtain special permission from the local authorities.

Turkey

The lack of clarity regarding treasure hunting/detecting has made many people shy away from this country. Turkey does require that you get a permit if you want to use a metal detector, even on the beach. To treasure hunt you first need to apply for a permit from the nearest museum administration or the nearest government office. The administration will issue a certificate and also provides a witness officer who will accompany you during your searches.

Also if you decide to bring a metal detector to Turkey remember this: Any detector that is valued up to EUR 430 and is for your personal use can be brought into the country without having to pay customs duty or any other tax; if your equipment is costlier, you might have to keep it at the customs department's warehouse and collect it when you are leaving Turkey.

Greece

Like most European countries you must have a permit to treasure hunt, but in Greece, you must also have a license for owning the equipment. This license is issued by the Greek Ministry of Culture.

Another thing you need to know is that the process of issuing of the permits in Greece can be long and drawn out and take anywhere between three to seven months.

As you can see there are some restrictions in every country, but as long as you are following the rules you will do just fine.

With all this said, if your exciting treasure hunt still seems like a great idea, start the planning phase. Check and see what lost treasures are still out there and what is needed to look for the one you want to pursue. Check and make sure it's not on private property and get permission from that country.

Unless you're lucky enough to have a buried treasure in the backyard, planning a treasure hunt sometimes requires camping out, especially if the target area is a considerable distance away.

Once the treasure target area has been determined and you've gotten permission if needed, it's time to load up the camping and treasure hunting gear and move out. As in all the chapters on conducting a legend trip, I have compiled a list of items needed for this adventure at the end of the chapter. Locate campgrounds or a hotel close to the target area. If camping, I'll go over some of what you need to do.

Find campgrounds that are close to the treasure target area and locate a campsite close to the area, or maybe get permission from the landowners to camp out there. With this kind of legend trip, there is usually only one area to look at. If it's a considerable distance to hike to the target spot, never go rucking or hiking alone. If finding a partner is difficult, wait until someone is available. Many of the stories of lost treasure locate the caches in the woods and sometimes around a body of water like a lake or river, so you'll want to be careful.

Setting up a base camp is pretty much the same as for doing all outdoor legend trips. Make a checklist of everything needed for the trip. More detailed advice is found in Chapter 4 under the "Base Camp" heading. Make variations to the equipment list based on the environment and weather expected during the hunt.

Once base camp is set up, if it's still daylight scout around the target area. If using a treasure map or code, it's best to do this during daylight hours. Compare the treasure map with an updated map of the area. It is also great to have a GPS.

It there is enough time, take the team to the target area. It's easier than going back and explaining it on a map. Make sure everybody knows what they should look for and point out where the treasure is supposed to be.

Whenever leaving the campsite, always have somebody stay back to keep an eye on the gear. Now, if this treasure is located in a broad area, and there are enough team members, consider breaking into teams to cover a more significant search area. Have the team's AORs marked on a map, so the base camp keeps track of them. Also, if somebody gets hurt, the person at base camp can call for medical aid and have it come to the base camp. Have the team move around on foot versus using vehicles. They might miss some clues just riding around. They can have a vehicle at the AOR to use to come and go from base camp.

Each team needs to have a working radio with fresh or extra batteries or a cellphone. Have the teams do radio checks before they move out to their AORs. If a team loses contact, they should return to base camp immediately and either get a new radio or a working cellphone. Have them report any wild animal like panther or bear tracks, or human activity. You might not be the only ones looking for the treasure. Some treasure hunters are not too keen on having other people out there, so be careful. Go over all of this with everybody, before each team moves out to its AORs. Depending on the size of the investigation area, each team should take water and food. Always take a survival kit because they will be hiking around the AORs and these kits have first aid items like bandages and antiseptic wipes.

If conducting the treasure hunt near water, watch out for everything around. For example, if a team needs to move through the swamps to get to their AOR, they need to watch out for hidden dangers like cypress trees. Their roots do not grow straight down, but rather to the side and up. This happens because most of the time, the swamp is flooded, and the roots grow up above the waterline. These roots are called knees. They look like stalagmites and can be sharp. These are especially dangerous at night. It is best to keep the teams on dirt roads at night. Also, there are sinkholes, which you can't see, and you can't tell how deep they are, which presents a dangerous situation. Make sure you go over all of this with the team before you enter the area.

During the first walk around or recon, choose a rallying point, especially if using vehicles. A rallying point is a designated area where everyone will meet back up after the investigation. It is usually near the main road and in the middle of all the AORs. Once it starts to get dark, return to the campsite and have the teams do the same. Go over what the teams saw. Sometimes based on the recon, changing AORs could be a good plan of action. Then get a good night's sleep to get ready for the next day's adventure.

The next morning, when it is time to move out, have the teams load up the vehicles and boat/canoe(s), and proceed to their AORs. Have them double-check their radios, cameras, and gear before they leave. Each team should have a metal detector, if serious about finding this treasure.

Equipment

Metal Detector

This is a key piece of equipment. This device is an electronic device that gives an audible or other signal when it is close to metal. There are ones that are used by law enforcement personnel to detect hidden weapons. The ones I'm talking about are the handheld units with a sensor probe that can be swept over the ground or other objects to detect buried metal objects like gold or silver. The first ones developed were for the military to find land mines in World War I. Today these devices come in a wide range of sizes and prices. They can be found in toy stores and sporting goods stores. Most metal detectors are "all-purpose" detectors that will find everything from coins, jewelry, metal relics, to gold. If looking for a buried treasure cache, a deeper seeking detector is needed, which costs about $600.00, but it does send a signal down further than an all-purpose. If new to this kind of legend trip, go with an all-purpose detector and see how it goes. The best advice is don't run out and buy all the equipment, wait until you're sure legend tripping is a preferred path. One option is to purchase a used good quality metal detector. Good quality devices can be found on Internet auction sites.

Shovel

Believe it or not, this is one piece of equipment people seem to forget about. They remember the metal detector, but when they go out to do a search and find something, they don't have any tools to dig up what's buried. They end up using their hands. Shovels are easy to find. Folding shovels are good to have. They are cheap and easy to carry. When the detector goes off, take out a shovel, unfold it, and dig up what's buried.

Brush

This can be a small paintbrush. Sometimes the treasure is a delicate item, and you need to remove it slowly from its resting place. Also, some items are too big to remove to clean up around it. A clue to the treasure might be a carving on a large boulder or rock and you need to clean up around it to get a better look at it. A brush is a good item to use. I like to use a small paintbrush. They are not expensive, and they do the trick.

When a team is out, one member of the team can lead the way while the other works the metal detector. If another member is available, they can look for clues as well as monitor the radio. Each team should stay on paths or dirt roads as much as possible.

When it comes to rivers, walk along the shoreline and look for anything that might have washed up, but you need to watch out for quicksand. It's not easy to see. Work the shallow waters with an underwater detector and find things that have been pushed closer to shore by storms. It might be better for some teams to stay on dirt paths and roads. This increases the chance that nobody will get lost, and it's easier to backtrack to the rally point. When in the woods, be careful of what is around. In the eastern part of the country, which is very hilly, there are a lot of cliffs

I have stated this in each legend trip where you go into the woods. I do not apologize for repeating myself on this subject. There are dangerous animals you need to be aware of and should be considered when venturing into the woods. The most dangerous animals are bears, large wild cats, wild pigs, alligators, snakes, and certain insects. You should avoid these dangers at all costs. In Chapter 4, I go into detail on each of these animals. I am not an expert on animals, but I do know there are wild ones out there. There are popular stories about attacks on humans by animals, and there is some truth to those stories. Do not underestimate any kind of wildlife, even small foxes and armadillos.

After a couple of hours, if nobody has found anything, call them in and reassign AORs so teams don't get bored looking at the same thing all day. Call them in when the sun goes down, and it gets dark.

If a team finds some kind of clue, they should immediately call it in and check it out. If warranted, they should have the rest of the teams come to that location.

When all teams back, inventory gear. If on a team and be getting back to base camp late, as a safety measure, call on the radio and let the base know you have stopped and are searching for something. Give them the location as well. It only takes a couple of seconds to do this. If a team does not show up at the prescribed time, don't panic.

First, call them on the radio and see where they are. On the way back, a team might be distracted by something and stop. If they don't answer (radio/cellphone) and it has been a while, then send only one team with a member who knows the area.

Remember, there is still treasure out there, and some maps, too. A lot of people, especially groups like outlaws, pirates, and the Spanish, left clues to their treasures carved in rocks and on rock bluffs. Finding these types of clues, and even an entire map, is almost as exciting as working the map to a hole. It's also something that happens quite often, but if not looked at it properly, one might not realize when a clue is directly in front of them. When most people see a map or a clue carved into a rock or bluff, they assume it is some type of graffiti because they aren't looking at it the way it was intended to be seen. Good luck with this legend trip, and I hope you find something.

Here is the equipment list I use when I go out legend tripping for treasure:

Treasure Hunt

- Camera—one that has IR capabilities
- Camera stands and pods
- GPS
- Cold weather clothes
- Backpack (with items mentioned previously in the backpack list)
- Metal detector
- Shovel (folding)
- Binoculars
- Poncho

Chapter 13

Museums and Roadside Oddities

You must carry along with you a lively imagination and plenty of romance in your soul. Some of the most wonderful things in the world will seem dull and drab unless you view them in the proper light.
—Robert L Ripley

When it comes to legend tripping, it's not just about the legends that you're investigating. It's about everything from the beginning and middle to the end. What I mean by this is plan to do stuff en route to the legend trip. Nothing is saying you can't stop along the way and look at places on the way. I encourage it. Sometimes the journey is just as exciting as the destination.

They are what I call day legend trips. These are places you can visit during the day or nighttime, but you can't camp out or stay there. Examples are mysterious places like haunted castles and abbeys. You can pay and visit them, but you can't stay and conduct an investigation. Most would think that this isn't very exciting. My answer is day legends can be and are just as exciting as other legend trips. You'll find you will feel the same excitement doing this as you would if you were looking for cryptids or ghosts.

It is fascinating standing on a mountain and watching mysterious lights dance around. Are they lights from UFOs or from Indian spirits wandering the mountains, looking for their lost loves? What about visiting a site and standing where a flying saucer crashed, and its occupants died, only to have the military spirit them away to some hidden warehouse? There are all kind of different day legend trips to do.

Halloween is a great time to go legend tripping. A lot of haunted places around the world have special ghost hunts and tours. I'm not talking about haunted houses at amusement parks, which are set up with people in costumes or electronic devices. I mean real—or supposedly real—haunted places.

Also, some people can only make day trips as their schedules allow. Me, I like to incorporate day legend trips into my other ones. In other words, if I'm heading up to New York for a lake monster legend trip, I'll check and see what's on the way and make a day of legend trips.

Museums

Nicknamed the "Modern Marco Polo," Robert L. Ripley traveled to more countries than any other person in his lifetime and reported on some of the most fantastic people and places. And it all started with a cartoon drawing called "Chumps and Champs," or as we now know it, "Believe It or Not."

When you hear the word "Ripley," most people conjure up the weird, the strange, and the fantastic. Since the early part of the twentieth century, Robert L. Ripley had been presenting these strange and fantastic people and places from around the world in his daily cartoon Ripley's Believe It or Not. Over 10,000 cartoon panels appeared in publications since the 1920s when Ripley first started drawing them.

Today there are over thirty-two Odditoriums (museums) and aquariums bearing Ripley's name in such places as Gatlinburg, TN, San Antonio, TX, Myrtle Beach, SC, and Pattaya, Thailand. Even though Ripley passed in 1949, Ripley's Entertainment, based in Orlando, Florida, keeps Ripley's legacy alive with these Odditoriums and annual books logging the weird and fantastic things found each year.

Ironically, a young, gifted artist from Santa Rosa, California with aspirations to play professional baseball would later become one of the richest, most famous men in the United States. As a youth in school, I read and marveled at Ripley's exploits around the world and always imagined myself traveling the world like him. I think I read every Ripley book in our local library. Later, I visited Ripley's World of the Unexplained in Gatlinburg and became an immediate fan of cryptozoology, UFOs and the paranormal. Sadly, that museum closed in 1986 due to poor attendance but it is now open as part of an extensive entertainment complex. When I was in the military and deployed, I always had a Believe It or Not (BION) book to keep from getting homesick. Today I

An early 1940s photograph of Robert Ripley in his office.

always make it a habit to find the nearest BION Odditorium when I'm traveling. To date, I've been to twelve, and I still have all my BION books. In 1933, Ripley opened the first Odditorium at the Chicago World's Fair that featured unusual items he had collected, along with performances by sideshow acts like contortionists, sword swallowers, and a girl who had been born without arms or legs. As the expression goes, "Seeing is believing."

Shortly after Robert L. Ripley died in 1949, John Arthur purchased many of Mr. Ripley's oddities at a public auction of his estate. Mr. Arthur would later open a new, permanent Believe It or Not museum in St. Augustine, Florida in 1950.

Whenever I go traveling, especially with my family, I look to see if there is a Ripley's Odditorium on the way or close by. The entrance price is not expensive, and there is a lot to see.

The great thing about Ripley's is that they're all different, including the outside design. My favorite Ripley's is the one located in St. Augustine. The castle was the scene of a double murder and is now said to be haunted. Ripley's Believe It or Not in St. Augustine also has a ghost train to take tourists to locations in the city that are said to be dwellings of the paranormal. I have also had the privilege of visiting Ripley's warehouse in Orlando.

If a trip is going to take more than a day while traveling to a different state, plan a pit stop to look at things along the way. That is why roadside oddities are so popular, and this is where these museums come in. Some of the museums have a section on local legends and mysteries. The roadside stops can be fun.

Here is a list of the current Ripley's Believe It or Not Odditoriums that are open.

Europe

Denmark, Copenhagen—This Ripley's museum is a smaller one located close to the city hall and next to a museum of H. C. Andersen.

Amsterdam, The Netherlands—The Ripley's Believe It or Not! Amsterdam museum opened on June 23, 2016, at the Dam Square, Dam 21, in a building that belongs to the Heritage of Amsterdam. It has more than 500 exhibits.

Lancashire, England—This Ripley's museum opened in 1972. It was the first, and is based in the popular holiday destination of Blackpool Pleasure Beach. Like Ripley's Odditorium in St. Augustine, Florida, it too is reputed to be haunted. The legend behind the ghostly happenings involves the skull of a young girl that was loaned to the company for public display. While it was on display, guests started reported feeling cold and icy in a specific area, despite the park insisting the temperature in the attraction was acceptable. Some guests reported seeing a ghostly figure of a young lady dressed in a black gown standing next to the 'cursed' skull. The owner suddenly and tragically passed away a week after the skull was removed from display.

Asia

Shanghai, China—This Ripley's museum opened in June 2013 and is located at Huangpu River.

China announced that a new Ripley's museum was being built in Harbin, China.

Bangalore, India—This Ripley's Museum is at the Innovative Film city.

Genting Highlands, Malaysia—This Ripley's museum was orginally located in the First World Plaza. It reopened in March 2018, as Ripley's Adventureland with three other Ripley's attractions, all located on level 4 in SkyAvenue.

Jeju Island, South Korea—This Ripley's museum opened in 2010 and is located at the Jeju Jungmun resort. Visitors to the museum will be awed by a large selection of hard-to-believe pieces, including part of the Berlin Wall from 1989, meteorites from Mars, and a life-size model of man that's part unicorn.

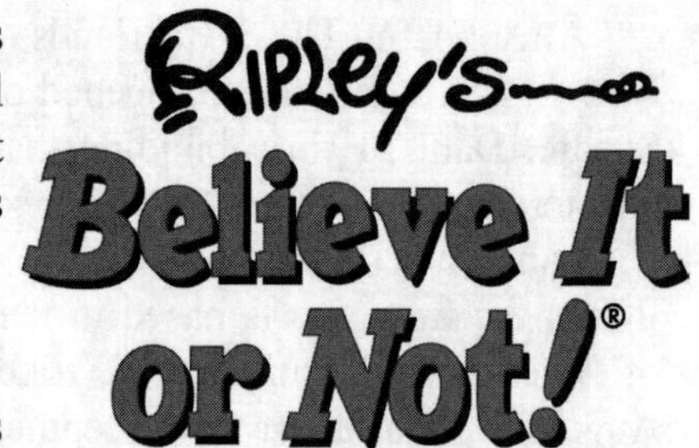

Pattaya, Thailand—This Ripley's museum is in Royal Garden Plaza in Pattaya. It appears as if an airplane has crashed into it.

Australia

Gold Coast—This Ripley's museum is located at the popular tourist destination Surfers Paradise. It reopened in the new Soul Centre on January 22, 2010, featuring a band of human oddities playing songs at the entrance.

Canada

Niagara Falls—This is the second oldest Ripley's Museum in the world and is one of two in Canada. The museum is shaped like the Empire State Building fallen over, with King Kong standing on top of it, which is the largest and most valuable museum for the company.

Cavendish, Prince Edward Island—This Ripley's museum is located in a concentrated area of tourist attractions adjacent to the Prince Edward Island National Park. A lighthouse (the top broken) features the Ripley's sign.

Mexico

Mexico City—Opened in 1992, this Ripley's museum is shaped like a medieval castle and has 14 exhibition halls within it. This was the first of three locations to open in Latin America.

Guadalajara—Opened in 1994, this Ripley's museum is a small one like Mexico City's location. It is near downtown.

Other museums

The Museum of Vampires and Legendary Creatures was

created by Jacques Sirgent, who dedicated much of his life to researching vampires, esoterism, and occidental folklore. The museum features a spooky history of Paris (where it is located) and the cemeteries where vampiric rituals were once practiced, as well as cannibal sorcery, medieval Christian hierarchy. There are collectibles, old books, and art that will creep you out.

The Jack the Ripper Museum in London allows you to get a better look at the serial killer. You can take a "Jack the Ripper Walk," where you can follow in his footsteps, seeing recreated scenes from his crimes and getting the perspective of the victims. You can read old newspaper accounts of the murders, see original autopsy photos, and more. It's a terrifying experience.

In Scotland, there is a Loch Ness Centre and Exhibition that allows you to learn so much more. The presentation takes you through seven themed areas that cover 500 million years of history, myth, and legend that are undeniably creepy.

The Museum of Witchcraft and Magic located in London is, obviously, about witches. You can see glass spirit bottles, skulls, witches' charms, and other pagan artifacts. You can even book a witches' workshop. There's also lantern-lit evening tours, which make the whole experience even scarier.

Here is a scenario for a legend trip that turned into something else.

The evening sun slowly descends to the treetops as you scan the edge of the woods for any sign of movement. For some reason, this early night seems quieter than most. A slight wind has picked up in the field, bringing a much-needed coolness to the air. As the mist appears as serpents coiling around the bushes, there is still enough light to make out the towering pine trees that line the field. As you scan the dark woods, you stop and stare, hoping to catch a glimpse of a large hairy figure that was just seen out here days earlier. You think of the thrill of being one of the few to actually see this mysterious animal called bigfoot.

Tonight you are one of those who have come to this cryptid animal's domain to see and possibly film the legendary animal. This forest giant has been seen over a hundred times, but only the lucky few have been at the right place at the right time. You've come to this area, where the recent sighting was made by a driver who saw the animal walking around this field. You brought with you not only a flashlight but a camera with night vision. You tell yourself if bigfoot is out there, you're going to find it. But after hours of scanning the tree line, with no sign of movement, your enthusiasm starts to deteriorate with the realization that maybe the animal has moved to another location.

As you gather up your equipment, you suddenly catch movement out of the corner of your eye, and you quickly look towards it. At first, you see nothing but the large pine trees surrounding the field. But then you see something large moving just inside the tree line. You blink a couple of times to make sure your eyes are not playing tricks on you, which happens quite often at night. Again you see something shifting, and whatever it is, it is massive. You grab your camera and quickly head in the direction of the movement. As you get closer, you can see the large shape is moving deeper into the woods. You move faster now, not wanting to let whatever it is get away from you. As you make it to the tree line, you pause momentarily to scan the trees for any movement. There it is, heading away from you and moving rather quickly.

It might be your once in a lifetime opportunity not only to see this cryptid but to film it with your camera. You decide to go after it. At first, you find it easy to make your way through the woods, but as you venture deeper, darkness falls more rapidly. You stop after losing sight of the large shape and listen, but there is no sound.

Suddenly you hear something large moving away from you, again heading deeper into the forest. You head in the direction of the sounds. Whatever it is, it is still moving at a fast pace. You feel the excitement of the chase intermingled with the fear of losing your prize. You find yourself struggling to see around you but moving faster toward the movement and sounds. You can't let it get away from you!

The sound suddenly ceases, and you immediately halt and listen. There is not a single sound, not even the wind. You stare into the darkness of the woods. There is no light to let you see clearly. You bring your camera with the night vision to your eye and start scanning your surroundings. With the night vision, you can discern all the trees and bushes, but you don't see anything moving. The only sound you can hear is your breathing. You lower the camera and listen, but again, dead silence. Whatever it was you saw and heard is nowhere in sight. Like other investigators before you, bigfoot eluded you this night.

Now you look around preparing for your journey back to your vehicle when you suddenly realize you have become disoriented and are unable to determine your location. You're looking around at the way you came into the forest, but all the trees look the same.

What are you going to do now? You only have your camera with you and a flashlight. You didn't prepare for this situation. You thought this was only going to be a two-hour trip.

You look down at your cellphone and discover you have no signal here in the forest. You also realize you are not prepared to be out all night. You have no food or water and nothing to make a shelter. You don't even have a compass or knife! Your bigfoot investigation has now turned in a survival situation with you thinking, "What do I do now?"

The motto of Scouting is "Be Prepared." In the book *Scouting for Boys*, author and scout master Robert Baden-Powell explains the meaning of the phrase. "Be prepared" means "you are always to be in a state of readiness in mind and body to do your duty." Remember these two disciplines:

- Be prepared in mind by having disciplined yourself to be

obedient to every order, and also by having thought out beforehand any accident or situation that might occur, so you know the right thing to do at the right moment, and are willing to do it

• Be prepared in body by making yourself healthy and active and able to do the right thing at the right moment, and do it.

Here is what to carry in backpacks when I go out for the day on a legend trip:

- Camera with night vision
- Survival kit
- First-aid kit—including poison ivy cream, moleskin for blisters
- Foot powder (cold weather)
- Petroleum jelly (hot weather and swamps)
- Extra socks
- Canteen with cup
- Flashlight (two)—always carry a headlamp and an extra flashlight
- GPS (with extra batteries)/Map of the area
- Compass—in case the GPS stops working
- Poncho (for use in bad weather or as a shelter)
- Rain gear
- Back-up knife
- Water purifier pump
- Plaster casting kit
- Binoculars
- Trail camera
- 550 parachute cord
- Marking kit
- Bear mace
- Machete
- Food (beef jerky, trail mix, peanut butter crackers, and an MRE)
- Solar wrap used to recharge a cell phone or GPS
- Toilet paper/baby wipes (you will need them)
- Sunscreen/bug spray

Chapter 14

Bushcrafting and Outdoor Survival

Look deep into nature, and then
you will understand everything better.
—Albert Einstein

One of the things I like about legend tripping is camping. I love to go out and set up a tent way back in the woods, where there has been a sighting of a bigfoot-type creature. My wife, a photographer, will sometimes come along. She has taken hundreds of pictures of my legend trips. The best time to go is in autumn when it starts to cool off, and there aren't a lot of insects.

Since I started legend tripping, I have had the opportunity to go on monster hunts with many people. Some have been doing it for years, and some are new to the field. I've been with some that have never even gone camping and know nothing of the woods. Each time I found myself showing them how to set up their camps, make fires, and navigate in the woods. I don't consider myself an expert on outdoor camping, but I do know what I'm doing when I go out. Unfortunately, I've also had to look for people who have gotten lost when they set out into the woods. I have no problem helping people in need. However, ignorance of the forest shouldn't be an issue when it is general knowledge that the wilderness can be challenging.

I want to reiterate what I said in my first book, "If you are new to legend tripping, specifically monster hunting, DO NOT GO OUT ALONE!" Always have somebody with you; in fact, it's better to have two extra people. If one of you gets hurt, it's easier for the other two to aid the injured person and carry them back to the starting point. I find it better to go out with a fellow bigfoot hunter and someone familiar with the area. It is a good practice to check out a location during the daytime before you do it at night. Always let somebody know where you are going and when you expect to return, in case something should happen.

Every successful legend trip or expedition is the result of the people and the equipment involved. A well-planned-out legend trip is a successful and exciting one. I make no apologies about going into depth about putting together an equipment list. All the items I will go over with you are ones I have used and that have worked for me. With equipment, I look for dependability and not necessarily a name brand. You may have different items from what I use; what you prefer to take is up to you. You need to bring the equipment you are comfortable with and know how to use. Depending on where you are going and how long you are staying at the location, you may need to add items. I always make a list to ensure I don't forget anything. Some people like to take a lot of electronic equipment with them. Don't buy something because it looks neat. I want to keep it simple and not carry extra weight.

You don't have to bring a lot of gear with you when you venture into the woods. With legend tripping (monster hunting), you sometimes have to trek miles back into the woods where these cryptids prowl. Taking a lot of equipment can be exhausting and can take a lot of the enthusiasm out of the trip.

Bushcrafting is using the resources around you to survive and thrive in the outdoors. Being equipped with essential tools, i.e., a knife, makes outdoor living more comfortable and more efficient.

Believe it or not, one of the best outdoor survival books

available is the *Boy Scout Handbook.* This book has been in publication since the 1920s and is loaded with the most up-to-date survival information out there. Years of experience have gone into this handbook.

When it comes to outdoor survival, I couldn't have written anything better. Lt. Gen. Robert Baden-Powell, a commander in the British Army, started the Boy Scouts back in 1908; he implemented military discipline and structure but also taught outdoor survival for young men. Everyone I know who has a scouting background has a strong knowledge of the outdoors and self-reliance.

One of the first books written on outdoor survival was Larry Dean Olsen's 1967 book *Outdoor Survival Skills*. Olsen makes it clear that most of the skills he learned came from Native Americans. This book is the standard on the subject. The book is no longer in print, but you can still purchase it on the Internet.

One of the first bestsellers was the *SAS Survival Handbook* by John "Lofty" Wiseman. It is a fully illustrated and practical guide to outdoor survival. Lofty has made two instructional videos on outdoor survival and recently introduced a survival app for your cell phone, which is his book put into app form.

Two outstanding books on the subject of bushcrafting is Dave Canterbury's *Bushcraft 101* and *Advance Bushcraft*. Mr Canterbury shares a lot of valuable information and skills that he has tried and perfected. A must for anyone wanting to get into bushcrafting.

Bushcrafting has been around since pioneers first ventured into the great outdoors. It recently gained in popularity, thanks to the Internet. You type in "bushcraft," and you will find hundreds of videos from around the world. The people in these videos refer to themselves as bushcrafters. They show different outdoor scenarios, the different food they prepare, and the items they bring with them. There is valuable information in these videos.

When it comes to bushcrafting video series, two of the best are "Kent Survival" and "Simon, a Bloke in the Woods." Both can be found on Youtube. In the "Kent Survival" videos, British bushcrafter Andrew Davidson ventures out to remote areas in England. He also camps and ghost hunts in haunted locations around England. Andy is a very down to earth gentleman and offers very informative and entertaining adventures. He gives you the full low down on the area he is at, along with the history. He also prepares some excellent and easy to make meals to enjoy outside.

Simon Jacklin is the host of the "Simon, a Bloke in the Woods" video series. Also a Britsh bushcrafter, Simon roams many parts of England, sometimes on foot, sometimes in a canoe, and sometimes with his dog Maggie. Like Kent Survival, the videos are very informative and a lot of camping tips are presented. Simon creates most of his bushcrafting equipment, especially his tents. He shows you step by step how he constructs them, and then takes them out for a field test. Like Andrew, Simon gives you the complete background and history of the area he is camping in. A couple of the videos feature both Simon and Andy together on canoe trips, where they wild camp along the river route.

In both video series, Andy and Simon test new camping and bushcraft equipment. Andy also features videos of MREs (meals ready to eat) from different countries.

Today more and more people are going out hiking and are going on monster hunts. Every year, hundreds of hikers go missing in the woods.

According to the National Missing and Unidentified Persons System, or NamUs, a national database for missing people, over 90,000 people are missing in the US at any given time. That averages out to about 750,000 per year.

In 2019, 1,600 hikers went missing in the wilderness. Unfortunately, some of them died, and some still have not been found. Investigations into these disappearances show the hikers often didn't properly think through what they would need or what could go wrong.

Outdoor survival should be considered a priority and incorporated into every legend trip plan. But I can't stress this enough. Preparation and outdoor survival skills are priorities when it comes to legend tripping. Your safety and that of your family and teammates should be a top concern and is where outdoor survival and self-reliance come into play.

While I have taken outdoor survival courses, I do not consider myself an expert on the subject. To date, I have not been in a survival situation. I attribute that to proper planning and preparation. I always prepare for the unexpected, especially if I'm going into the woods. I always keep safety and survival in mind when preparing for a legend trip into the swamps or woodlands. What can go wrong will.

I once had a couple of neophytes on a trip. I had them on my team when we went walking around the woods at night. I found out they did not know how to navigate at night. They didn't understand how to use a compass. I had to show them how to do it, and they ended up having a great time hiking through the woods that night.

Another time, I went on a bigfoot expedition, and two of the members didn't bring a sleeping bag or tent. I asked them why not, and they replied it doesn't get cold enough at night in Florida. They related that they had been watching these outdoor survival shows and were going to rough it with the skills they had learned on the shows.

I later observed them trying to start a fire. After retrieving some big logs, they tried to light them with a small plastic lighter. I could see that they didn't have any idea what they were doing. They tried to justify their actions by letting me know that they had seen it done on a television show. After numerous fruitless attempts to get a fire started, I showed these agitated outdoor survivalists how to do it.

I noted above that they all didn't bring any sleeping bags. One of them remarked that they were going to bury themselves with leaves. I knew the campfire was not going to be enough to keep my adventurers warm at night. Luckily, the park rangers were kind enough to give me some sleeping bags that some campers had left behind.

Later I had them on my team when we went exploring the woods at night. I found out they, like my other neophytes, did not know how to navigate at night and didn't understand how to use a compass. One of them told me that they were going to use the stars to navigate. They couldn't find the North Star. Fearing that they would get lost, I had them follow close to me that night.

At the end of our adventure, they came to me and said that they had a great time and learned a lot. It was a successful legend trip.

Bottom line, don't ever plan to rough it in the wild. That is how people die. I always take a sleeping bag and tent with me whenever I go camping. You have to always plan for the unexpected. If you think something cannot go wrong, it will happen.

If you or your team have never been camping, then you should do a campout at a local campground with facilities (i.e., showers and bathrooms). Sleeping outside for the first time is quite an experience. Also, you may want to attend an outdoor survival course; if one is available in your area, I highly recommend it. They can be expensive, and if you can't afford to go on a course, there are plenty of books on the subject. If you go this route, you need to practice outdoor survival skills before you go into the woods. Once you are out in the wild, there is no turning back. Some people refuse to go to the bathroom outside, and one of your team members might be one of them. You need to find this out before your legend trip.

There are also plenty of survival shows on television. I like watching survival shows, and I am friends with a couple of the shows' hosts. They provide useful information, and you can learn a great deal from watching them. One thing I have learned is to make sure you and the family know every plant out there—especially poison ivy and oak.

The next chapter lists the equipment you will need for a legend trip, but when it comes to outdoor survival, I feel it necessary to talk about individual pieces of equipment you must have, and I want to go into detail on why and how to use these items. The items I believe are a must for an outdoor legend trip are knives, survival kits, first aid kits, water, and safety necklaces. The last thing I want to mention is being in proper shape, and as you will see, this does fall into outdoor survival.

The first thing I want to talk about is knives. A knife is one of the most critical items to have whenever you go into the woods or swamps. Remember, a knife should be considered a tool and not a weapon. Small children should not have knives until they know and understand the importance of knife safety.

History has shown us that the knife was first designed as a tool and not a weapon. They are only as good as the person who owns it and takes care of it. Every camping and survival book I have read says, "You've got to have a good knife." All I can add is it's true. Every time I have gone out camping, I've had to use a knife for some task.

There are all different kinds of knives and all with various uses. The purpose of this discusion is not to get you to buy a particular type of knife, but I have learned a couple of lessons in my military career about the kinds of knives not to buy. When the Rambo movies came out, everyone had to buy one of the survival knives. I bought one, and it looked so cool, and it had everything I would need to survive in the wild—or so I thought. The knife broke the first time I used it.

After this embarrassing episode, I now do not own or carry a big fancy survival knife. I will not buy a knife because some famous person has his name on it or endorses it. I don't choose a knife for its decorative looks. I carry a knife that is strong, dependable and has everything for a survival situation.

At the end of World War II, returning American soldiers introduced the Swiss Army knife to the American public, and they have been popular ever since. My dad gave me my first Swiss Army knife, and I carried one for most of my childhood into my teens. Then I was introduced to the multi-tool. To this day, I take a multi-tool with me. I even purchased a multi-tool for each of my sons. I knew they would need it. There are one hundred different versions of multi-tools made by various companies. Be careful, some of them are cheap knockoffs and will break the first time you use them.

As you can imagine, there is quite a selection to choose from when it comes to knives. You need to select the type of blade you are going to be comfortable using. I know people who spend a lot of money on a certain kind of knife and then don't know how to use it properly. I continue to test knives new to the market, but only if I think they are worthy of a try. If you have a knife, you have been using for years, and it works for you, then, by all means, continue to use it and carry it with you. Again, I'm not trying to push any kind of knife on you.

Here is a quick lesson on knives. There are two kinds of knives. The fixed blade is a knife with an edge and handles which are connected or are one piece, an example of which would be the army bayonet and the Ka-bar. The other style is the folding blade knife that has a blade that will retract into the handle, and the best-known examples are the Swiss Army type and pocket knives. Outdoors, I prefer the fixed blade. As noted above, when I was young, I owned a Swiss Army knife, and it was pretty handy. But with the introduction of multi-tools, the Swiss Army knives are not as popular anymore.

Mora knives, from Sweden, have recently gained in popularity. When my good friend Kevin Jackson gave me one, I was hesitant to use it because it doesn't look like an outdoor knife. It looked like a steak knife with a dark green handle. I'm not gentle with blades.

I need a dependable one to withstand constant use.

The little knife has held up to everything I have put it through. It's not a fancy-looking knife but hasn't broken, and it keeps its edge after continuous outdoor use. You cannot use it to chop down medium-size trees, and if you are not careful, you can bend it.

Another little knife that is reliable and extremely handy to have with you is the Opinel knife from France. Since 1890 the Opinel company has manufactured a line of eponymous wooden-handled knives. Each knife blade is made of high carbon steel or stainless steel. Opinel knives have a unique locking ring on the handle that prevents the blade from folding down when in use. They come in a variety of sizes, the most popular being the No 7. There are currently 12 of the wooden-handled carbon knives available, and they are not expensive. They are tough enough to cut rope and branches. But the most popular use with bushcrafters is in preparing food.

I'm not endorsing any knife. My point is that you should not judge a knife by its appearance. You need to find a knife that you are comfortable with and that meets your individual needs.

Today most knife blades are made in the Orient, and sometimes the quality is poor. They break the first time you use them. Not all knives made in the Orient are of poor quality. I own a handmade parang from Malaysia, and I think it is a great knife.

When picking out a knife, make sure it has the metal tang, which is an extension of the blade, that runs through the entire handle. Some of them don't, and they break easily. They are called rat tail knife and claim to be full tang knives. Stainless steel is good metal, and it will not rust easily. You'll know you've got a cheap knife when it rusts the first time you take it outdoors.

I carry three knives with me. I have one that I got when I was in the military, and I secure it on my belt. I have a Mora knife inside my rucksack, and the third knife is my Opinel, which I carry with my cooking gear. Always have backup blades in case you lose your primary knife. Also, have a multi-tool, which comes in handy when you need to fix equipment or make vehicle repairs.

It would be wise to teach your children how to handle a knife if you want them to carry one. Teach them to use a knife the way it is meant to be used. Don't let them have one until they are old enough and responsible enough to carry it. Make sure they understand a knife is for hunting down and killing a bigfoot. My sons were ten years old when I started letting them carry their knives on legend trips, and those were pocket knives. Small pocket knives, in my opinion, are not particularly great for continuous outdoor use. They are useful around the house, for fixing everyday things, but not out in the woods. I have one to use as a backup knife to use on the small stuff to keep my primary knife's blade sharp.

Water is the second thing I want to talk about, and I think it's pretty obvious why. Let's be real: You can't survive without it. A lot of weekend hikers and legend trippers do not take enough water with them. They think they are just going to be in the woods or forest for a couple of hours, and why carry around a large canteen? This is a disaster in the making. Dehydration can be dangerous and a showstopper.

There is a survival saying: A human can live three minutes without air, three days without water, and three weeks without food. Because of this, water needs to be a top priority on your packing list. If you are out in the woods and run out of water, you're going to have to end your legend trip and go back. It happened to me with a friend, and now I don't go legend tripping with him anymore. I don't buy cases of water; instead, I buy big collapsible water containers. It is a lot cheaper, and it gives you more room in your vehicle. Plus, you won't have all those empty plastic containers.

I always take a canteen with me, and I make sure it is filled up with water before I go out hiking. I prefer the two-quart military-style canteen. It is easier to carry than some of the new styles of containers. I also take water purification tablets and iodine, in the event that I have to get my water from a stream or creek. I always put the water containers in a cooler with ice. There is nothing better than coming back to some cold water after a hike. I'm not a big fan of energy drinks. They only work for a short period, plus, you have to deal with those empty plastic containers. I stick to just water. There is water flavoring you can buy, and it does a great job making yucky water taste good. Make sure you don't put it in water that needs to be treated. I don't use it all the time.

A trick that I picked up from Cody Lundin's book *98.6 Degrees: The Art of Keeping Your Ass Alive!* is to put 550 cord or rope in a loop secured with duct tape. If you have to lower your canteen into a creek or stream, the loop makes it more accessible. In the southeastern part of the country, you have to be careful of alligators, and you might not want to get too close to the banks, so this helps out. Lundin's is a great book, with practical and useful ideas when you are out into the wild and surviving.

I recently purchased a water purifier pump I carry with me. It was not expensive, and I now have another way to get clean water if ever I need it. Make sure you also pack iodine, either liquid or tablets, to purify water if you have to. Some of these purifying tablets on the market do not kill all the bacteria, like Giardia, and once bacteria get into your system, you can't find a bathroom quick enough. You can also purchase Iodine Tincture Solution, which is two percent iodine and about forty-seven percent alcohol. Bottles of this solution should be available at your local drugstore, and a two-ounce bottle is usually three dollars or less. Just to let you know, iodine tastes awful, but it does make the suspect water safe to drink. Keep the iodine in a tear dropper for easy use. You can keep the iodine with the firstaid kit; just make sure you know exactly where it is when you need it.

You need to find a source of water like a pond, lake, river, or stream if you run out of water. Please remember that clear water is better than cloudy water, and flowing water is better than still water. Even if the water looks exceptionally pure and clean, you should always purify it before drinking. Looks can be deceiving! If you can't boil the water (which is the best way to purify water), add five to ten drops of Iodine Tincture Solution per 32 fluid ounces (about one liter) of water. The exact number of drops is a personal choice. I'm a fan of eight drops. If you are filling up a bottle or container that is not thirty-two fluid ounces or one liter, change your measurements accordingly. A two-liter bottle will require twice the number of drops. How much you use depends on the water source (if your source is a lake or some other still body of water, you will want to add closer to ten drops; if the source is flowing, you can add fewer) and the clarity of the water (you should add closer to ten drops if the water is cloudy). Then you need to wait at least five minutes before you start drinking it. Be ready; it is still going to mess with your system. Have the toilet paper ready?

The third thing that is a must is a survival kit, and I do stress the importance of having one with you. I carry a survival kit, and so does every member of my family. Though it is considered pretty standard, it has everything I need in a survival situation. There are plenty of excellent survival kits available on the market today. Most are priced at about thirty dollars and come in small, compact containers. There are even zombie survival kits and end-of-the-world survival kits. Whatever one you purchase, make sure you can carry it with you. I'm not going to endorse any particular one. Most of them have the same stuff. Remember, though, a survival kit is only as good as the person who owns it. In other words, you can have all this fancy stuff to help you in a survival situation, but if you don't know how to use it, the kit is worthless to you.

Before you go into the woods, make sure you know how to make a fire with the stuff in the kit. It's better to learn how to use it before you are in a real survival situation. Learning to make a fire is not an easy task, and it takes practice. I added a sewing kit to my survival kit, because of my habit of ripping my clothes or losing a button. You don't want to turn your trip into a survival situation, but it can happen. You can read stories about people who went on a day trip and found themselves in a survival situation. If you prepare accordingly and make sure you bring everything you need, then it won't happen. I recently downloaded a survival app on my cell phone. It looks pretty good and has a lot of information, but I have not tried it yet. I hope I won't have to use it, but it's there if I need it.

When it comes to survival situations involving young kids, the only things useful to them in a survival kit are the emergency blanket and a signaling mirror. The most important to relate to them is that when they find themselves disoriented, they should stay where they are. The safety necklace (described below) is a must for young members of the team or first-time outdoor legend trippers.

The fourth must-have item is a first aid kit. If you are bringing the whole family, you have two options. You can bring a large one for everybody, or you can have the family members each carry a small individual kit. Most first aid kits are pretty standard, with alcohol and Band-Aids, but you will have to personalize them depending on the kind of trip you are taking. Some survival kits have small first aid kits in them. If you are taking specialty medicine of any sort, you need to make sure you bring it and notify everybody with you that you are taking it. For example, if you are allergic to bee stings, then you need to bring your EpiPen (epinephrine injection). I have hay fever, so I always bring my antihistamine medicine with me just in case. I don't have it as bad as when I was a kid, but you never know, and the worst time to forget it is when you are in the woods, and your eyes start to itch.

Most standard first aid kits do not have poison ivy cream. Make sure you bring some. It would be a good idea to add moleskin to your kit, in case you or your team get blisters walking around. Petroleum jelly is good to have in tropical weather. You can also waterproof gear with it. I add cough drops to my first aid kit. They are effective in the morning when you get a weird cough and sore throat, called camper's cough. Most people do not take enough plasters or Band-Aids with them. Some hikers think they will only need one, the whole time they are out there. Wrong; you need to change the Band-Aid once a day, and if you are in a survival situation, you don't know how long you are going to be out there. Put a drop of iodine on the cloth part of the Band-Aid, and it will speed up the healing. One word of caution: Some people are allergic to iodine because it contains shellfish. You need to know every member's medical background and see if they are allergic to anything.

The fifth must-have item is a flashlight, which is essential in a survival situation at night. Humans are not nocturnal. I always make sure I bring a couple of them with me. One is a small pocket light I carry on the pocket flap of my jacket. I like to wear a headlight at night. It makes monster hunting more manageable, and it leaves your hands free to operate your camera. And it makes going to the bathroom outside a lot easier. I always make sure I carry a couple of light sticks I can break open and use in case my flashlight stops working.

When you go legend tripping at night, you need to be proactive on this. If your light source goes out and you are in the middle of the woods, you are screwed, and you're going to end up lost for hours. If you are bigfoot hunting, it is good to have a red or blue lens flashlight. It doesn't give off an intense light, and it helps your eyes adjust more quickly to the darkness—a technique I learned in the military. I even installed a blue light in my Jeep for the same reason.

The last thing I want to talk about is ensuring every team member has a safety necklace. When we all go into the woods, I always make sure each person has a safety necklace around his or her neck. The items on it are a whistle, a penlight, and a couple of optional things I will talk about later. Though some hikers and outdoorsmen like to secure these items to a shoulder pad of their backpack, I found this isn't always a good idea. When you are out rucking, and you come to a stop, the first thing you do is take off your ruck. Most people, myself included, will take off the ruck to go to the bathroom. Now your safety items are away from you and on the ruck, and this can be bad at night. It is easier to have them on a necklace, which is readily accessible to you at all times.

I remember one night in the military when we were out at night doing a mission. One of my soldiers took off his rucksack to go to the bathroom. He heard a loud noise and took off running. We had to stop everything to locate his rucksack. It took us all night, and we finally found it when the sun came up. I have all first-time legend trippers' sleep with their safety necklaces on when we are camping. You never know when you are going to have to urinate, and it's usually at night. I go over each item on the safety necklace and explain its importance to the trip participants. The first item is a whistle. Be careful, a lot of them you can't hear from a certain distance. I highly recommend storm whistles.

The US Coast Guard introduced a whistle that emits a sound that can be heard over the high winds of a hurricane or other storm. They were appropriately named "storm whistles" and are now considered standard on all diving gear. Storm whistles are a little more expensive than average ones, but when it comes to you and your teammates' safety, the extra cost is well worth it.

The second item on the necklace is a small penlight. I try to get a variety of colored lights and assign a different one to each family member, so I know who it is I'm seeing at night. They come in pretty handy when you have to go to the bathroom outside. I tell everyone to use the light in conjunction with the whistle at night, so we can find someone who is lost. A night vision scope can easily see the lights.

The next items are optional on the safety necklace. A compass is significant to have when you know how to use it. They are easy to find and are very inexpensive. Be careful of cheap ones. They don't work right. Small kids really won't use one. They understand that the arrow points to the north but don't understand the importance of a compass. Of course, this trip might be a great time to teach them.

You might want to have a small folding knife on your safety necklace. As I have mentioned, I don't really like folding knives, but it is good to have one as a backup knife because they are light and compact. Do not purchase cheap ones at a dollar store. You never know what you are going to have to cut yourself loose from, and cheap knives do not hold up. If you have small children, you might want to reconsider putting this on their safety necklace. Children love to play with stuff, and knives are not a good idea. Secure the whistle, light, and compass (blade is optional) on an orange 550 paracord.

The last thing I want to emphasize about outdoor survival is being in the right shape when you go into the woods for your legend trip. If you're going to go hiking or even climbing up hills, then you and your team members need to be in decent shape. One way to accomplish this is to go out and start walking around. Most state parks have walking trails, so take the family and walk one of the trails. Not only are they getting in shape, but they are also getting used to the outdoors.

Legend tripping is an excellent way to get your kids outside and exercising. If they are not used to it, I recommend you start with just a day-long legend trip. Be patient, and don't push your kids too hard. If you feel you or they are not in the right shape, then don't wear a backpack, but you do need to have water with you. Your first outing may not involve a lot of walking, and that's OK.

Be prepared to have plenty of stops to help them get used to being outdoors. Make sure they have the right footgear (see Chapter 15, Tools of the Trade). Bring plenty of bug spray; you are going to need it.

You also have to be aware of what time of day you are going hiking. In some places during the summer months, it is not wise to go hiking in the middle of the day due to the heat. Do not plan long walks during the hottest part of the day. Hike in the morning before it gets hot. I go hiking in the morning or the early evening when it starts to cool down.

Also, don't bring any unnecessary gear. I have seen many people bring a lot of survival gear and knives. They carry heavy packs with them and end up getting tired quickly and can't finish the expedition. If you are going up any mountains or hills, you need to prepare yourself to do this. A heavy pack is not a good thing to have when you are rucking up hills. You are going to lose your team and friends if you have to end the expedition because of that.

I like to go rucking on weekends through the woods with at least fifty pounds in my backpack. When it comes to hiking and climbing in the outdoors, you can't just hope you're in the right shape. On a side note, *never* go hiking or rucking alone.

Your team is your priority out there, and you should always make sure they are prepared and won't panic if anything goes wrong. You need to carry the right equipment, which I will go into in detail in the next chapter.

Expect the unexpected, even if it is only a day trip. People have gotten lost and died on day trips. Make sure you make this a priority in your legend tripping plan.

You need to remember, "go prepared." You can journey out on your legend trip and discover something you wish you had brought, but as long as you have the basics that I mentioned above, your trip will be exciting and enjoyable. Never treat any journey into the woods as a simple day trip. Always prepare for the worst. That way, it will give you peace of mind, and you can concentrate on finding bigfoot and other legends.

LEGEND
TRIPPER

Chapter 15

Tools of the Trade

No matter what you are out to research, i.e., cryptid creatures, haunted places, or lost treasures, a well-planned-out adventure trip is a successful and exciting one. I make no apologies about going into depth about putting together an equipment list. Every successful trip or expedition is a result of not only the people but also the right equipment.

With equipment, I look for dependability and not a name brand. You may have different items from what I use that you prefer to take. I do not endorse any specific product in this book. All the items that I will cover are those that I have used and that have worked for me. You must bring equipment that you are comfortable with and know how to use.

On every one of my adventures, I either add or remove items from the equipment list. I pack according to what and where I'm researching. When it comes to new equipment, I always try it out first, make sure it is in good working order.

Also, make sure that your equipment is worth the money you're paying for it. Take for instance, a person who first tries out golfing. He goes out and buys an expensive set of golf clubs and then finds out he can't stand the game. Now he's stuck with expensive golf clubs. I talk more about this in the ghost hunting part of the book.

Legend tripping should not be an expensive experience, but spending some money is a requirement of any adventure or hobby. You need to plan and look around for the right equipment. It doesn't have to be expensive, but remember, "You get what you pay for." You need the right equipment to go on a good legend trip and have a great experience. It doesn't have to be expensive, but don't go out and buy really cheap stuff, especially clothing.

As I said, it is essential to make an equipment list. If you already have camping equipment, then going out and buying a lot of stuff won't be necessary. If camping is a pastime, then everything required for a bigfoot hunt will be readily at hand. My wife purchased a lot of her ghost hunting equipment at the hardware store. She paid a fraction of the price that some online ghost hunting stores are charging for the same items. Also, go to some of the online bidding websites and check out some of the equipment they have there. Just because an item is new and expensive does not necessarily mean that it is better than the used item. I have purchased name brand items, after trying cheaper versions that did not hold up. When deep in the woods, you need reliable equipment.

I will go over items and equipment that I feel are important to have on any legend trip.Pay particular attention to my side notes.

One of the important things I want to talk about is money. Part of planning is to make sure there is adequate money or put some aside for the trip. I pack up my credit card for trips. I also carry some international traveler's checks in case my credit card gets lost. Always keep a stash of cash to put gas in the vehicle. If you are vising another country, this is extremely important.

On a side note: Always put the money/debit cards in a safe place. If you are traveling with family members, don't have one person carry it all. Do not carry a purse. It's an easy target for thieves. Also, do not place money in the outer pockets of your backpack. Keep it in a waterproof container or pouch.

When you are visiting another country, there may be items that you can't bring on the plane, for example, a canoe. Keep in mind that it can be expensive paying for checked baggage, so you might not even want to bring all the equipment that is transportable. Also, you can't carry certain items in your carry-on bags, like a knife. Put it in your checked luggage.

Equipment for your Legend Tripping Adventure

Camera: It is an essential piece of equipment on a legend trip. You need to have some device to record the experience. There might be a lake monster or ghost, and a camera is necessary to get a picture or video of it. The best part of legend tripping is recording the experience. When it comes to cameras, don't buy cheap. Most cameras are digital now, and it is effortless to download the pictures right onto the computer. I recently purchased a small digital camera that has IR capability from a ghost hunting store. The IR means infrared, and it takes pictures with night vision and is a must when looking for cryptid creatures, ghosts, or other nocturnal legends.

Most cellphones on the market today have excellent cameras installed in them. My wife uses her cellphone most of the time, and the picture resolution is remarkable.

By looking at some of the online retail sites, finding a decent camera at a reasonable price is made much more accessible. I find most of my equipment online using these non-specialty websites.

On a side note: When on a legend trip, take a whole bunch of pictures. The background of the picture could reveal more than the original target. Also, video each other and talk about the legend trip and the stories behind the legends. I know it sounds weird, but imagine being on one of those reality shows. Make sure to bring extra batteries and car chargers, so the cameras are ready.

Equipment for Camping

For a legend trip that requires camping, you will need this gear:

Clothing: When it comes to "what to wear" on a legend trip, it is not about fashion. Make sure the clothing is comfortable, not heavy, quick-drying, and—most important—durable! Like I said earlier,

"You get what you pay for." I once bought some cheap clothing items, and they fell apart the first time I washed them. Never again will I buy cheap clothing.

I am meticulous about the clothing I buy because I am pretty hard on clothes. I've torn my clothing numerous times. Regardless of the brand names, I purchase outdoor clothing that I know is going to stand up to trips into the woods or swamps. I don't dress up as if I were going to be on television. I rarely wear camouflage or hunting items. I purchase clothing that is durable and comfortable. I don't have anything against camouflage clothing; I wore it for more than twenty-one years in the Army. I just don't see the necessity of wearing it. I like light-colored (usually tan) clothing that will dry quickly and keep me cool when it gets hot.

There are numerous outdoor companies that produce clothes that are reasonably priced. Some of it can be kind of expensive, though, and I recommend looking for seasonal sales. My wife found good deals on the clearance rack. I see people going out and buying expensive clothing and gear for their first adventure. Make sure legend tripping is something you find exciting and enjoyable before investing too much money. Clothing should be the last thing to worry about when deep in the woods on a legend trip. During the summer season, make sure the clothing is durable and lightweight. During the winter season, it is vital that the clothing keeps the cold out and keeps you warm and dry. Today you can purchase clothing that will keep you both warm and dry and is lightweight.

If going on a monster hunt, you will need to wash your clothes in anti-scent detergent found in outdoor stores, as well as the anti-scent dryer sheets, because even the no scent dryer sheets have a scent. It also keeps some insects off of you.

On a side note: Make sure to take rain gear with you whenever hiking or in the woods.

GORE-TEX can be expensive, but it does work, and it will also keep wearers warm during cold nights. I still have my original

GORE-TEX rain jacket from the military, and I still use it. Yes, it is camouflage, but I don't use it for that reason. I use it to keep warm and dry during inclement weather. I recommend buying these jackets at a military surplus store where they are used but cheap.

On a side note: If purchasing any GORE-TEX gear, make sure to take care of it and be careful when cleaning and storing it. Prolonged exposure to the sun will dry out the fabric membranes making it useless in the rain and cold.

During the colder season, don't go out with this television survivalist attitude and think you're roughing it. Without the right gear in cold weather, you can and will die. I recommend fleece shirts and caps, a warm coat, and gloves.

A lot of people don't think about how cold it can get at night. An example would be in the desert. While deployed to Afghanistan, I found it blazing hot during the day and below zero at night. Be prepared for the change in temperature at all times. A poncho will help to keep the cold out and is easy to carry with you.

When hiking in cold weather, do not wear a coat, but put it on during stops to stay warm. When hiking, body heat will keep a body warm.

On a side note: During hunting season, wear items that have orange in them, so you don't get mistaken for a deer and get shot. Hunting accidents happen every year because of people not wearing the right clothing.

When hiking in the woods, I carry a small orange backpack and hat. I have an orange cord on my walking stick, and even my cell phone has an orange case. My croslite clogs have an orange band on them.

Another reason for putting orange tape on my gear is so that I don't lose any of it when I'm out at night. If it was camouflage and I dropped it (especially at night), I would never find it again. On one of our outings, a friend of mine could not find his sleeping bag, which, of course, was camouflage in color. It turned out it was right next to him the whole time.

A lot of hunters wear orange gear. Deer are supposedly color blind, but wearing it helps in that other hunters do not mistake each other for deer or other animals. In areas that allow hunting, I highly encourage possessing items with orange on them.

On a side note: A lot of new survival gear is bright in color. During a survival situation, it can easily be seen and utilized as a signaling device.

Headgear: I am not a big fan of hats. I'm not saying I don't wear them; I'm just saying I don't like to wear them. But, I do understand the importance of wearing them in extreme hot weather climates. Headgear offers protection from the harmful UV rays of the sun.

A boonie hat is a wide-brim hat commonly used by military forces in hot tropical climates. This headgear offers protection for your entire head and neck.

When I first started monster hunting in Florida, I didn't wear a hat. Hiking a trail during July, I ended up getting sunburned on the top of my head and neck. It was a painful lesson. Skin cancer caused by the harmful UV rays of the sun is difficult to cure.

Now, I take along a hat if I know we'll be walking around in the sun. But when I'm in the deep swamps, I wear a simple tan baseball cap. It is light and comfortable. I do recommend some form of headgear when doing any kind of trip in the sun. Some people like to wear head wraps, and they are effective in keeping the sweat out of the face, but they do not keep the sun out of our face, or the harmful UV rays that can cause skin cancer. Ensure that every member of the team has some kind of headgear.

In cold weather, I bring what the military calls a "watch cap." It is like a large sock for the head. It gets its name from being worn while standing watch on a ship or at a guard post. It is beneficial to wear one in a sleeping bag during a cold night. It also helps keep the body heat in when hiking in the winter.

On a side note: Pick out headgear that you will wear; do not buy it because it looks good.

Gloves: These may not be needed all the time, but prove handy when chopping wood with an ax or machete. They are good to have when roughing it through the high bush or grass. There are thorny bushes out there, and wearing gloves makes it easier to get through. Inexpensive work gloves are sufficient, so please ignore expensive combat gloves.

Sunglasses: They are good to have on extremely sunny days. Get a strap to put on the back so you won't lose them. Make sure everybody in the team has sunglasses. Some people pay a fortune for them and some just buy cheap ones. I don't like to wear expensive ones, for fear of losing or breaking them. You can also purchase sunglasses that are bifocal, and you can use them for reading. In my travels, I have gone through many pairs of sunglasses. I buy ones that are durable but not expensive.

Footwear: I wear hiking boots on my adventurers that are broken in and comfortable. Because of this, I can walk for miles in them. Proper footgear can make or break the legend trip. Do not wear new footwear on expeditions where you are going to be hiking long distances. Otherwise, have some moleskin for blisters. Add foot powder to the packing list. If getting feet wet is a possibility, bring petroleum jelly to stop the development of foot fungus frequently found in tropical environments.

On a recent outing in the swamps, I joined some bigfoot hunters. We ended up walking a couple of miles in water up to our knees. Everyone developed "trench foot" except me. That is because, before departing, I covered my feet with petroleum jelly. I always pack extra moleskin and petroleum jelly for my team and me, just in case. A good rule for hiking is to use foot powder for cold weather and petroleum jelly for tropical weather.

Snake boots, otherwise known as snake proof boots, are boots designed to protect your feet and ankles from snake bites when hiking in areas inhabited by venomous snakes. I wear snake boots when I'm walking through the deep swamps. They, unfortunately, are not designed for long-term hiking. I prefer to wear my hiking boots whenever I can.

On a side note: Snake boots are expensive and will cost about one-hundred bucks on average. They are cheaper during the off-season. I only use them when I have to or when my wife makes me.

The lower southeastern part of the United States, is home to rattlesnakes and cottonmouths. Both are incredibly poisonous and aggressive. A bite from one of these reptiles will quickly end the legend trip. In the interest of safety, you need to stay away from areas that might have snakes.

Another type of footwear I always bring is my Crocs clogs. I like to wear them when I am not hiking or out in the woods. Made of a foam resin called croslite, they are incredibly comfortable. Crocs come in a variety of colors and styles and are inexpensive.

They are great to put on in the morning when first waking up. These clogs are also great to change into after a long hike or ruck march. They help my feet relax. They are better than typical sandals because they cover up the toes and are not slippery on boats and canoes. The straps on my Crocs sandals are orange and they're easy to find when I need them.

On a side note: Watch out for cheap imitations of the clogs. They're not made from the same material and do not hold up.

Socks: This item is as equally important as footwear. Make sure the socks fit properly and do not rub when they get wet. Most standard white socks are terrible when wet, and fungus develops quickly because of the cotton. I wear nylon socks that were made for hiking and dry quickly. They help prevent foot fungus and blisters and aren't too expensive. Correctly sized hiking socks will help prevent blisters.

Tent: There are a large variety of tents in different sizes and made for different environments. Make sure to buy a tent that is the right size. Do not take a tent made for two people if your whole family is coming. That is when family togetherness becomes very uncomfortable. Also, don't purchase an inexpensive tent. You will find that they won't hold up to any inclement weather. You may have to spend some money, but you will want a tent that is going to hold up in any kind of weather.

If you are visiting another country, you might have to rent or purchase one. In some countries, they can be expensive.

For my adventures, I utilize three different tents. I have a small one-person tent that I use when taking long hikes, and the weight that I'm carrying is a factor. It is lightweight and easy to set up, even in the dark. I use my hiking pole to set it up or tie the peak to a low-hanging tree branch. It stands up well in bad weather and high winds. It also has a built-in mosquito net. The second tent is my two-person tent. I take this tent when my wife comes out with me, and we are doing some long-range hiking and camping. It is a lightweight teepee design and I also use my hiking stick as a guide pole or tie the peak to a low hanging tree branch. My wife likes the roominess to it while I like how small it is to carry. Like my one-person tent, it is also effortless to put up. My third and last tent is the large tent that I bring out when my wife and I are staying for an extended period, and we can also accommodate more people. We use this tent as a base camp tent. It sets up to two rooms or sections and is high enough to stand erect inside. It is easy to set up and take down. It does take up a lot of room, and it does have some weight to it. It is blue, so it's easy to see in the woods.

Like I said at the beginning, there are different kinds of tents for different environments and the number of occupants.

Sleeping Bags: There are different kinds of sleeping bags for different temperatures. If they're out and it gets freezing, but their bag is for summertime use, campers end up wearing all their packed clothes to keep warm. When it comes to a good night's sleep, you need to invest in a suitable and reliable sleeping bag. The military has excellent sleeping bags, and you can purchase them at military surplus stores. I recently purchased one that could handle the different climates. It consisted of two actual sleeping bags, a small one for mild temperatures, and a larger one for cold temperatures. For extreme cold, take the small one and put it into the larger one, creating an extreme cold weather sleeping bag. The best two things about the sleeping bag are that it folds to a tiny size for my rucksack, and it only cost sixty dollars. When purchasing a sleeping bag, look at the tag, and see what temperature range it is suitable for. Here are the three sleeping bag temperature categories:

+30° F to +55° F Sleeping Bag: For summertime backpacking and camping adventures at low to moderate elevations.

+5° F to +29° F Sleeping Bag: Referred to as a "three-season" bag. It provides more versatility than any other category.

-40° F to +4° F Sleeping Bag: Designed for mountaineering and winter camping trips. If your adventure involves snow and ice, then you will need this bag.

Air Mattresses: These inflatable mats make sleeping outside a lot more bearable. My wife refuses to go camping without them. You will find them in the camping section of any store, and they are not expensive. I also have a self-inflating mattress that I bring. Let's be real, a good night's sleep is incredibly important; otherwise, the whole legend trip turns into a bad experience and puts everybody in a bad mood. Get the body off the cold ground at night; it's not healthy. For me, there is nothing better than a comfortable bed after a nighttime ruck march. Also, you might want to put a groundsheet or tarp down so that your mat does get ruptured on a sharp rock

On a side note: Make sure to bring a repair kit in case a team member gets a leak in their mattress. I don't know why, but it always seems to happen.

Lanterns: I highly recommend the battery-operated ones over the kerosene ones. They come in a wide range of sizes, and they are not expensive. Always remember to bring extra batteries and replacement light bulbs. If you are visiting another country, I recommend cheap battery operated ones that you can pack in your luggage

On a side note: I always bring two lanterns, just in case one gets broken.

Bug Spray: When it comes to bug spray, all I can say is purchase a lot of it. Make sure everybody on the trip has his or her bug spray. It has been my experience that unless the bug spray contains DEET, it will not work, or it won't work for long. Mosquito repellers are battery-operated devices with a cartridge insert that works around camps when there are only a few of the irritating insects around or in the tent. A while back, I tried one out in the woods, and I still got covered in those bloodsucking insects. I ended up putting bug spray on. They work well in tents, but make sure the tent is well ventilated and has an open mesh at the top, even though they're DEET free.

Mosquito Net: This is a great thing to bring if you're going into the swamps or woods. Mosquitoes will drive anyone crazy when they're trying to sleep at night. A net doesn't cost a lot and will pack into a small ball to carry in either a pocket or backpack. It can provide added protection if secured over the tent. When out in the swamps, throw it on for additional bug defense. You can purchase them at any outdoor store or military surplus store.

Cleansing/Baby Wipes: One item that I swear by and always bring is baby wipes. When going to the bathroom outside, either in the woods or in a portable toilet, toilet paper is not enough. Wipes are great to clean the hands before eating, and cleaning all parts of the body when a bath or shower isn't available. In today's military, all soldiers bring baby wipes with them. Don't get the scented ones without expecting funny looks from the teammates. Now, stores sell wipes for camping.

On a side note: Do not litter when out in the woods. Used wipes attract flies and other critters. Take out what you brought in.

Food: I like to take freeze-dried meals or military meals called MREs (Meals Ready to Eat). It's easier than carrying around huge coolers of food. You can purchase a cooking stove at a reasonable price, and it is fun to cook over the campfire. Because of wildfires in some countries, their campgrounds prohibit campfires. A camping stove will come in handy. Waking up on the first morning will be an enjoyable experience for those camping for the first time. I say that facetiously. For me, a good hot cup of coffee is the way to start the morning, so I always make sure I bring coffee with me. You can also purchase portable fire pits, which you can also cook over. They break down to a minimal size for easy toting in your backpack. Some of them can be expensive.

Snacks: Trail mix, energy bars, and beef jerky are great to take along for hikes and rucking. As any parent knows, when kids get hungry, they also get irritable. They then have one thing on their minds, and that's food. On a side note: When packing in snacks, make sure to bring plenty of water.

Machetes: These large knives are good to have in the jungle or swamps, but if you're only going out to the jungle once a month, don't invest in an expensive one. A while back, I ordered a commercial parang machete online. I thought it was just what I needed in the jungle and swamps. When it arrived, I found it to be too heavy, and it gave me blisters every time I used it. I ended up dropping it off a cliff in Ecuador, and I almost followed.

I noticed that our Ecuadorian guides had cheap machetes, which they sharpened razor sharp. They had no problems cutting through the jungle with them. Now I don't buy fancy machetes. I purchased one in a sporting goods store at a reasonable price. If I go back to South America, I won't be taking an expensive machete with me. Just because it looks neat, doesn't mean that it is practical. Also, items like knives and machetes will have to be in your checked luggage if you want to travel on an airplane with them.

Bear Mace: If worried about the local wild animals, I suggest bear mace rather than a gun, as most public park areas prohibit guns. When on an outing with the family, it might make everybody uncomfortable knowing a member of the team is armed. Also, if exploring on private or government property with a gun, the person carrying the firearm can be charged with poaching. Poaching comes with a hefty fine, and firearms get confiscated. If caught trespassing with only bear mace, the fine can only be for trespassing. It happened to me, and I was able to talk my way out of it, with only a butt-chewing from the Fish and Wildlife people. I think the Fish and Wildlife officers were amused when I told them I was bigfoot hunting. Bear mace is not that expensive, and it will do the trick if a bear, panther, or wild pig sneaks up. Snakes hate the stuff as well.

Adults, and not children, should always carry the bear mace. I made the mistake of allowing my son to carry it, and he ended up using it on me. For the record, he stated he thought I was a bigfoot. I think he just wanted to see how the stuff worked. Boy, I was irate. That mace burned for two days. I will never make that mistake again.

Most countries will not allow you to enter the country with bear mace. You might be able to purchase it in the country you're visiting. If you are traveling by air, you will not be able to take this on the plane, period.

Fishing Gear: Bring it just in case there is a chance to fish. It will be something to do during the day when waiting for the evening. There is nothing worse than being bored, and a bored family is less likely to return for another legend trip. If catching fish for dinner, it will save money down the road. You can use fish or fish guts as bait for the trail camera. Just make sure to stay in compliance with state law when fishing. Most fishing permits may be purchased online. Fishing poles are a great thing to add to the packing list. Fishing itself is enjoyable, and I have found that for some reason when father and son are alone out there, there is better communication. I don't know why, but there is something about a father and son fishing trip; sons seem to understand the bonding factor with fishing, and start to open up and communicate. If skeptical, give it a try. It works. My sons and I have some excellent conversations when we're out fishing.

Fishing Poles: I always bring my "Pocket Fisherman" pole with me. You can take this small compact fishing device anywhere (I sound like a commercial), and it is inexpensive. I purchased this many years ago for my father for Christmas. While we were cleaning out his garage, he found it and gave it to me. It works great, and I've caught quite a lot of large fish with it.

Side note: If going fishing in another country, make sure to adhere to their laws and regulations, and have a fishing license.

Rope: This should always be part of the gear when camping. Rope must have a thousand uses. I use it to cross rivers or streams and to secure gear. I like to bring 550 paracords with me. This is actually parachute cord, but it is extremely strong and can hold 550 pounds, hence the name 550 paracords. I like to use it for my safety necklaces, and I also replaced my bootlaces with it. I use it when I put up my hammock and to help secure my trail cameras to trees. You can watch outdoor survivalists use paracord with animal traps survival shows. I use orange-colored 550 paracords so that it's easy to see in the woods. It comes in all different colors. Side note: Bring bungee cords. Like 550 cord, bungee cords have a hundred different uses. They make setting up a shelter a lot easier.

Duct Tape: This firm and durable tape also has a hundred different uses. I bring dark green tap—and orange, of course. You can use it to fix tears in tents and tarps. I had to use it on my GORE-TEX rain jacket one time, and it worked like a charm. I use the orange tape to mark individual items of equipment.

Flares: Flares are a good thing to have if you're a diehard legend tripper and go miles into the wilderness. If a weekend warrior, like most family guy, are, then keep flares in the car. If I bring the family, I stay close to the main paths so I don't get into a survival situation. If canoeing downriver to another site, flares might not be a bad idea.

Some countries prohibit you from owning these items. You cannot take one on a plane, either in checked or carry-on luggage.

Emergency Locators: These are a must for diehard legend trippers that go deep into the wilderness, miles from any human population. If you are lost or run into a survival situation, simply push the button, and it notifies emergency personnel of your location. The only problem is that they are expensive. Most cell phones have an emergency locator app on them. Some parents have added the app to keep a heads up on their kid's location. Once the child is eighteen, the service is not allowed. Only emergency services and police authorities are allowed to use them to locate individuals.

Side note: If the batteries run out, the cell phone only records the last position when the cell phone was working. Stay put when this happens if that is at all possible.

Cold Wrap Towel: This is a new item that is gaining in popularity. The towels are made of absorbent material and are so cool when wet. They are great when you're sweating your butt off; they take the sweat off and feel cool against the skin. Side note: The towels need to be kept damp to work correctly.

Global Positioning System (GPS): I recently purchased a GPS, and now I make sure I always bring it with me. They are great and easy to use. A lot of cell phones now have GPS on them. My wife loves using hers, and she can always tell me where we are. They are good to use at night when location is difficult to determine. Make sure there are good batteries in them.

I remember one time when I was bigfoot hunting in Florida, near the Suwannee River. My friend and I were setting up a trail camera. After we put the camera up, I looked around in the darkness, and I couldn't see where we were or how far we had gone from the dirt road. I remember panicking, for I couldn't tell where I was in the swamp. It was so dark in the swamp, and every palm tree looked the same.

My friend pulled out his GPS and switched it on. It turned out the dirt road was just to our left and about ten feet away. I kicked myself for not getting a compass reading before we went into the swamp that night, but I didn't think it was going to be hard to find the road again. Boy, was I wrong! Now, I have a GPS app on my cellphone, and I always take a compass reading when I go in the woods and swamps. Side note: GPS depends on the use of satellites, and if the weather is cloudy and overcast, the reading may not be accurate. Always bring a compass and map as a backup.

Solar Battery Rechargers: Another new item I just bought is a solar battery recharger. Whoever invented this little item is a genius. They make them small enough to carry in a cargo pocket or rucksack. Just make sure to have rechargeable batteries. I use it for my cell phone and flashlight.

Binoculars: These are another great item to bring along. Binoculars can be expensive, so make sure to look online before buying. I found a great pair at a garage sale. If there are younger kids, then purchase a relatively cheap pair for them. It gets them into the mood and ready for adventure. It also gives them something to do when they are riding in the car, and they feel part of the experience.

Backpacks: Last but not least, have a backpack or rucksack to carry the gear. There is a new term, "bug out bag," which refers to a portable emergency bag, usually a backpack, that's thoughtfully filled with critical gear and supplies needed to survive a multi-day journey to a safe location in the event of a crisis.

I don't keep my bag ready for a crisis. I like to have a bag with all the stuff I use on a legend trip. It does have critical survival gear and some supplies, but only because I want to be prepared for anything while I'm out in the woods. I carry my trail camera and evidence-collecting equipment, in case I find something, as well as casting powder for large footprints.

I have my family members each put together a bag of stuff for a legend trip, and they have designed their bags according to what they feel they need. My sons always make sure they have their music listening devices. There are plenty of suitable backpacks on the market. I have two packs. The ruck that I carry for day trips is one I had in the military. It is the one I'm used to, and I find it comfortable. The second one is a large backpack for when I go rucking back into the woods, and I expect to camp over time. I bought it used on the Internet. If one is needed, I suggest first looking on the auction websites before buying anything new. Some backpacks can be expensive.

Recreational Vehicles (RVs) or Campers: These are great to use, and there is some added comfort. If you are like my wife and sleeping in a tent on the ground is a deal-breaker for adventure, then maybe an RV is the right way to go. They are great but expensive to rent. I don't like them because I can't take them back to the areas where I bigfoot hunt. You can set up at the nearest campground, and then either hike or bicycle over to the area you want to investigate.

In some countries, you can only park RVs at designated campgrounds, and that will cost money. RVs are great for long-distance legend trips if tent camping is out, although if an RV is used instead of hotels, it may cost the same or more. RVs take a lot of fuel, and setting one up at camp can prove to be a challenge. They should make solar-powered RVs.

I recently purchased a pop-up camper, and we now have a reason to go legend tripping. It wasn't expensive, and it meets all our needs. Now when we go out, we don't have to worry about getting a hotel room. We all think it's fun to take the camper out and set up in the woods for the weekend.

They also make little campers called "teardrop campers," which can go into areas where a standard-size camper won't fit. The problem is that they are expensive and only (sort of) fit two people. My wife doesn't like them. Handy types can buy a set of plans to make one of their own but they require a trailer frame to build on. When I have to set up in an area where a camper can't go, I just take my tent. It's a lot easier and less expensive.

Vehicles: When on a legend trip, one of the essential items is the one most don't think about. I'm talking about your vehicle. When it is not working, your legend trip will come to a halt.

I own a four-wheel-drive vehicle. I have always owned this kind of vehicle. They have always been dependable, and when I go out into the wetlands, I don't get stuck. The point I am trying to make is to take the right kind of vehicle for a legend trip. Some vehicles can't handle off-roading, and that is a disaster ready to happen. I'm not recommending that you purchase an off-road vehicle. I am saying make sure to take the vehicle only where it can safely go. I have had to pull numerous vehicles out of the mud because the driver took the vehicle where it wasn't equipped to go.

It's straightforward: if the vehicle (for example, a minivan) can't go off-road, then stay on the hardtop. Either that or park it and walk. Check out the vehicle before departing for a trip, especially the tires. Make sure the spare tire is inflated and the right size. I always carry a vehicle emergency kit in the back. They cost about thirty dollars, and they o come in handy.

Bringing an ATV can add to the legend trip. Not only are they fun to ride, but they can increase the search zone.

On a side note: Be careful riding them. ATVs do not have a good track record, and people have died in accidents on them. I know a person who got his ATV stuck out in the swamp, and it is still out there. It's in a spot where a recovery vehicle can't get it.

Inflatable Boat or Canoe: A boat is nice to bring if there is room. Be careful when taking it out. Make sure there are no alligators in the water if using an inflatable raft. Some lakes and streams have sticks poking up that can puncture them, too. I am the proud owner of a hovercraft. I bring it on occasion just to have something fun to do if the trip turns out to be a bust. Always have a backup plan for entertainment and fun when bringing children. It is fun to go canoeing, and the family gets some exercise and sees things. Always locate nearby places that rent boats and canoes. It might be something to think about, especially if the area where you are going to be has a lake, river, or creek.

Side note: For safety, make sure all members have life vests and safety necklaces.

Equipment for Monster (Bigfoot) Hunting

The next listed items are for a monster (bigfoot) hunt.

Night Vision Goggles: These are nice to have, but they can be expensive. I bought a set online for fifty dollars. They work, but only for about fifty feet in front of you. Even though the device is a toy, eye reflections from animals are easily seen from more than one hundred feet away. My camera also has night vision capabilities, and with it, I can see a lot further than fifty feet. It's a small camera that I can carry in my breast pocket, which makes it easier to grab when I need it. I'm not a big fan of using night vision devices to maneuver through the woods. They limit your depth perception which can result in tripping over plants or branches. I like to get my eyes adjusted to the dark and go from there.

Side note: If it gets too dark, I pull out my flashlight and use that. As I stated before, I don't like tramping around the woods because I end up making too much noise.

Trail Camera: If going on a monster or ghost legend trip, please get one. Called a "trail cam" for short, it is a camera that has an automatic device that triggers when something walks by. It is suitable for bigfoot and ghost hunting. Trail cams used to be expensive, but are now available from any outdoor store for a reasonable price.

I like to find a game trail (a path made by some animal through the brush) and put the trail camera on a tree with a good field of view. I then spray it with a chemical that takes away the human smell. I leave it out there for about two weeks or a month, long enough for the human scent to go away. I go back and retrieve it and check the pictures. If I get nothing, then I move it to another location.

Side note: I have had trail cameras stolen, so I now always put a lock on it.

Camouflage Netting: I like to conduct most of my monster investigations in the early morning or early evening. From my research, I have observed that a lot of bigfoot sightings take place during this time frame. These cryptids are nocturnal, so this is the best time to see them. I have acquired some netting that I like to bring. Believe it or not, I bought it at a toy store. Sometimes I will sit in a tree stand (used for hunting) and put the camouflage over me and wait. The camouflage helps break up my human pattern or silhouette. I also wrap my trail cameras in it when I set them up in trees. It disguises them better. It doesn't matter what clothing you're wearing unless hunting for deer or other animals. Visibility is a safety guideline when in the habitat of certain animals such as panthers and hogs—and people; if they can see you, the animals and hunters will leave the area, and no one gets shot accidentally. I can't stress enough how important it is to be visible to hunters. Every year somebody gets mistaken for a deer and shot. One of our former vice presidents shot somebody during a hunting trip, thinking the person was a deer.
Luckily the person lived.

Footprint Casting Kit: I bring one of these when I go out monster hunting, just in case I find the footprint of an unidentified animal. The kit should consist of the following items:

- Plaster casting powder: can be purchased from any hardware store. I recommend you double the amount you would take. Purchase two of the eight-pound tubs and carry a Ziploc bag of plaster powder when you go deep into the woods. These cryptids have broad feet, making large prints. It will take a significant amount of casting powder to make a casting.

- Rubber gloves, because the process can be messy
- Water—using too much, the cast takes forever to dry, and the material is not as firm. If you use too little water, the plaster becomes a thick paste that can damage the casting.
- Soft brush
- Large plastic or bendable copper strip (2" x 24" or two pieces of 2" x 13")
- Hairspray (in an aerosol can)
- Measuring tape

Evidence Kit: Conducting research also involves collecting evidence. You might not believe this, but you can purchase a good evidence kit at a hobby store. With the popularity of TV shows involving crime scene investigations, evidence kits are now readily available and not expensive. They have everything needed for hair samples or scat (animal poop). It is costly to have DNA samples sent off and professionally examined. I leave that for the monster-hunting TV shows, which have the money.

The evidence kit should consist of the following items:

- Plastic tackle box—to keep the kit together
- Plastic bags of assorted sizes – for collecting hair or scat samples
- Rubber gloves
- Tweezers
- Small shovel
- Plastic medicine containers
- Measuring tape

Side note: Make sure the evidence kit includes gloves to protect the evidence and the hands. Also, do not leave any trash after collecting the evidence.

Trail Markers: These are brightly colored strips of cloth or plastic that hunters use to mark their area in the woods or swamps. They are great for marking the trail at night. They can also be used to find the way back to a main road or trail. I use them during my scouting trips during the daytime. They are inexpensive and easy to see at night. Some of them are reflective, and can be seen at night with a flashlight. They are very effective in dense, wooded areas. You can retrieve them during the daytime so they can be used again.

Parabolic Listening Device: It looks like a toy gun with a satellite dish on the front of it, and it comes with a set of earphones, also referred to as a Bionic Ear. It is excellent for listening to noises, especially at night. I can plug it into my wife's voice recorder and tape what I am listening to. The only problem is that it is bulky and hard to pack away in my backpack. Great to use at a static post with the vehicle, but when rucking into the woods, it is not easy lugging it around.

Portable (Walkie-Talkie) Radios: These are great items to bring, and they help keep track of everybody. They are available at most sporting goods stores, and they are great to have when the group separates into smaller teams. I make sure the base camp has a radio and is always in communication with all the teams.

Equipment for Ghost Hunting

When it comes to ghost hunting, there is a lot of fancy equipment out there to buy. Type in "ghost hunting equipment" on the Internet and look. My wife, who loves conducting paranormal investigations, bought all of hers, except for the camera, at a hardware store. We have ghost hunting friends who own a lot of equipment for ghost hunting. Tracy thinks it is too time-consuming to lug all that equipment around and set it up. It never fails that at least one piece does not work right or is missing a power cord.

We did an investigation in an old shut-down school, and it turned out there was no power source for the equipment. We ended up just using just our cameras and recording devices. We still got great results with my wife catching a voice on her recording device. It is still just theory whether the ghost hunting equipment works or not. Ghost hunting has not turned into a money-making endeavor, so I don't recommend spending a fortune on all the fancy gizmos. You can purchase a lot of these items at any hardware store. Here are some items needed to conduct an effective paranormal investigation:

EMF Reader and Temperature Reader: An EMF (electromagnetic field) reader picks up on the electronic signature given off by any electrical fixture. Ghost hunters swear by them. Many online ghost hunting stores sell them for much more than the hardware store.

The temperature reader looks like some space-age laser gun. Point at any object with the red light dot, and it will relate the temperature given off by the object. They are great to use when monster hunting at night to see if anything is out there.

Sound Recorder: My wife always brings one with her ib paranormal investigations and is always ready in case we run into a haunted location.

During a ghost hunt, my wife will find a spot, hit record, and leave it there. She will retrieve the device later and listen to the recording and see if she can hear anything. She claimed success when we did an investigation on an old school.

Standard 35mm Camera: Believe it or not, these old film cameras pick up lots of things that some digital cameras won't. The significant part is that they are very inexpensive. The only thing is you have the film developed, which costs money.

Night Vision Game Camera: They work on great all the different kinds of legend trips from monster to paranormal hunts.

There are different versions out today. Some are expensive, and some are affordable. I do not invest in the expensive ones because they can get stolen once placed out in the woods or forests. I have even put a lock system on one, and still had it stolen. Also, if buying the inexpensive ones, purchase more than one, and saturate an area with trail cameras. Some bigfoot hunters believe that bigfoot can see the IR and stays away from the cameras, so that is something to think about

Here is a list of other tools and devices that paranormal investigators use on investigations. I'm going over this just to briefly share what they are and how to use them, so if you go out ghost hunting with experts, the equipment will be familiar to you. Do not purchase these items unless you are serious about ghost hunting and will continue doing paranormal investigations.

Thermal Imager: This is an excellent tool to have on a monster hunt or paranormal investigation, but unfortunately, they are costly. They are for serious monster/paranormal hunters who have the money to buy them. I have used the expensive types in the military, but I don't own one. I found out that most television shows rent them because of the cost; they do break, and they are expensive to have repaired. The good news is that the prices are dropping, and there is one that is durable enough for outdoor use. I recently purchased one which attaches to my cellphone.

Full IR Camera/DVR Set Up: DVR (digital video recorder) systems with night vision can be a powerful way to capture significant paranormal evidence.

Using multiple cameras will record and cover large areas for long periods with one easy set-up.

Dowsing Rod: These L-shaped rods have been used for centuries by different cultures. The word "dowsing" means to use a rod or pendulum to find something. In the past, farmers would use these devices to find water and minerals. In our modern day, large oil companies, police forces, mining operations, and farmers employ skilled dowsers.

After World War I and during the Vietnam War, soldiers equipped with rods were able to locate booby traps and underground tunnels. Dowsing rods have now found a new use by paranormal investigators as a way to communicate with ghosts or spirits. An investigator will hold the rod and ask the spirit questions.

Questions can be answered either with a "yes" or "no," or the spirit will direct the rods at an object or person. The rods are inexpensive and easy to find on the Internet.

Laser Grid Pen: This high-powered laser emits a grid of green dots useful for detecting shadows or general visual disturbances during an investigation. Set it in front of a running camera to catch potential evidence when something goes through the dots.

EM Pump: An electromagnetic (EM) pump creates a low-level magnetic field to help provide energy. The theory is that spirits use it to manifest or communicate. Investigators believe that since the frequency and duration changes, it acts as a beacon or trigger device.

Motion Sensor: This device will detect any movement and alert you with a blinking light (for visual alerts and video documentation), or you have the choice of a pleasant chime or piercing alarm when not near the unit. Just place it in any room where movement can be detected, and it will give an alert when something happens.

REM Pod: This new item for ghost hunting uses a mini telescopic antenna to radiate its independent electromagnetic field around the instrument. The EM field reacts to materials and objects that conduct electricity. Based on source proximity, strength, and

EM field distortion, four colorful LED lights can be activated in any order or combination. This device is expensive and is for the serious paranormal investigator.

Ghost Box: This device utilizes various environmental cues through software to give the spirits a voice while a spirit box emits raw radio frequencies. These are popular in paranormal television shows. Like the REM Pod, this item is expensive, and it is for serious paranormal investigations.

In closing, in this chapter, I have gone over everything you will need to look for cryptids, ghosts, and mysterious places. While most investigators rarely forget their research equipment, they do tend to forget some of the items they need for camping.

Here is a gear checklist to assist you on your next outdoor adventure. Always inspect and ensure you have all your gear. I still use this list when I prepare to go out camping.

❒ Sleeping bag
❒ Sleeping pad
❒ Pillow
❒ Tent, hammock, or tarp including guylines and stakes
❒ Tent repair kit
❒ Ground cloth
❒ 550 paracord
❒ Camping chairs
❒ Headlamp and flashlight
❒ Camp lighting
❒ Cell phone
❒ Portable/solar battery pack
❒ Matches, firestarters or tinder
❒ Knife
❒ Machette or parang

- ☐ Axe with sheath
- ☐ Folding saw
- ☐ Folding shovel
- ☐ Personal water bottle with water purification device
- ☐ Stove and fuel
- ☐ Pot and frying pan
- ☐ Camp coffee maker
- ☐ Spatula
- ☐ Plates, bowls, and cups
- ☐ Eating utensils
- ☐ Cooking oil
- ☐ Salt, pepper, seasonings
- ☐ Cutting board
- ☐ Multi-tool with bottle opener, can opener, corkscrew
- ☐ Dishwashing basin/biodegradable soap/sponge/dishtowel
- ☐ Trash & recycling bags
- ☐ Personal water bottle
- ☐ Toothbrush, toothpaste, dental floss
- ☐ Sunscreen
- ☐ Prescription drugs
- ☐ Hand sanitizer
- ☐ Needle kit
- ☐ Bug protection
- ☐ First aid kit
- ☐ Rain gear
- ☐ Cold weather clothing
- ☐ Bear mace

Chapter 16

Legend Tripping Organizations Around the World

When you travel to another country and you want to check out the haunted places, or where there were sightings of UFOs or strange animals, you need to find the local experts. Even here in the US, if I go to a different state I contact someone from that area to help me out.

Here are a list of organizations around the world that research and investigate the unexplained. I have listed them by country (except for those in Africa) in alphabetical order. The organizations are sorted by cryptozoology groups, then paranormal groups and then UFO research groups. While there are more groups, especially in Great Britain, if they did not have a website, I did not include them.

MUFON (Mutual UFO Network) is an international organization with investigators located all over the world.

Africa

The South African Society for Paranormal Research
http://s-a-s-p-r.ning.com/
Gauteng Paranormal Society (GPS)
http://www.facebook.com/GhostHuntersOfGauteng
Phoenix Paranormal South Africa
http://www.phoenixpsa.co.za/

Australia
Australian Cryptozoology Research Organization
http://acro-research.blogspot.com/
A.P.F.I.- Australian Paranormal Field Investigators
http://apfiinvestigations.jimdo.com/
Ghost Hunters Down Under (GHDU)
http://www.ghdu.com.au/

Belgium
Paranormal Investigation Research Service Belgium
http://s-r-i-p-b.be/Activa-Cortex/index.php

Brazil
Paranormal Research and Investigation Group
http://www.gpip.com.br/

Canada
The British Columbia Scientific Cryptozoology Club
http://www.bcscc.ca/blog/
British Columbia Paranormal Research Society
http://www.bcparanormal.org/
Canadian Haunting and Paranormal Society
http://www.chapsparanormal.ca/

Denmark
Overnaturligt.dk
http://www.overnaturligt.dk/
Roskilde Ghost Hunters
http://www.rghs.dk/
Scandinavian UFO Information
http://www.sufoi.dk/

Egypt
White Masked Metaphysics
http://www.whitem.webs.com/

Great Britain (England, Scotland, and Wales)
Black Country Paranormal Society
http://bcps.moonfruit.com/
Bristol Ghost Club
http://www.bristolghostclub.org.uk/
International Fortean Research Society
http://forteans.com.s3-website-us-east-1.amazonaws.com/
The Centre for Fortean Zoology
http://www.cfz.org.uk/
The British Big Cats Society Official Website
http://www.britishbigcats.org/
The Ghost Club
https://www.ghostclub.org.uk/
British Paranormal Association
https://issuu.com/bpa-tam
British American Paranormal Society Forum
http://www.britishamericanparanormal.com/
British Paranormal Club
https://www.british-paranormal.co.uk/
The British Paranormal Society
http://britishparanormalsociety.co.uk/
National Paranormal Association
https://nationalparanormalassociation.blogspot.com/2013/03/the-uk-ghost-survey-map.html
Scottish Ghost Adventures
http://scottishghostadventures.com/
Gwynedd Paranormal Society
http://gwynedd-paranormal-society.co.uk/

The Bwgan Paranormal Society
http://thebwganparanormalsociety.webs.com/
British UFO Research Association (BUFORA)
http://www.bufora.org.uk/

Finland
The Finnish Ghost Hunter Group
icaros.von.windt@gmail.com

France
Spirit Investigation Paranormal Group
http://www.facebook.com/groups/GSIP54/
The Believers
http://www.facebook.com/TheBelieversNews
Study and Information Group on Unidentified Aerospace Phenomena
http://www.cnes-geipan.fr/

Germany
Paranormal Germany
http://paranormalgermany.webs.com/
Paranormal Society
http://www.paranormal-society.de/

Greece
Paranormal Research Crew—Greek Ghost hunters
http://www.ghosthunters.gr/
The After Dark Project
http://theafterdarkproject.blogspot.gr/

Hungary
P.OK Paranormális Oknyomozók
http://p-ok.eu/

India
Archaeological Haunting
http://archealogicalhaunting.blogspot.in/
GIFT Paranormal Society
http://www.giftindia.org/
Indian Paranormal Team
http://www.indianparanormalteam.com/
Indian Specter Paranormal Society
http://specter-paranormal-society.weebly.com/
Paranormal Society of India
http://www.paranormalsocietyofindia.com/

Indonesia
Avanoustic | Unexplained Mysteries
http://www.avanoustic.com/
International Rama Wijaya Associates
http://www.ramawijaya.com/

Italy
Italian Ghost Hunters League
http://www.italianghosthuntersleague.it/
Gruppo Internazionale Paranormale Speciali Investigatori
http://gipsifiles.com/

Japan
Ryukyu Islands Paranormal Investigations & Research Society
http://www.rip.xbuild.com/

Malaysia
Malaysian Paranormal Research
http://www.malaysian-paranormal-research.org/

Mexico
ParaNormal Club
http://www.facebook.com/groups/PNCMX/

Netherlands
Ghost Hunters Overschie
http://www.ghosthuntersoverschie.com/
Ghosthunting Netherlands
http://www.ghosthunting.nl/

New Zealand
Strange Occurrences Paranormal Investigators
http://www.strange-occurrences.com/

Norway
UFO-Norge
http://www.ufo.no/

Peru
Grupo Dharma Paranormal
http://www.dharmaparanormal.com/

Philippines
RPN-Paranormal Society of the Philippines
http://www.facebook.com/rpnpagadian
Poland
Professional Team of Ghost Hunters
http://ghosthunters.com.pl/

Singapore
The Supernatural Team
http://www.facebook.com/THESUPERNATURALTEAM

The Singapore GHOST Club
http://ghostclubsg.blogspot.com/

Spain
Ghost Area - Area de Fantasmas
http://www.ghostsarea.com/
Ovnispain (UFOs)
http://www.ovnispain.com/

Sweden
Archives for the Unexplained
http://www.afu.se/

Turkey
Istanbul UFO Museum
http://siriusufo.org/geziciufomuzesi/index.html

Russia
Kosmopoisk
http://kosmopoisk.org/

United States
The International Cryptozoology Society
http://cryptozoologymuseum.com/international-cryptozoology-society
Bigfoot Research Organization
http://bfro.com
The World Explorers Club and Magazine
http://wexclub.com

LEGEND TRIPPING
ADVENTURE OUTSIDE THE BOX!

Chapter 17

Your Adventure Begins Now!

Your time is limited, so don't waste it living someone else's life. Don't be trapped by dogma—which is living with the results of other people's thinking. Don't let the noise of others' opinions drown out your own inner voice. And most important, dare to follow your heart and intuition.
—Steve Jobs

"It is all about the experience." I don't know who said it first, but he or she is right. Legend tripping is all about an excellent experience. Now that you've finished reading this book, you are all psyched up to go out and look for bigfoot or maybe do a ghost hunt. I have related my knowledge of legends and mysteries, and I've set out all the tools needed to have a successful and safe adventure.

You have the legend trip planned and all the gear loaded in the vehicle. You and your team are off on the adventure. I need to bring up one point about leadership. Being retired military, I have always found that somebody needs to be in charge at all times. Somebody has to be there to make the command decisions and stick with those decisions. I'm saying that when you're actually walking into the woods or swamps, is not a good time to change plans. Being flexible is always a factor, and plans change due to unforeseen events. An example of this would be arriving at a chosen campground to find it is closed or full. Always have a backup plan or an alternate place to go.

One time, we got to a campground and found it full, so we had to drive around and find another place to camp. It ended up taking us all day, and we lost one day of walking around. But as the leader, you need to be ready for things like this. If something goes wrong (and it will), fix it and continue. In other words, don't stand around mad and complaining about it. Go to Plan B and continue with your adventure.

The first step is to find a legend to go check out. Find out everything you can about it, then make a plan that includes location, gathering up the family, or calling some friends to join in. Pack the gear and then head out. I wish you all the luck, and I hope you find the truth behind the legends you're investigating.

Once traveling with your team or family down the highway on the way to adventure, what else can you do to create the right mood for this legend trip? The answer is to bring reading material related to the subject of the legend trip. You can look on the Internet for sites like YouTube and look for shows about it. As I mentioned, back in 1977, there was an excellent show called *In Search Of.* Actor Leonard Nimoy was the host, and the show dealt with mysteries and the unexplained. The show ran for six seasons, with episodes about bigfoot, the yeti, UFOs, lake monsters, ESP, witchcraft, the Oak Island Money Pit, the Bermuda Triangle, and Coral Castle. The show is now available on DVD and on YouTube, where it is easier and cheaper to watch. The shows are well done and help set the mood.

Another good thing to bring along are books on the unexplained, which help educate the family. There are books on almost every legend and mystery. Some of these books are out of print but can still be found on Amazon.

Before you go out, I want to emphasize safety. Children watch what adults do and say. Adults—know to be careful; what children see, they imitate. When on a legend trip, never take unnecessary risks. Do not try to show off in front of the family. There are numerous horror stories where the father was doing just that, and an incident happened, and sadly, in some cases, a family member died. As a parent, put safety first. Set the example of safe practices and behaviors. If a sign says it's private property, then set an example for the kids: stay behind the fence. If the leader acts safely, then the rest of the family will follow suit. If not, you will spend most of the trip worrying about something happening or somebody getting hurt. Explain to the family or team that safety is the top priority.

Today's youth are stimulated with video games and not outdoor vacations. The reaction of today's teenager to going camping is "whatever." But instead of telling them that, tell them it's a monster hunt, and they will get excited and look forward to the expedition and doing something out of the ordinary. I believe the youth of today are craving adventure. They like video games because in the game they are participating in an adventure. Legend tripping is a way for them to have a real adventure

If looking for something exciting to do with the family or scout group, maybe going on a legend trip might be the thing. With legend tripping, I know I am doing two good things: I'm getting out there and getting exercise and not being a couch potato. The second thing is I'm doing what I enjoy doing—looking for legends. I hope you find as much excitement on your legend trips as I do on mine. Don't be deterred and discouraged if nothing is found the first time out. Patience pays off in this field.

Albert Einstein said it best:

> The important thing is not to stop questioning. Curiosity has its reason for existence. One cannot help but be in awe when he contemplates the mysteries of eternity, of life, of the marvelous structure of reality. It is enough if one tries merely to comprehend a little of this mystery

each day.

If the chosen location offers a tour, take it. The tour guides know their job and location better than most historians, and can share personal experiences and anecdotes not found in a guidebook or website. The Loch Ness tour is an excellent one.

There is no reason not to do this. I'm not fond of hearing about people being too busy to go out camping. You should plan at least one legend trip a month. It will create an adventurous mood at home. You can also go online and look for a group that goes legend tripping, i.e., monster or ghost hunters. If this doesn't work then form a group or take the family. As I said, not a lot of money is needed to trip locally. Just make time and a plan to go out and experience stuff.

One thing I learned during my time in the military is that life is short, and without adventure or challenge, it's boring. People, in general, like to have excitement in their lives. To me, there is nothing worse than getting old and having regrets about what you didn't do.

Sometimes, when I hear of a bigfoot sighting or a recent haunting, I contact some friends or a family member and head to the location as soon as I can. I always keep my gear in my vehicle just in case I get a call.

I have now shared with you my bucket list of places that I plan on visiting and legends that I plan on investigating. While this is the end of my book, it is only the beginning of your adventure into the mysterious and unexplained world we live in.

GET OUT THERE AND EXPERIENCE ADVENTURE OUTSIDE THE BOX.

GO LEGEND TRIPPING!

References

Names for Bigfoot Relatives Around the World | Explore. https://exemplore.com/cryptids/Names-for-Bigfoot-Around-the-World
Yowie - Wikipedia. https://en.wikipedia.org/wiki/Yowie_(cryptid)
Southern Sasquatch Expeditions: Know your Creatures…
https://www.thetravel.com/places-destinations-fans-witches/
Bigfoot Cousins Claimed in Many Countries | Live Science.
https://www.livescience.com/8766-bigfoot-cousins-claimed-countries.html
Southern Sasquatch Expeditions: Know your Creatures…
https://southernsasquatchexpeditionsblog.blogspot.com/2017/12/know-your-creatures-cryptozoologys.html
Exploring Canadian Monsters: New Brunswick | Mysterious…
https://mysteriousuniverse.org/2018/05/exploring-canadian-monsters-new-brunswick/
Sasquatch | The Canadian Encyclopedia.
http://www.thecanadianencyclopedia.ca/article/sasquatch

Chapter 3
Werewolf Legends from Around the World | Historic Mysteries. https://www.historicmysteries.com/werewolf-legends/

Werewolf Legends from Around the World | Historic Mysteries. https://www.historicmysteries.com/werewolf-legends/

Mystery 'werewolf' creature terrifying families in Hull…
https://www.mirror.co.uk/news/weird-news/mystery-werewolf-creature-terrifying-families-7979525

Ratman of Southend | Cryptid Wiki | Fandom.
https://cryptidz.fandom.com/wiki/Ratman_of_Southend

Creepy Creatures From Around The World - Everything After ….
https://www.dictionary.com/e/s/humanoid-monsters-creepy-creatures-worldwide/

Chapter 4
Cadborosaurus
https://zeenews.india.com/news/eco-news/cadborosaurus-spotted-in-alaskan-waters_720913.html

Loch Ness Monster
https://www.dailyrecord.co.uk/news/weird-news/loch-ness-monster-new-picture-4586604
http://www.nessie.co.uk/index.html
http://www.lochnesssightings.com/index.asp?pageid=506195

Morag
http://de-and.fun/Attraction_Review-g1096818-d8481778-Reviews-Loch_Morar-Morar_Mallaig_Lochaber_Scottish_Highlands_Scotlandnrxiq763vwd.html

OgoPogo
https://www.livescience.com/42399-ogopogo.html

Champ
https://www.lakechamplainregion.com/heritage/champ

Muyso
https://en.wikipedia.org/wiki/Monster_of_Lake_Tota

Yacumana
https://bizarre-and-amazing.blogspot.com/2017/04/yacumama.html
https://www.livinginperu.com/terrifying-legends-peru-3-yacumama-sachamama/

Lagarflojot Worm
https://grapevine.is/news/2012/06/11/another-american-network-searches-for-lagarfljot-worm/

Lake Como Lariosauro
https://www.aroundturin.com/lake-como-bellagio/

Lake Tianchi Monster
https://en.wikipedia.org/wiki/Lake_Tianchi_Monster

Lake Van Monster
https://mysteriousuniverse.org/2019/03/the-mysterious-lake-monster-of-turkey/

Nahuelito.
http://www.strangemag.com/nahuelito.html

Chapter 5

Mermaid Legends
https://www.mentalfloss.com/article/75471/9-mermaid-legends-around-world

https://www.livescience.com/5642-mermaid-sightings-claimed-israel.html

https://www.connollycove.com/the-legend-of-the-selkies/

https://www.smithsonianmag.com/smart-news/how-13th-century-mermaid-bones-came-be-displayed-japanese-temple-180962209/

Chapter 7

The 32 Most Beautiful Haunted Destinations Around the World https://www.architecturaldigest.com/gallery/most-beautiful-haunted-houses-slideshow

24 Spooky Places to Visit Around the World | Nat Geo
http://www.natgeotraveller.in/24-spooky-places-to-visit-around-the-world/

21 Most Haunted Places in the World
https://www.hauntedrooms.co.uk/21-most-haunted-places-in-the-world

Tower of London ghosts | Spooky Isles.
https://www.spookyisles.com/haunted-tower-of-london/

15 Haunted Forests Around the World - Condé Nast Traveler. https://www.cntraveler.com/gallery/haunted-forests-around-the-world

Top Most Haunted Places To Visit Around The World Top Most
https://www.factworldzz.com/top-most-haunted-places-to-visit-around-the-world/
The world's most haunted castles and mansions
https://www.businessinsider.in/thelife/news/7-of-the-worlds-most-haunted-castles-and-mansions-and-a-look-at-their-dark-histories/articleshow/71844785.cms

Chapter 9

5 Famous UFO Sightings Across the World
https://www.travelchannel.com/shows/expedition-unknown-hunt-for-extra-terrestrials/articles/5-famous-ufo-sightings-across-the-world

Best places to go alien spotting this World UFO Day
https://besttraveltale.com/travel/best-places-to-go-alien-spotting-this-world-ufo-day/

https://www.independent.co.uk/travel/news-and-advice/ufo-day-aliens-tourism-sci-fi-space-travel-roswell-a8977861.html

Dragon's Triangle
https://history.howstuffworks.com/history-vs-myth/devils-triangle-been-swallowing-up-ships-for-centuries.htm

Burle Triangle
https://criticalbelievers.proboards.com/thread/18298/burle-triangle?page=1

Stonehenge
https://www.english-heritage.org.uk/visit/inspire-me/blog/blog-posts/2016/30-things-you-might-not-know-about-stonehenge/

Westbury White Horse
https://en.wikipedia.org/wiki/Westbury_White_Horse

Skellig Michael and Skellig Islands
https://www.skelligmichaelcruises.com/

Angkor Wat – Smarthistory.

https://smarthistory.org/angkor-wat/

Louvre Pyramid
https://science.howstuffworks.com/engineering/architecture/louvre-pyramid.htm

Machu Picchu
https://artsandculture.google.com/entity/m0krfy

Most Mysterious Places on Earth
https://www.farandwide.com/s/most-mysterious-places-4fc481db2838490b

12 Bewildering Hills Where Gravity
https://www.atlasobscura.com/lists/gravity-hills

https://www.businessinsider.com/what-really-happens-on-a-gravity-hill-2016-4

The Story Behind Italy's Cursed Gaiola Island.
https://theculturetrip.com/europe/italy/articles/the-story-behind-italys-cursed-gaiola-island/
https://www.amusingplanet.com/2013/09/the-cursed-island-of-gaiola.html

The Curse of Peche Island.
https://www.nailhed.com/2014/09/forbidden-fruit-curse-of-peche-island.html

Seven of the World's Most Cursed Islands
https://www.atlasobscura.com/articles/seven-cursed-islands-from-around-the-world

Palmyra Atoll, Daksa Island, Lazzaretto Nuovo: Islands ....
https://www.news.com.au/travel/travel-updates/health-safety/cursed-five-gorgeous-uninhabited-islands-with-truly-terrifying-histories/news-story/84a617f938d9dc3799c43e8508e657c9

30 Haunted Places to Visit Around the World - Czech ....

https://www.czechleaders.com/travel/30-haunted-places-to-visit-around-the-world

Phnom Kulen, the Most Sacred Mountain
https://theculturetrip.com/asia/cambodia/articles/a-brief-history-of-phnom-kulen-the-most-sacred-mountain-in-cambodia/

Padmanabhaswamy Temple
https://www.beyondsciencetv.com/2017/06/15/the-mysterious-sealed-temple-door-no-one-can-open-last-door-of-padmanabhaswamy/

Akshardham Temple, Delhi
https://www.tripadvisor.com/ShowUserReviews-g304551-d626913-r179355327-Swaminarayan_Akshardham-New_Delhi_National_Capital_Territory_of_Delhi

Chapter 11

30 of the world's most valuable treasures that are still ....
https://www.livescience.com/60436-most-valuable-treasures-still-missing-lost

Top Ten Lost Treasure of the World | Historic Mysteries.
https://www.historicmysteries.com/lost-treasure/

Treasure Hunting: So you want to be a treasure hunter?. https://okietreasurehunter.blogspot.com/2010/09/so-you-want-to-be-treasure-hunter.html

15 Amazing COUNTRIES to Enjoy Metal Detecting!!.
https://detectingschool.com/best-countries-for-metal-detecting/

Spooky Places: 10 Destinations For Fans Of Witches | TheTravel.
https://www.thetravel.com/places-destinations-fans-witches/

BIGFOOT NATION
A History of Sasquatch in North America
By David Hatcher Childress

Childress takes us on a tour of Bigfoot Nation—the apparently real world of bigfoot around us in the United States and Canada. Surviving in the shadows and suffering from loss of habitat, bigfoot has had many encounters with humans, many of which are chronicled here. In these meetings, bigfoot has been found to be curious, dangerous and even amorous, depending on the circumstances. He appears in commercials and movies, on roadside billboards and stamps. In fact, bigfoot is everywhere, on the fringes of modern society, creeping into our dreams.

320 Pages. 6x9 Paperback. Illustrated. $22.00. Code: BGN

OBELISKS: TOWERS OF POWER
The Mysterious Purpose of Obelisks
By David Hatcher Childress

Some obelisks weigh over 500 tons and are massive blocks of polished granite that would be extremely difficult to quarry and erect even with modern equipment. Why did ancient civilizations in Egypt, Ethiopia and elsewhere undertake the massive enterprise it would have been to erect a single obelisk, much less dozens of them? Were they energy towers that could receive or transmit energy? With discussions on Tesla's wireless power, and the use of obelisks. Chapters include: The Crystal Towers of Egypt; The Obelisks of Ethiopia; Obelisks in Europe and Asia; Mysterious Obelisks in the Americas; The Terrible Crystal Towers of Atlantis; Obelisks on the Moon; more. 8-page color section.

336 Pages. 6x9 Paperback. Illustrated. $22.00 Code: OBK

THE TESLA PAPERS
by Nikola Tesla, edited by David Hatcher Childress

David Hatcher Childress takes us into the incredible world of Nikola Tesla and his amazing inventions. Tesla's fantastic vision of the future, including wireless power, anti-gravity, free energy and highly advanced solar power. Also included are papers on: •The Secret History of Wireless Transmission •Tesla and the Magnifying Transmitter •Design and Construction of a Half-Wave Tesla Coil •Electrostatics: A Key to Free Energy •Progress in Zero-Point Energy Research •Electromagnetic Energy from Antennas to Atoms.

325 PAGES. 8X10 PAPERBACK. ILLUSTRATED. $16.95. CODE: TTP

HESS AND THE PENGUINS
By Joseph P. Farrell

Farrell looks at Hess' mission to make peace with Britain and get rid of Hitler—even a plot to fly Hitler to Britain for capture! How much did Göring and Hitler know of Rudolf Hess' subversive plot, and what happened to Hess? Why was a doppleganger put in Spandau Prison and then "suicided"? Did the British use an early form of mind control on Hess' double? John Foster Dulles of the OSS and CIA suspected as much. Farrell also uncovers the strange death of Admiral Richard Byrd's son in 1988, about the same time of the death of Hess.

288 Pages. 6x9 Paperback. Illustrated. $19.95. Code: HAPG

www.AdventuresUnlimitedPress.com

THE LOST WORLD OF CHAM
By David Hatcher Childress

The mysterious Cham, or Champa, peoples of Southeast Asia formed a megalith-building, seagoing empire that extended into Indonesia, Tonga, and beyond—a transoceanic power that reached Mexico and South America. The Champa maintained many ports in what is today Vietnam, Cambodia, and Indonesia and their ships plied the Indian Ocean and the Pacific, bringing Chinese, African and Indian traders to far off lands, including Olmec ports on the Pacific Coast of Central America. Topics include: Cham and Khem: Egyptian Influence on Cham; The Search for Metals; The Basalt City of Nan Madol; Elephants in North America; The Cham and Lake Titicaca; Easter Island and the Cham; the Technology of the Cham; tons more. 24-page color section.

328 Pages. 6x9 Paperback. Illustrated. $22.00 Code: LPWC

ADVENTURES OF A HASHISH SMUGGLER
by Henri de Monfreid

The son of a French artist who knew Paul Gaugin as a child, de Monfreid sought his fortune by becoming a collector and merchant of the fabled Persian Gulf pearls. He was then drawn into the shadowy world of arms trading, slavery, smuggling and drugs. Infamous as well as famous, his name is inextricably linked to the Red Sea and the raffish ports between Suez and Aden in the early years of the twentieth century. De Monfreid (1879 to 1974) had a long life of many adventures around the Horn of Africa where he dodged pirates as well as the authorities.

284 Pages. 6x9 Paperback. $16.95. Illustrated. Code AHS

NORTH CAUCASUS DOLMENS
By Boris Loza, Ph.D.

Join Boris Loza as he travels to his ancestral homeland to uncover and explore dolmens firsthand. Chapters include: Ancient Mystic Megaliths; Who Built the Dolmens?; Why the Dolmens were Built; Asian Connection; Indian Connection; Greek Connection; Olmec and Maya Connection; Sun Worshippers; Dolmens and Archeoastronomy; Location of Dolmen Quarries; Hidden Power of Dolmens; and much more! Tons of Illustrations! A fascinating book of little-seen megaliths. Color section.

252 Pages. 5x9 Paperback. Illustrated. $24.00. Code NCD

THE ENCYCLOPEDIA OF MOON MYSTERIES
Secrets, Anomalies, Extraterrestrials and More
By Constance Victoria Briggs

Our moon is an enigma. The ancients viewed it as a light to guide them in the darkness, and a god to be worshipped. Did you know that: Aristotle and Plato wrote about a time when there was no Moon? Several of the NASA astronauts reported seeing UFOs while traveling to the Moon?; the Moon might be hollow?; Apollo 10 astronauts heard strange "space music" when traveling on the far side of the Moon?; strange and unexplained lights have been seen on the Moon for centuries?; there are said to be ruins of structures on the Moon?; there is an ancient tale that suggests that the first human was created on the Moon?; Tons more. Tons of illustrations with A to Z sections for easy reference and reading.

152 Pages. 7x10 Paperback. Illustrated. $19.95. Code: EOMM

ORDER FORM

10% Discount When You Orde[r] 3 or More Items

One Adventure Place
P.O. Box 74
Kempton, Illinois 60946
United States of America
Tel.: 815-253-6390 • Fax: 815-253-6300
Email: auphq@frontiernet.net
http://www.adventuresunlimitedpress.com

ORDERING INSTRUCTIONS

- ✓ Remit by USD$ Check, Money Order or Credit Card
- ✓ Visa, Master Card, Discover & AmEx Accepted
- ✓ Paypal Payments Can Be Made To: info@wexclub.com
- ✓ Prices May Change Without Notice
- ✓ 10% Discount for 3 or More Items

SHIPPING CHARGES

United States

- ✓ Postal Book Rate { $4.50 First Item; 50¢ Each Additional Item
- ✓ POSTAL BOOK RATE Cannot Be Tracked! Not responsible for non-delivery.
- ✓ Priority Mail { $7.00 First Item; $2.00 Each Additional Item
- ✓ UPS { $9.00 First Item (Minimum 5 Books); $1.50 Each Additional Item

NOTE: UPS Delivery Available to Mainland USA Only

Canada

- ✓ Postal Air Mail { $19.00 First Item; $3.00 Each Additional Item
- ✓ Personal Checks or Bank Drafts MUST BE US$ and Drawn on a US Bank
- ✓ Canadian Postal Money Orders OK
- ✓ Payment MUST BE US$

All Other Countries

- ✓ Sorry, No Surface Delivery!
- ✓ Postal Air Mail { $19.00 First Item; $7.00 Each Additional Item
- ✓ Checks and Money Orders MUST BE US$ and Drawn on a US Bank or branch.
- ✓ Paypal Payments Can Be Made in US$ To: info@wexclub.com

SPECIAL NOTES

- ✓ RETAILERS: Standard Discounts Available
- ✓ BACKORDERS: We Backorder all Out-of-Stock Items Unless Otherwise Requested
- ✓ PRO FORMA INVOICES: Available on Request
- ✓ DVD Return Policy: Replace defective DVDs only

ORDER ONLINE AT: www.adventuresunlimitedpress.com

10% Discount When You Order 3 or More Items!

Please check: ✓

☐ This is my first order ☐ I have ordered before

Name

Address

City

State/Province | Postal Code

Country

Phone: Day | Evening

Fax | Email

Item Code	Item Description	Qty	Total

Please check: ✓

- ☐ Postal-Surface
- ☐ Postal-Air Mail (Priority in USA)
- ☐ UPS (Mainland USA only)
- ☐ Visa/MasterCard/Discover/American Express

Subtotal ▸	
Less Discount-10% for 3 or more items ▸	
Balance ▸	
Illinois Residents 6.25% Sales Tax ▸	
Previous Credit ▸	
Shipping ▸	
Total (check/MO in USD$ only) ▸	

Card Number:

Expiration Date: Security Code:

✓ SEND A CATALOG TO A FRIEND: